REUTERS GLOSSARY
OF
INTERNATIONAL FINANCIAL
&
ECONOMIC TERMS

Edited by
THE SENIOR STAFF OF REUTERS LIMITED

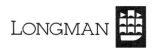

REUTERS GLOSSARY OF
INTERNATIONAL FINANCIAL & ECONOMIC
TERMS 3rd edition

Published by Longman Information & Reference
Longman Group Limited, Westgate House, The High,
Harlow, Essex CM20 1YR, United Kingdom.
Telephone: (01279) 442601
Facsimile: (01279) 444501

First Published 1982
Second edition (first Longman edition) 1989
Third edition (second Longman edition) 1994
A catalogue record for this book is available from the
British Library.

ISBN 0-582-24871-X

Printed and bound in Great Britain by
BPC Wheatons Ltd, Exeter.

FOREWORD

Reuters is the world's leading supplier of financial and economic information to the professional markets and produces news services in 17 languages.

To maintain consistency in our worldwide coverage there is a need for clear and concise definitions of the often highly technical terms our journalists may encounter or employ.

This is the third edition of the glossary and it has been entirely reworked. It will be of value not only to journalists and traders but to anyone interested in the mechanics and terminology of today's markets. We hope you find it useful.

I would like to thank all those who have helped to compile this book.

Mark Wood
Editor-in-Chief

INTRODUCTION

This book, the third edition of Reuters Glossary of International Financial & Economic Terms, has been completely revised and updated since the last edition was published in 1989.

The new Glossary contains nearly 3,000 definitions, an increase of 30%. For the first time it covers the expanding and influential field of derivatives, giving definitions concerning futures, options, option strategies and swaps.

Other subjects are foreign exchange, treasury, money and capital markets, sovereign and corporate debt, mortgage-backed assets, equities, commodities, energy, macro-economic terms and technical analysis.

The Glossary has an easy-to-use alphabetical format. Entries are cross-referenced where necessary.

We aim to provide Reuter customers and staff with a useful reference and training tool and also to explain for a wider public some of the specialist financial terms found in newspapers and in business life.

The Glossary was compiled by Reuter journalist Frank Nunnay-Elam and Reuter Geneva training executive Tracey Shaw. The entries have been checked by other senior Reuter journalists and by expert participants in the financial markets.

Responsibility for the contents rests entirely with Reuters but we are grateful for the kind help and for comments from the following individuals and organisations:

Fédération des Bourses Européennes, Brussels.
Association Cambiste Internationale.
Nick Gilbert, managing director, European Representative Office, Chicago Merchantile Exchange.
Union Bank of Switzerland, Geneva
Jeremy Huddle, BHF Bank, London.
Leif Carlsson, Micke Lundin, Nordbanken, Gothenburg.
Guy Kingsbury, GK Associates, London.
Christian Dummett, Abbey National Treasury Services, London.
Steve Pickering, Trader ApS, Denmark.
Kai Fisher, NationsBank, London.
Equity Systems Pty Ltd., Sydney.
Peter Hill, Nomura Bank International PLC, London.
Richard Knight, Paul Kirk, Canadian Imperial Bank of Commerce, Toronto.

The sections covering key interest rates for G10 nations and Switzerland are taken from the *Reuter Guide to Official Interest Rates* by Ken Ferris and Mark Jones (Reuters Financial Television), published in 1994 by the Probus Publishing Company.

We are indebted to McGraw-Hill International (UK) Limited for permission to use extracts covering money supply in the G5 countries from *Market Movers* by Mark Jones and Ken Ferris, published in 1993.

John Bartram
Reuters International Quality Editor, Economic News

A Shares See Ordinary Share.

A/B Pass Throughs Pass through certificates which are divided into senior and subordinated certificates. Senior holders have priority over cash flows from the underlying pool of mortgages.

ABEDA Arab Bank for Economic Development in Africa. Makes loans and grants to sub-Saharan African nations to finance development projects. Based in Khartoum.

Abu Dhabi National Oil Company See ADNOC Prices.

Acceptance House An acceptance house "accepts" a trade bill at a specified date in the future, meaning it pays the trade bill at a discounted rate. See BAs.

Accommodation Platform Platform or semi-submersible oil rig built or adapted to offer full accommodation for offshore oil or gas platform personnel.

Account The period during which deals on a stock exchange are done for settlement on the due account day. The number of days in a period varies in different countries.

Account Limits A financial and contractual relationship whereby an investor is allowed to use the services of a bank, investment bank or an exchange dealer for investment or speculative purposes and agrees to a set maximum amount of credit and possibly a defined period.

Account Trading The practice of buying and selling securities in a single account period so that settlement is effected by one net payment. Mostly been the practice in the U.K., France, Italy and Belgium.

Accounting Standards Board U.K. accounting body. See FASB.

Accreting Principal Swap A swap with an increasing notional principal amount. See Amortising Rate Swap.

Accretion Applies to a range of instruments where the notional principal grows in amount over the life of the underlying instrument. Opposite to Amortisation.

Accrued Interest The interest accruing on a security since the previous coupon payment date. Coupons are paid to the holder of the security on the payment date so if it is sold between times the buyer must usually compensate the seller for the interest accrued until the value date, either calculated within the price or as a separate payment. A bond can trade with negative accrued interest from the ex dividend date until the next coupon payment (in the case of a new buyer). See Simple Interest.

Accumulation / Distribution Analysis A technical analysis which measures the difference between the cumulative amount of buying pressure (accumulation) and the cumulative amount of selling pressure (distribution).

Accumulation occurs when the close is higher than the previous close. The contribution to the total accumulation is then the difference between the close and the true low where the true low is the minimum of the low and the previous close.

Distribution is assumed if the close is lower than the previous close. The contribution to the total distribution is then the difference between the true high and the close where the true high is the maximum of the high and the previous close.

A buy or sell signal is then indicated when a divergence between the analysis and the price is confirmed by a relevant trend.

ACI See Association Cambiste Internationale.

Acidization Process whereby acid is injected into reservoir rock, thereby enlarging the pore spaces and increasing the flow of oil.

ACP See Lomé Convention.

Acre Land measurement used in the U.S. and the U.K. which equals 43,560 square feet. One square mile has 640 acres. A hectare measures 2.471 acres.

Acreage Allotment U.S. government limitation on the planted acreage of some crops. See Acreage Reduction Program.

Acreage Reduction Program In the U.S., a voluntary government programme in which a farmer retires part of his acreage and usually receives no payment. However, his offer may enable him to take part in other government programmes where payment is made.

Across the Board In tariff negotiations this involves uniform percentage reductions or increases in duties on major categories of items. The opposite position is item by item tariff negotiation.

Acting in Concert Investors working together to achieve the same goal, e.g. to buy all the stock they need to take over a company or purchase sufficient shares to hold a majority or to buy the minimum needed where they can legitimately make an open bid to shareholders to buy outstanding shares. Sometimes acting in concert can be considered illegal. Also known colloquially as concert party. See Warehousing.

Actuals Also called physicals. Refers to the physical commodities available for shipment, storage and manufacture. Physicals which are available for delivery are traded for cash on a spot or forward basis as opposed to futures contracts which are traded on margin.

Ad Hoc Repurchase Tender   In Germany, a very short maturity repurchase tender offered by the Bundesbank, in times of extraordinary liquidity needs, to fine tune the money market. Such repos are offered only to banks operating in the money markets and for same day settlement. Also known as a quick or fast tender.

Ad Valorem   Latin, meaning "according to value". A tax or duty levied as a fixed percentage of an item's value as opposed to a fixed unitary levy such as a stamp duty.

ADB   African Development Bank, based in Abidjan and founded in 1964. Also stands for Asian Development Bank, based in Manila and founded in 1966.

Adjustable Rate Mortgages   ARMs. Interest rates are adjusted periodically at predetermined intervals in accordance with changes that occur in an agreed index. Can have a rate cap from one period to the next and a rate cap through to maturity. Also known as a floating or variable rate mortgage.

Adjustable Rate Note   A note, linked to U.S. Treasury yields, with no early redemption feature. For example, a 12 year bond could bear a fixed coupon for two years and then be reset every subsequent two years until maturity to yield a fixed margin over U.S. Treasuries. Investors are limited to a two year risk on interest rate movements but are able to obtain an annual return higher than on two year deposits.

Adjustable Rate Preferred Stock   A type of preferred share whose dividend is not fixed but set periodically to reflect changes in interest rates. The rate is normally fixed at a slight premium to a benchmark rate, often as the result of a Dutch auction by investors. When adjusted more regularly it is fixed against a shorter term rate and is called a Money Market Preferred Stock.

Administration   A legal procedure under the U.K.'s 1986 Insolvency Act that allows insolvent companies to be reorganised and refinanced. It is often used to effect better realisation of assets than Liquidation. This would include repackaging of the business and its sale. The administrator - appointed by and reporting to the court - manages the affairs of the company on behalf of all its creditors. At the same time, this procedure restricts the rights of secured creditors, finance and leasing companies.

Administrative Receivership   In the U.K., this is a statutorily controlled procedure where the unpaid holder of a floating charge debenture appoints a receiver to take control of and manage the charged assets - normally comprising the whole of the company's business and assets. The receiver is empowered to trade and dispose of the company's assets as a going concern. It is an important method by which medium and large companies are reorganised and the means by which the business (as opposed to the legal entity) of many insolvent companies is allowed to continue.

ADNOC Prices   Official monthly selling prices of Abu Dhabi crude oil of Murban, Lower Zakum, Upper Zakum and Umm Shaif as issued retroactively by the state Abu Dhabi National Oil Company (ADNOC). Used as a benchmark in spot trading of Abu Dhabi crude.

ADR   See American Depositary Receipt.

ADS   American Depositary Share. See American Depositary Receipt.

Advisory Funds   Funds managed by a fund manager who has permission from the investor to take decisions without consultation. The manager can have control completely or within set limits.

Aeration   A method of preservation where air is blown into stored grain to prevent spoilage.

AFESD   Arab Fund for Economic and Social Development. Participates in financing of economic and social projects in Arab states and countries. Offers loans on easy terms. Encourages investment of public and private capital to aid the Arab economy. Established in 1968 in Kuwait.

Affiliate   Two companies are affiliated when one owns less than a majority of the voting stock of the other or if both are subsidiaries of a third company.

Afloats   Commodities on board, underway or ready to sail.

AFRA   Average Freight Rate Assessment. Calculated monthly by the London Tanker Brokers Panel. It is the average cost of transporting oil in several different sizes of tankers.

African Development Bank   See ADB.

African Petroleum Producers Association   Established in 1986 to stabilise prices and maintain cooperation among regional producers. Members are Algeria, Angola, Benin, Cameroon, Congo, Ivory Coast, Egypt, Gabon, Libya, Nigeria and Zaire. Based in Nigeria.

After Hours Dealing   Takes place after the official close of business on the trading floor of a stock exchange. No set length of time is allocated for after hours dealing, particularly with the advent of electronic screen trading.

After Sight A Bill of Exchange drawn after sight is payable when it has been accepted and when the acceptor has written an acceptance date on the bill.

AG German company title, meaning Aktiengesellschaft, a joint stock company.

Against Actuals See Exchange for Physical.

Agencies In the U.S. many federal agencies issue short term paper and notes, offering a rate of interest 15-60 basis points higher than similar government securities. See Government Agency Bonds - Germany, Government Agency Bonds - Japan.

Agency Broker The equivalent of the old style stockbroker. Transacts business on a customer's behalf, passing through the securities at cost price and makes profits on commissions charged.

Agency Cross Trade Involves an agency broker - one who acts solely as an agent - buying shares from one party and passing them on to one or more buyers at the same price. He makes his profit from commission.

Agency of the Ministry of Finance - Netherlands Issuer of government debt in two forms: sinking fund issues and bullet bonds. Generally known as Dutch state loans or guilder bonds. Due to the stable exchange rate between the Dutch guilder and the German mark and the large volume of trade handled between the two countries, the Dutch government debt market is often regarded as an alternative to the German bund market. Foreign investors hold almost half of the government bonds outstanding.

Agent Bank Bank appointed by members of an international lending syndicate to protect the lenders' interests during the life of a loan.

Aggregate Demand Total demand for goods and services in the economy. Comprises demand from firms and government for investment goods, demand from local and central government for goods and services, demand from consumers and firms in other countries for goods and services such as exports.

Aggregate Risk Total exposure of a bank to any single customer for both spot and forward contracts.

Aggregate Supply Total supply of goods and services in the economy available to meet aggregate demand. It is made up of domestically produced goods and imports.

Aggressive Growth Fund A type of investment fund in the U.S. which invests in the shares of very speculative companies.

Agio Difference in value between two currencies. Also used as a term to describe the percentage charged on changing paper into cash or moving from a weak into a strong currency. In gold, it represents the added value of a coin over its gold content.

AGM Annual General Meeting. Called sometime after the financial year-end inviting shareholders to vote acceptance of the company's annual report, balance sheet and final dividend and to vote on any resolutions. By law, the shareholders receive details of all the foregoing within a set period before the meeting. On the day of the meeting, shareholders usually hear comments on the company's business prospects in the early months of the new financial year.

ALADI Asociación Latino-Americana de Integración (Latin American Integration Association). Wide-ranging inter-governmental body. Basic purpose is to establish reciprocal trade arrangements in the region and to set up a Latin American common market. Formed in 1980 to replace its precursor body, the Latin American Free Trade Association (LAFTA) which was founded in 1960. Member nations are Argentina, Bolivia, Brazil, Chile, Colombia, Ecuador, Mexico, Paraguay, Peru, Uruguay and Venezuela. Based in Montevideo.

Alexander's Filter An analysis which measures the rate of rise or fall in prices by a percentage price rise or fall over set periods. Buy signals are interpreted by a sufficiently fast rate of increase while sell signals are indicated by a fast rate of decrease.

Alfatoxin Carcinogen produced by mould. Seen on stored maize, for example.

ALIDE Asociación Latinoamericana de Institucíones Financieras de Desarrollo. Latin American Association of Development Financing Institutions. Promotes cooperation among regional development financing bodies. Has 144 members from 25 nations. Based in Lima.

All or None Limit order requiring that no part of an order be executed unless all of it can be done at the specified price.

Allotment Allocation of securities from a new issue. Shares can be fully allotted, i.e. everyone receives what they applied for, or a sliding scale of pro rata allotments is made when an issue is very popular.

Allotment Letter Informs an applicant of his allocation of shares in a new issue offer. The letter, which is in bearer form, has value as it can often be sold, particularly when it is generally believed that the shares of a new issue will open higher at start of trading than the sum paid for them in the offer.

Allowances Discounts or premiums to par allowed for commodity grades or delivery locations which differ from the basis grade or location specified in a futures contract. Also known as differentials.

Alluvial Deposit Sand, gravel or earth which sometimes contains metallic minerals and which has been washed away from its original location by the action of water.

Alpha-Beta Trend A technical analysis which aims at avoiding some of the false signals associated with crossing moving averages. The centre of a trend channel and of a trading filter is calculated by a forecasting technique based on the alpha-beta filter. The trend channel is defined by an upper and lower band where each band is a user-specified number of standard deviations of price from the channel's centre. The channel's width therefore varies with price volatility. An investor should be long when the trading filter is below the lower band, short when it is above the upper band and out of the market when it lies between the two bands.

Alternative Currency Option An option granting the holder the right to settle in one of two currencies (but not both) against a base currency at preselected strike prices.

Alternative Order Limit order to do either of two alternatives, e.g. either sell or buy a particular financial instrument at a limited price.

Alumina See Bauxite / Alumina.

Aluminium The most widely used metal after iron (including steel). It is a lightweight base metal used in the construction industry, resistant to corrosion, a good conductor and easily worked. Aluminium can be recovered as scrap. Major producers of primary aluminium include the U.S., the Commonwealth of Independent States, Canada and Australia. See Bauxite / Alumina.

American Depositary Receipt Usually issued by a bank in the U.S. to facilitate trading in a foreign share. The original shares are held by the bank and the ADR certificate is bought and sold as a bearer document. The ADR holder is entitled to all dividends and capital gains but not to voting rights. Also known as an American Depositary Share (ADS). See European Depositary Receipt.

American Depositary Share See American Depositary Receipt.

American Option An option giving the holder the opportunity to exercise at any time over the life of the contract, up to and including the expiry date. A variation, called semi-American, is where options can be exercised on just a set number of dates before expiry. See European Option.

American Petroleum Institute See API.

American Society for Testing Materials See ASTM.

AMEX Major Market Index Compiled by the American Stock Exchange. A price weighted average of 20 blue chip industrial shares which have their listings on the New York Stock Exchange and 17 of which are in the Dow Jones Industrial Average. The index follows the pattern of the DJIA in portraying the price trend of major industrial shares. In this price weighted index the high price issues exert more influence than lower price shares. Calculated in real time, i.e. as share prices change. The Chicago Board of Trade deals in futures on the index.

AMEX Market Value Index A market value weighted index that tracks the overall trend of over 800 components including shares listed on the American Stock Exchange, American Depositary Receipts and warrants. Dividends paid are reflected in the index on the basis that they have been reinvested (return index). Calculated in real time, i.e. as share prices change. AMVI options are listed on the AMEX.

Amortisation The reduction of principal or debt at regular intervals. This can be effected by a Purchase Fund or Sinking Fund. Can also be used, for instance, on depreciation and write-offs of intangibles. Opposite to Accretion.

Amortising Rate Swap A swap whereby the notional principal on which interest payments are based decreases over the life of the swap. See Accreting Principal Swap.

AMSTEL Club Grouping of finance houses from European countries which make reciprocal arrangements to finance trade, especially for the smaller exporter. Official title is Amstel Finance International AG.

Amsterdam/Rotterdam/Antwerp See ARA.

Andean Pact A group originally of five Latin American nations formed to found a free trade area. In 1978 the group set up an Andean Reserve Fund to help nations with balance of payments problems. The group widened in 1988 and the fund became a Latin American Reserve Fund. Aims to develop economic and social integration. Member nations are Bolivia, Colombia, Ecuador and Venezuela. Peru is an observer member. Based in Lima.

Anhydrous Ammonia Dry ammonia containing no dissolved water. One of the most important petroleum derived raw materials used in the chemical industry.

Animal Feed Ingredients These include:

-Manioc (tapioca or cassava). A root crop with a high energy value.

-Maize gluten or corn gluten. A by-product from maize starch extraction with high protein content.

-Molasses. Mainly a binding agent for dry feedstuffs, also improves taste. Produced when making sugar from cane and sorghum.

-Brans and sharps. Residues derived from milling cereals and having a similar nutritive composition to wheat and barley grains.

-Fruit waste, especially citrus. A dry concentrate made from the peel, pith and seed of fresh fruits. Its large amount of nitrogen-free extract makes for a useful energy source.

-Oilseed meals, including cotton meal, soybean meal, groundnut meal, sunflower meal, rape meal, sesame meal, corn meal, copra meal, palm kernel meal and linseed meal.

-Beet pulp. Remainder of the sugar beet root after the sugar has been extracted during processing. Main value is its energy content which is easily digested by ruminants.

-Brewing and distilling waste. Residue of grain after brewing and distilling. The spent grains form a useful cheap ingredient.

-Rice bran. A residue from which oil has been extracted. A popular filler ingredient.

Annual General Meeting See AGM.

Annual Rate Compares the average level in the current year with the average in the previous year. The benefit of this measure is that it smoothes out unusually large or small changes that may have occurred for a short while during the year.

Annual Report A status report on the current condition of a company. Issued once a year before the Annual General Meeting for shareholders' examination.

Annualised Rate Plots the change in an indicator over the whole year if the latest monthly or quarterly figure is presumed to persist for the rest of the year.

Annuity An investment that pays a given stream of interest for a fixed period of time.

Annuity Swap An interest rate swap whereby spasmodic payments are exchanged for a flow of regular payments of equivalent present value.

Anti-Trust Laws U.S. federal legislation to prevent restraint of trade and act against monopolies.

APEC Asia-Pacific Economic Cooperation. Aims to develop regional trade and cooperation. Members are Australia, Brunei, Canada, China, Hong Kong, Indonesia, Japan, Malaysia, Mexico, New Zealand, Papua New Guinea, the Philippines, Singapore, South Korea, Thailand, Taiwan and the U.S. Chile is scheduled to join in 1994.

API American Petroleum Institute. U.S. oil industry institution. Provides key weekly data on U.S. petroleum consumption and stock levels.

API Gravity Universally accepted scale adopted by the American Petroleum Institute for expressing the specific gravity of oils. It serves as a rough measure of quality. The higher the API gravity number, the richer the yield in premium refined products. Saudi Arabian Light is 34 degrees API while Algerian Saharan Blend, an even lighter crude, is 44 degrees.

Appraisal Drilling Drilling carried out to determine the extent, reserves and likely production rate of an oil or gas field.

Appraisal Well A well drilled to appraise the extent of the reservoir following a discovery well.

Appropriations Committees U.S. Congressional committees which prepare individual spending bills.

Approved Delivery Facility Any bank, stockyard, mill, store, warehouse, plant, elevator or other depositary recognised by an exchange as approved for the delivery of commodities tendered against a futures contract.

ARA Amsterdam/Rotterdam/Antwerp area. An oil cargo that is offered cost and freight ARA implies that ports within this area can be considered.

Arab Common Market Exists within the Council of Arab Economic Unity. Members are Egypt, Iraq, Jordan, Libya, Mauritania, Syria and Yemen.

Arab League Voluntary association of 21 sovereign Arab states designed to strengthen existing close ties and to coordinate policies.

Arab Monetary Fund Based in Abu Dhabi. Encourages Arab nations' economic integration and development. Provides loans and loan guarantees. Members comprise 20 Arab countries.

Arab Oil Embargo In 1973 Arab oil producers led by Saudi Arabia curbed oil sales to the Western nations in reaction to Western support for Israel in a Middle East war. The Organisation of Petroleum Exporting Countries took advantage of buyer confusion to wrest control of pricing from the Western oil companies and to quadruple crude prices. See IEA.

Arabica / Robusta Types of coffee bean. Arabica has a more mild flavour and is regarded as better quality. It is grown on high ground mostly in Central and South America but also in East Africa and India.

Robusta is grown in Ivory Coast, Indonesia, Uganda, Zaire and West African states. Instant coffee manufacturers use a blend of both coffees to meet required taste standards.

Arbitrage Simultaneous purchase and sale or vice versa of the same or similar financial instruments in the markets with a view to making profits from the difference in prices.

Arithmetic Index A weighted index that takes each component and calculates a mathematical average.

ARM See Adjustable Rate Mortgages.

ARO See Average Rate Option.

Aromatics Group of hydrocarbon fractions that can be transformed into numerous chemicals. Principal aromatics are benzene, toluene and xylene.

Around Par Foreign exchange term used in the forward market when the Points are quoted either side of par; one side of the quotation being at a discount, the other side at a premium. "One around par" (-1/+1) would mean one point to be deducted from, and one point to be added to, the spot price.

ARP Stock See Adjustable Rate Preferred Stock.

Arrears Reset Swap See In Arrears Swap.

ASCS Agricultural Stabilization and Conservation Service. The U.S. Department of Agriculture's main administrative arm, with offices in every agricultural producing county. It is responsible for signing up producers for agriculture programmes and keeping track of participation. It monitors U.S. owned farm stocks and sets prices for Payment in Kind redemption rates.

ASEAN Association of South East Asian Nations. Seeks enhanced economic progress and increased stability in the region. Members are Brunei, Indonesia, Malaysia, the Philippines, Singapore and Thailand. Formed in 1967. Based in Jakarta.

Asian Clearing Union Provides clearing arrangements whereby members settle payments for intra-regional transactions among participating central banks on a multilateral basis. Aim is to save using foreign exchange and also to promote use of domestic currencies among developing countries' trade. The Central Bank of Iran is agent for the organisation. Members are the central banks of Bangladesh, India, Iran, Myanmar (Burma), Nepal, Pakistan and Sri Lanka. The unit of account is the Asian Monetary Unit.

Asian Currency Unit Separate accounting unit used in Singapore by some banks licensed to deal in non-resident deposits.

Asian Development Bank Founded in 1966. Based in Manila. Has 36 members within the region and 16 others. Offers loans for economic development and loans and grants for technical assistance.

Asian Dollar Market This equivalent to the London based Eurodollar market has expanded in Singapore as a base for Asian funds inhibited from moving to London by the cost of fund transfers. The market is based throughout Asia but tends to concentrate in Singapore which is popular due to its interlocking time zone with Sydney, Hong Kong, Tokyo and London.

Asian Monetary Unit Accounting unit for the Asian Clearing Union with its value tied to the Special Drawing Rights issued by the International Monetary Fund.

Asian Option See Average Rate Option (ARO).

Ask A market maker's price to sell a commodity, security, currency or any financial instrument. A two-way price comprises the bid and ask. The difference between the two quotations is the spread. Also known as offer.

Aspartame A non-calorific artificial sweetener.

Asphalt A solid hydrocarbon found as a natural deposit. Crude oil with a high asphalt content is refined to remove the lighter fractions such as naphtha and kerosene and leave asphalt as a residue.

Asset Backed Bond A bond whereby the borrower pledges an asset, such as a property mortgage or the interest and repayments from a loan, to enhance the credit quality of a bond. See CMO.

Asset Backed Securities Securities collateralised by assets, not mortgages, such as car loans and credit card receivables.

Asset Stripping Seeking a profit by buying a company, often when the market price is below the value of the assets, and then selling off all or some of the assets.

Assets / Liabilities Assets are tangible items of value such as factories, machinery, financial instruments and intangibles such as goodwill, the title only of a newspaper or a product's brand name. Liabilities are items of negative value that cover tangibles such as assets which hold a high risk factor and intangibles such as a financial obligation.

Asset management, also known as liability management, is the function of controlling cash flows or the duration and maturity of assets and liabilities so as to reduce interest rate risk and aim for optimum return.

Assignment The notice given to an option writer that an option has been exercised by the option holder. See Exercise.

Associate Formed when two or more companies engage in partnership or joint venture projects.

Associated Gas Natural gas found in association with oil, either dissolved in the oil or as a cap of free gas above the oil.

Associated Liquids Liquid hydrocarbons found in association with natural gas.

Association Cambiste Internationale (ACI) The ACI is a non-commercial organisation based on the fellowship of cambistes (foreign exchange dealers) with the sole aim of furtherance of the profession. Located in Paris.

Forex organisations have been formed in various countries. These groups are linked by affiliation to the ACI. Each national organisation is fully autonomous within the framework of the ACI charter and bye-laws.

The ACI issues a code of conduct setting out the manner and spirit in which business should be conducted so that the market and its participants maintain their reputation for high standards of professionalism, integrity and ethical conduct. See Forex, Forex Club.

Association of Coffee Producing Countries Coordinates policies of all the producing countries, including production and marketing, aims to increase coffee consumption and supports programmes to maintain prices. Operates an export Retention Scheme. Members account for more than 85 percent of the world's coffee exports and include Brazil, Colombia, five Central American nations, Kenya, Ivory Coast, Indonesia and Uganda. Based in Brazil.

Association of Tin Producing Countries Operates supply controls to support tin prices and reduce stocks. Group comprises Australia, Bolivia, Indonesia, Malaysia, Nigeria, Thailand and Zaire. Brazil and China attend meetings as observers but do conform to supply controls. See ITC.

ASTM American Society for Testing Materials. Responsible for issuing many of the standard methods used in the oil industry.

ASX All Ordinaries Index Capitalisation weighted arithmetic index comprising some 300 companies quoted on the Australian stock exchange. Of the 300, the leading 100 constitute 85 percent of the index by market capitalisation. Futures and options are traded on the Sydney Futures Exchange.

At Best A buy or sell order indicating it should be carried out at the best possible price available at that moment.

At the Money A term used to describe an option whose strike price is the same or very close to the prevailing underlying forward market price. For very short term options, the strike price can be measured against the prevailing cash price of the underlying, known as at the money spot. At the money options have a Delta of around 0.5.

At Your Risk Dealers' language indicating that the quoted rate is subject to change at the risk of the receiver. Also known as your risk or risk.

ATX Index Austrian Traded Index. Arithmetic weighted index which includes all shares - currently 19 - which are continuously traded as distinct from those whose price is fixed once a day. The index is real time, i.e. it is calculated every time one of the 19 shares is traded. Options and futures are traded on the OTOB, the Oesterreichische Termin und Optionen Börse.

Auction A public sale of a security whereby the issuer invites authorised dealers to make bids in price or yield until the full amount of the issue is sold. See English Auction, Dutch Auction.

Auction Rate Preferred Share A share which is similar to a money market preferred stock in that the dividend is set at regular intervals (on a very short term basis) but the dividend rate has to be accepted by the shareholders. If the shareholders reject the dividend rate, the issuing company has either to increase the rate to one acceptable by the shareholders or repurchase the shares at par value.

Auditor's Report The company's balance sheet report, as presented to shareholders, carries a report from a firm of auditors which states that in their opinion (if it is so) the accounts give a true and fair view of the state of affairs of the company (on the date given on the balance sheet). See Qualified Accounts.

Aussie Dealers' language for the Australian dollar.

Austrian Traded Index See ATX Index.

Authorised Capital The maximum number of shares that can be issued under the firm's articles of incorporation. This can only be increased with the shareholder's approval.

Avails Short for immediate availabilities of crude oil, product or tankers awaiting charter at a given time. It is also a volume of refined petroleum products available for purchase on the spot market.

Aval A bank guarantee for debt that has been purchased by a forfaiter.

Average Freight Rate Assessment See AFRA.

Average Life The average time which the principal amount on a loan remains outstanding. The average life on a bullet bond is equal to its maturity, whereas on a bond with a Sinking Fund feature, the average life will be shorter.

Average Rate A figure, calculated from the rates of a series of deals, that indicates the price level required to create a zero profit and loss on closing out an existing position.

Average Rate Option (ARO) An option whose settlement value is based on the difference between the strike and the average of the spot rates over the life of the option. The averaging can be agreed to be taken at any point in the life of the option and readings can be at any specified interval and frequency. Also known as an Asian option.

Aviation Turbine Kerosene Medium light fuel burned in jet and turbo-prop aircraft engines. Also called jet fuel or jet kerosene.

Avoirdupois A weighing system where one ounce avoirdupois equals 28 grammes. There are 16 ounces avoirdupois to the pound (weight). See Troy Ounces.

B Shares See Ordinary Share.

B/S Buy after sell limit order. Two orders treated as one, the first order being to sell. If done, the buy order becomes valid. See S/B.

Back Office A department of a bank or a firm operating in financial markets that processes deals executed and handles delivery, settlement and regulatory procedures. See Front Office, Middle Office.

Back to Back Arrangement where a trader buys a cargo knowing that he has a specific buyer for that cargo. The trader, in effect, acts as a middle man.

Back to Back Loans Arrangement whereby a loan in the currency of one country is set against a loan in another nation's currency. It can be used to avoid or overcome exchange risks and controls. Also known as parallel loans.

Back-Up Facility Typically a bank line of credit used to provide back-up liquidity should an issuer be unable to roll the outstanding commercial paper. This back-up will be typically a standard line agreement or a Swing Line.

Backing and Filling Numerous small rises and falls in a market which is usually speculative but which shows no major overall change in price levels.

Backpricing Price setting method in the metal market whereby a consumer with a long term contract has the option of fixing the price for a proportion of his contract on the valid London Metal Exchange settlement price. There are two types: known, where the LME settlement price is established at the close of the second morning ring and is accepted as the cash market price for the next 24 hours; and unknown, where the customer books metal at the next close of the second morning ring without knowing what that price will be.

Backwardation The relation between a spot price and a futures market where the price for the futures is lower than the spot price. Opposite to Contango.

BAF Bunker Adjustment Factor. A surcharge imposed by shipping conferences to cover bunker fuel price fluctuations.

Bagasse Residue from crushing sugar cane.

Baht The Thai gold bullion bar weighing 0.47 ounces or 15.4 grammes.

Baker Plan Outlined at the 1985 Seoul meeting of the International Monetary Fund by U.S. Treasury Secretary James Baker. The plan proposed that commercial banks lend a further 20 billion dollars over 1986-88 to the 15 largest debtor countries. Multilateral lending by official financial institutions would increase by 50 percent above 1985 levels to nine billion in the same period with a major part played by the World Bank. The 2.7 billion dollar IMF Trust Fund would be used as new borrowing facilities for the poorest sub-Saharan African nations with an annual income per head of less than 500 dollars.

Balance of Payments Record of one country's net transactions with the rest of the world over a given period, including trade, services, capital movements and unilateral transfers.

Balance of Trade Monetary record of a country's net imports and exports of physical merchandise.

Balance Sheet A summary of the assets and liabilities of a company presented by that company at a given date, often at the end of the company's financial year. It is not an exact statement of the financial position but reflects this as fairly and accurately as possible.

Balanced Budget The situation in a government's budget where its expenditure matches revenue. Also known as a neutral budget.

Balanced Fund A type of investment fund where the main objective is to preserve capital, therefore investing in bonds, preferred and ordinary shares. See Closed End Company, Mutual Fund.

Ballast Bonus Lump sum paid to cover a voyage in ballast, i.e. without a cargo.

Balloon Loan   A loan which consists of regular monthly payments with one large (balloon) payment at maturity. Most of these loans have a term of between 3 and 5 years.

Balloon Payment   A large final payment.

Baltic Exchange   London freight market engaged in matching cargoes to ships and vice versa and covering both seaborne and air freight. Deals with dry cargo. Also deals in second hand ship sales. Tanker brokerage is often done by the same firms, although it is a telephone/telex market.

Baltic Futures Exchange   Formed by bringing together all London futures markets which were physically situated on the Baltic Exchange, the traditional centre for dry cargo shipping. It includes the Baltic International Freight Futures Exchange (BIFFEX), the Soybean Meal Futures Association (SOMFA), the London Meat Futures Exchange (LMFE), the London Potato Futures Association (LPFA) and the London Grain Futures Market (LGFM). Now attached to the London Commodity Exchange. See LCE.

Bands   In the U.K., the maturity bands in which the Bank of England is willing to purchase eligible bills in the money market. The maturity bands of the bills being offered are defined in terms of the remaining and not the original maturity of the bills. They comprise: Band 1 - 1-14 days, Band 2 - 15-33 days, Band 3 - 34-63 days, Band 4 - 64-91 days.

Bank Bill   A bill of exchange issued or accepted by a bank. It is thus more acceptable than a normal trade bill of exchange as the risk is less while the discount is also smaller. See Bills of Exchange.

Bank for International Settlements   The BIS is an international financial institution based in Basle, Switzerland. Its objectives are to promote the cooperation of central banks, to provide supplementary facilities for international financial operations and to act as agent with regard to international financial settlements.

Its functions include:
- acting as a principal forum for regular meetings of central bank governors of the Group of 10 nations; for periodic meetings of central bank experts on matters relating to gold and foreign exchange markets, payment and settlement systems.
- acting as a permanent secretariat for the Basle Committee on Banking Supervision.
- agent for the private ECU clearing and settlement system.
- acting as a banker to central banks by accepting deposits in gold or currencies and making advances.

The BIS was established in 1930 and its balance sheet is reported in gold francs.

Bank Limit   Commercial banks often impose limits on how much of a debt portfolio can comprise securities of one particular borrower as a means of good asset and risk management.

Bank of England   The central bank of the U.K. located in London, originally founded in 1694. The Bank was nationalised under the Bank of England act in 1946 and is legally under the control of the U.K. government. There is no official schedule for policy meetings. Colloquially known as the Old Lady of Threadneedle Street.

Bank of Japan   The central bank of Japan, known colloquially as the Nihombashi Cavalry as it is headquartered near the Nihombashi Bridge in Tokyo. Not to be confused with the Bank of Tokyo, which is a major commercial foreign trade bank.

Bank Release   Document issued by a bank after being paid on a bill of exchange thus allowing the purchaser of the goods to take delivery.

Bank Return   Weekly or monthly statement issued by a central bank showing its financial position in summary form.

Bankers Acceptance   See BAs.

Banking Day   A day when commercial banks in any city are open for business.

Banknotes   Central banks are responsible for the issuing of banknotes and oversee design and printing. This also applies to coinage. The bank withdraws notes and coinage when they are being replaced or, simply, worn.

BANs   See Bond Anticipation Notes.

Bar Chart   A chart that collects and represents price information on a vertical bar. The top of the bar is the highest price and the bottom of the bar the lowest. A dash on the left hand side of the bar denotes the open price and a dash on the right hand side the close price.

Bare Boat Charter   A charter where the charterer provides the crew. Also known as demise charter.

Bareme   See Caisse de Stabilisation.

Barge   Non self-propelling vessel used as a base for drilling equipment, transporting cranes, support facilities and accommodation modules to lay underwater pipelines or to transport crude oil or its products over short distances such as inland waterways.

Barley   Barley follows corn to be the world's second most important feedgrain based on production and trade - albeit by a wide margin. It can grow in sub-arctic areas through to sub-tropical regions and has a greater tolerance to cold conditions because it has the shortest growing season among major cereals. Over half the production is used in livestock feed. It is a major component in hog feeding and also increasingly important in cattle feeding. It is used for alcoholic beverages and in food, such as soups, and milled into flour. Major barley producers are the Commonwealth of Independent States, Canada, the U.S. and France.

Barley Malting Malt is made when the grain's starch content has been converted to sugar through sprouting or growing. It is used in the brewing and distilling industry. A different type of barley is used for malting in the U.S. - where the need is for light, pale beer - from that in parts of Europe, notably Germany and the U.K., which have a demand for dark beer.

Barrels Volume measurement of liquid in the petroleum industry. Equal to 42 U.S. gallons or 35 Imperial gallons or about 0.136 tonnes depending on specific gravity which can range from 7.1 to 7.8 barrels per tonne.

Barrels Per Day Recognised world-wide as bpd. Measures the flow of crude oil production from a field or producing company or nation. May also measure the throughput of crude at a refinery or its capacity or output of refined petroleum products.

Barrier Option An option which is activated or de-activated once the underlying reaches a set level, known as the barrier. Can be categorised into trigger options: Down and In, Up and In; and knockout options: Down and Out, Up and out.

BAs The bankers acceptance, sometimes known as a Time Draft, is an order to pay a specified amount of money to the person who has accepted a trade bill at a specified date in the future. BAs are drawn on, and accepted by, a bank which assumes the responsibility to make payment on the draft on the day it matures. They are bearer form short term non-interest bearing notes sold at a discount, redeemed by accepting banks for full face value at maturity. See Bills of Exchange.

Base Currency The currency which forms the base of the quotation, i.e. the denominator expressed as a unit of one (or sometimes 100). For example, the base currency in the U.S. dollar/German mark quotation is the U.S. dollar whereas the base currency in the German mark/Swiss franc quotation is the German mark. See Quoted Currency.

Base Date Economic indicators have a base date and usually a starting number of 100. For instance, a base date for a relatively new index could be shown as 100 equals January 1, 1994.

Base Metals Major industrial non-ferrous metals other than precious metals and minor metals. See Copper, Lead, Tin, Zinc, Aluminium, Nickel.

Base Rate - U.K. The rate set by the U.K. clearing banks and used as a reference rate for customer loans.

Base Relative Spread This analysis charts the relative performance of the price of one instrument against another. The value given for the analysis differs depending on the interval chosen.

Basic Balance of Payments Current Account plus long term Capital Account.

Basic Petrochemical Basic raw material made from crude oil by steam cracking or reforming, e.g. ethylene, benzene.

Basis The difference between the cash price of a financial instrument or commodity and the price of the corresponding futures contract. See Basis Risk.

Basis Book A book of tables which converts bond yields for given maturities and coupons to the equivalent dollar price.

Basis Contract Forward contract with a guaranteed basis. A farmer, for example, can establish a basis contract with his country elevator during July by agreeing to deliver a set amount of bushels of his product for a period during September. He agrees that the price he receives will equal the price of the November futures contract on the day of delivery plus or minus a specific basis.

Basis Delivery Grade Grade of a commodity used as the standard for a futures and options contract.

Basis Point Unit of measure (one hundredth of a percentage point, i.e. 0.01%) used to express movements in interest rates or bond yields.

Basis Point Value The measure of a change in the price of a bond compared with a given change in interest rates. Quoted in U.S. cents. A bond with a basis point value of 0.04 would indicate the bond price will change by 4 cents per 1 basis point shift (0.01 percent) in the yield curve. Also known as dollar duration. See Modified Duration.

Basis Risk The risk that the price of the futures contract will vary from the price of the underlying cash instrument as expiry approaches. See Convergence.

Basis Swap An interest rate swap where both counterparties exchange floating interest rates but based on a different index, for example six month LIBOR versus three month LIBOR.

Basis Trading See Cash and Carry Trade.

Basket Option An option granting the holder the right to buy or sell more than two currencies against a base currency at preselected strike prices.

Batching Sequence The order in which product shipments are sent through a pipeline.

Bauxite / Alumina Bauxite is the ore from which Aluminium is produced. Alumina is the semi-finished product. Major bauxite producers include Australia, Brazil, China, the Commonwealth of Independent States, Greece, Guinea, Hungary, India, Jamaica, Surinam and former Yugoslavia. Major alumina refiners include Australia, China, the Commonwealth of Independent States, Jamaica and the U.S.

BBA See British Bankers' Association.

BBAIRS Terms Recommended terms and conditions applicable to interest rate and currency swaps, as determined by the British Bankers' Association.

BCI Milan stock market index run by Banca Commerciale Italiana Spa, a commercial bank. BCI general index covers all 318 shares in Milan. Updated once a day at the end of the session's trading. BCI-30, its associated index, covers 30 leading shares based both on capitalisation and market turnover. Updated every 10 seconds. These are the two most important stock market indices on Milan.

Bear A market player who believes prices will fall and would therefore sell a financial instrument with a view to repurchasing it at a lower price. Opposite to a Bull.

Bear Covering See Shortcovering.

Bear Market Market in which prices are declining or are expected to decline. Opposite to Bull Market.

Bear Spread An option strategy combining the purchase and sale of two puts (bear put spread) or two calls (bear call spread) with different strikes on the same underlying.

Bearer Form A security for which ownership is evidenced by possession of a physical certificate. Coupons are detached and presented for interest payments, with no other record of ownership being kept. See Registered Form.

Bearer Shares Shares owned by the holder of the certificate with no specifically named owner listed. Dividends are claimed by clipping coupons from the certificate and sending them to a paying agent. Bearer bonds are similar.

Bearish Holding a belief that prices will fall. A bearish sentiment in the market will therefore push prices lower. Opposite to Bullish.

Bed Layer of sediments or sedimentary rock of considerable thickness and uniform composition and texture.

Bed and Breakfast Deal Involves selling a share on a day shortly before the end of the tax year and buying it back again the following morning. This can allow shareholders to register a capital loss or profit (where valid) for tax purposes but also permits the repurchasing of shares if a rise is expected.

Beef Beef production usually accounts for at least 30 percent of annual U.S. farm income. Great Plains ranchers maintain large brood herds of feeder cattle. Calves are raised to 350/500 pounds or yearlings to 500/800 pounds, then sold to feedlots for finishing (fattening), on concentrated rations, to a market or slaughter weight of about 1,100 pounds. Feeding usually takes three to six months. Leading feedlot states are Texas, Oklahoma, Nebraska and Kansas. The Chicago Mercantile Exchange (CME) lists futures and options on live and feeder cattle. Contracts are used for normal pricing and hedging purposes. CME feeder cattle deliveries are settled in cash. Live cattle deliveries are made at five terminal markets. Cattle production is cyclical with steers taking about 18/24 months from birth to slaughter. Demand factors include competition from poultry, exports, retailer featuring and season.

Beet Pulp The remainder of the sugar beet root after the sugar has been extracted during processing. Highly palatable as an Animal Feed Ingredient. Chief value is its energy content which is easily digested by ruminants.

Beige Book See Tan Book.

BEL 20 Index This stock index for the Brussels bourse is based on 20 shares listed on the forward market and represents 72 percent of total market capitalisation and 78 percent of turnover on the Computer Assisted Trading System (CATS). Companies are ranked by market capitalisation and turnover. Derivatives on this price index are listed on the Belgian Futures and Options Exchange (BELFOX).

BELFOX The Belgian Futures and Options Exchange based in Brussels. Trading began in December 1991. Contracts traded include the Notional Government Bond future, the Three Month BIBOR Interest Rate future and the BEL 20 Index future and option. BIBOR is the Belgian Interbank Offered Rate. See LIBOR / LIBID / LIMEAN.

Belgian Futures and Options Exchange See BELFOX.

Belgian State and the Road Fund Both issue bonds which are fully guaranteed by the central government, known as State Bonds (BGBs) and Road Fund Bonds. A new type of fungible bond was issued in 1989 by the state, called OLOs. Short term instruments are also issued in the form of Treasury certificates.

Belgium - Key Interest Rates The rates to watch are:

Central rate - sets the tone for money market rates

End of day (overdraft) rate - sets the ceiling for money market rates

Emergency lending (special overdraft) rate - highest official rate

Discount rate - lowest official lending rate

Tender rate - usually the same as the central rate

Special deposit rate - sets the floor for money market rates

The key rate is the central rate at which the 15 primary dealers in government debt can borrow (or deposit) funds overnight in limited amounts via the central bank. It is usually equal to the tender rate and is thus similar to the Bundesbank's repo rate, but for a shorter maturity.

The end of day, or overdraft, rate is an overnight lending rate for all financial institutions established in the Belgo-Luxembourg Economic Union (BLEU) and is also subject to a volume limit set by so-called current account credit lines. It is equal to the central rate plus a margin. Both rates usually change at the same time. Under normal circumstances the end of day rate sets the ceiling for money market rates, though the emergency lending rate is the highest official rate.

The emergency lending, or special overdraft, rate is an overnight rate charged on the part of the overdraft exceeding the credit line, for all financial institutions established in the BLEU, with no volume limit provided that, as for other lending facilities, there is sufficient collateral. It is always higher than the end of day rate, sometimes by a very large margin. It is the Bank's highest rate, but is not commonly used.

The discount rate is a preferential rate at which financial institutions established in the BLEU can refinance commercial bills at the Rediscount and Guarantee Institute (RGI), which is then refinanced by the central bank. It is the lowest official lending rate.

The emergency lending and discount rates are not operational money market rates and thus are not used to steer money market rates. In practice, the two rates are generally not changed unilaterally, but in concert with German and/or Dutch rates.

The tender rate, at which the bank supplies structural liquidity to financial institutions established in the BLEU through seven day advances or repos, by way of an auction, is usually in line with the central rate. A change in the central rate is thus normally followed by a change in the tender rate. Changes in the rates may coincide when they fall on the day of an auction (currently Monday).

The deposit and the special deposit rates are the rates financial institutions established in the BLEU receive for placing excess funds overnight at the Rediscount and Guarantee Institute (RGI). The special deposit rate is the lowest rate paid on deposits. It sets the floor for call money and is currently the central rate minus 2.0 percentage points.

There are various ways in which the central bank can lend to the banking system to ease a money market liquidity shortage.

When central bank lending takes the form of advances (including overdrafts) charged at the central, end of day, emergency lending or tender rates, it requires collateral. This must consist of securities denominated in Belgian or Luxembourg francs which are traded on the stock exchange or on the money and capital markets. They must be issued or guaranteed by the Belgian or Luxembourg governments, or issued by regional or local Belgian or Luxembourg public authorities, or by international financial institutions of which Belgium or Luxembourg are members. Examples are Treasury certificates and linear bonds (OLOs).

The National Bank of Belgium sets interest rate policy. The central bank has statutory independence from the government. The bank's policy making body - the Regency Council, or Conseil de Régence - has responsibility for setting interest rates. The council includes the governor, the bank's directors and 10 other members, of which five must belong to Belgium's economic federations representing employers and unions. In practice, most interest rate changes are decided by the board of directors.

However, the government's policy of shadowing the German mark within the exchange rate mechanism of the European Monetary System has left the National Bank with little practical independence.

Bells and Whistles Additional features of a securities issue designed to attract investors and/or reduce issuer costs.

Below the Line An Exceptional Item recorded separately in a company's profit and loss account. It does not have to directly affect the balance sheet, i.e. the earnings figure. See Extraordinary Item, Financial Reporting Standard 3.

Benchmark Issue A security that is usually the most recently issued of good size, the terms of which set standards for the market. The benchmark issue is therefore the most liquid and has the highest turnover.

Benchmark Issue - Japan   The benchmark issue in the Japanese government debt market can be any one of the 10 year bond issues but it is not necessarily the current issue. It can keep this status for a year or even longer. The benchmark issue dominates secondary market trading volumes and liquidity.

Beneficial Owner   The investor who owns securities held in Street Name or Nominee Account. The beneficial owner has the same rights as an investor whose stock is in customer name, i.e. the holder of record. See Nominee Account.

Benzene   Key petroleum derived raw material used in the chemical industry.

Berne Union   Full title is the International Union of Credit and Investment Insurers. Seeks international acceptance of sound principles in export credit insurance, in credit terms for international trade and in foreign investment insurance. Members are 40 organisations in 32 countries.

Beta Factor   A factor measuring the share volatility relative to the overall market as measured by various stock market indices. When the factor is less than one, then a share is considered less volatile than the overall market. A factor greater than one indicates a share is more volatile.

BFI-Baltic Freight Index   Based on a specified number of dry cargo voyages, each weighted according to its importance in the market and historical data. This is the basis for the Baltic International Freight Futures Exchange (BIFFEX) contract.

BFIs   Bank Financial Intermediaries. The largest group of financial intermediaries, the other main group being NBFIs, Non-Bank Financial Intermediaries, which includes such institutions as building societies and insurance companies. The distinctions between these groups are increasingly becoming less obvious and are leading to the universal banking system.

BGBs - Belgium   Belgian government bonds issued by the Belgian state. These classical bonds are referred to by a number prefixed with a "2". BGBs have an average maturity of seven to eight years and are either bullet or more recently callable. Another kind of classical bond was introduced by the state in 1990 called Philippe Bonds. However, since 1989, OLOs have become the most liquid bond issue of the Belgian state.

BIBO Vessel   Bulk in, Bagged out. For example, a ship loaded with bulk white sugar which is then bagged en route so that the cargo can be landed in bags. Useful where ports do not have unloading facilities for bulk cargo or where the buyer is purchasing only a small amount.

Bid   A market maker's price to buy a commodity, security, currency or any financial instrument. A two-way price comprises the bid and ask/offer. The difference between the two quotations is known as the Spread.

Bid Market   A market in which there is more interest from buyers than sellers. Opposite to Offered Market.

Big Bang   Popular term for the change in U.K. Stock Exchange rules and practices throughout 1986, taking full effect on October 27 1986. Banks and insurance companies were allowed to own stock exchange subsidiaries, new electronic dealing systems were established, fixed commissions were eliminated and the hitherto strict segregation was ended between brokers (retail) and jobbers (wholesale). The merging of brokers and jobbers became known as Dual Capacity.

Big Board   Colloquial name for the New York Stock Exchange.

Big Figure   The stem of a rate. When giving a quotation, dealers may only refer to the points (in foreign exchange) or to fractions (in money markets). In the U.S., the big figure is known as the Handle.

Big Four   The four major Japanese securities houses who dominate the equities and bond trading in Japan. They are Daiwa Securities Ltd, Nikko Securities Ltd, Nomura Securities Ltd and Yamaichi Securities Ltd.

Bill Broker   See Discount House - U.K.

Bill of Lading   Describes for foreign trade purposes details of the goods being sent. A marine bill of lading can give the holder the right of possession to goods and acts as a receipt for them. In the U.S. and U.K., it is a negotiable instrument and a document of title.

Bill Pass   An individual purchase of Treasury bills by the Federal Reserve to provide reserves to the banking system on a permanent basis. See Outright Purchases.

Bills of Exchange   Very old financial instruments originally used to finance international trade. A bill of exchange is an order to pay a specified amount of money to the holder of the bill either at a set future date (a Time Draft) or on presentation of the bill (a Sight Draft). Also known as Eligible Bills, Commercial Bills, trade bills and BAs.

Binary Option   An option which pays out a fixed amount if the underlying reaches the strike level either at expiry or at any time during the life of the option. Also called all or nothing option, digital option, one-touch option.

Binomial Model An option pricing formula suggested by Cox, Ross, Rubinstein and Sharpe and used primarily in the calculation of American style options.

BIS See Bank for International Settlements.

Black & Scholes Model A widely used option pricing formula created by Fischer Black and Myron Scholes in 1973 for European style options.

Black Gold Bismuth appears in some gold, turning it black.

Black Sea Economic Cooperation Organisation See BSECO.

Blair House Crucial bilateral deal announced in 1992 between the U.S. and the European Community at Blair House, Washington, on oilseeds and farm trade subsidies which helped overcome a stumbling block in the Uruguay Round world trade talks.

Blister Copper Crude copper produced after the smelting process and too impure for direct industrial use except for some chemical purposes. Used in the electrolytic refining process for copper.

Block Trading Transacting large share lots, usually in the U.S., in excess of 10,000 shares among institutional buyers or sellers.

Blocked Accounts Bank accounts where withdrawals cannot be freely made, e.g. accounts frozen due to political or legal disputes.

Blowout Occurs when gas, oil or salt water escapes from a well, usually by accident, when the release of pressure in the reservoir rock is not controlled by the containment systems or the failure of those systems during drilling or production.

Blowout Preventor Hydraulically operated safety valve which automatically closes a well if the drill bit hits high pressure hydrocarbons.

Blue Book Data published annually by the Central Statistical Office consisting of a digest of U.K. national income and expenditure statistics.

Blue Chip Stock A generic term for shares of major companies with sound earnings and dividend records and above average share performance. In current parlance the description remains valid even when a long established blue chip company is suffering adversely. Blue chip stocks are also known as Income Stock.

Blue List Daily list published by Standard & Poor's, giving municipal bond prices.

Blue Sky Laws Laws passed by various U.S. states to protect the public against securities frauds. New issue offerings have to be registered and full financial details provided. The phrase apparently comes from a member of the judiciary who said that one particular share offer had about as much value as a patch of blue sky.

BOBLs See Bundesobligationen - Germany.

Bollinger Bands Used in technical analysis. Bollinger bands are lines plotted above and below the moving average of the closing prices. These bands narrow and widen in line with volatility - narrow in calm markets and widen in volatile markets. The narrowing of the bands often indicates the start of a new trend, which is confirmed when prices break and close out of the band. A close outside the upper band followed by a close within the band can signify a sell signal. Conversely, a close outside the lower band followed by a close within the band can represent a buy signal. Bollinger Bands may be used with any price chart but are most commonly used with the bar chart.

Bond A fixed interest security under which the issuer contracts to repay the lender a fixed principal amount at a stated date in the future and a series of interest payments either semi-annually or annually. This type of bond is called a bullet or straight bond. See Zero Coupon Bond, Call Feature, Put Feature, Sinking Fund, Floating Rate Bond.

Bond Anticipation Notes (BANs) Short term municipal securities (municipal notes). Used to even out irregular cashflows into the treasuries of the issuer. BANs are issued in anticipation of the borrower selling long term bonds. See Municipal Notes.

Bond Equivalent Yield The calculation which converts the yield of a money market instrument such as a Treasury bill into the equivalent yield of a Treasury bond.

Bond Indenture The complete contract specifying all the terms and conditions of a bond issue.

Bond Salesman Responsible for sales of bonds to investors such as financial institutions or the general public.

Bond Trader Trades a book of bonds on behalf of an institution, or occasionally for his own account. Also makes prices to customers via bond salesmen.

Bond Washing Selling a security cum interest and buying it back after the coupon is paid so as to convert the interest income into a capital gain. This is worthwhile only where lower tax rates apply to capital gains.

Bonus Issue See Capitalisation Issue.

Book Trader's record of purchases and sales in one or more financial instruments. See Unmatched Book, Matched Book.

Book Building   A method of selling international equities when an investment firm seeks bids for a new issue at indicative prices. When the book is complete it prices and sells the lot in a single day. Has also been used in Privatisation issues.

Book Entry   Securities registered by the issuer usually in computerised form and for which there are no physical issues. This method reduces paperwork expenses and simplifies transfer of ownership.

   EUROCLEAR and CEDEL, originally set up as clearing systems for Eurobonds, currently clear government bonds of several European countries in book entry form.

Book Price   The value at which the assets were originally entered in the books of the company, i.e. on the balance sheet.

Book Value   Book value is normally defined as cost less aggregated depreciation and is not normally a valuation.

Borrower's Option   An option to buy an FRA on a predetermined date in the future. Opposite to Lender's Option. Also known as Interest Rate Guarantee (IRG).

Borrowing   Used mainly in the London Metal Exchange to refer to the purchase of a nearby delivery date and simultaneous sale of a forward date.

Borrowing Requirement   Net amount of money needed by a government to finance budget deficits and maturing debt.

BOT - Italy   Buoni Ordinari del Tesoro are Italian Treasury bills with maturities of three, six and 12 months, issued at a discount. These issues are the most popular investment instrument among Italian retail investors. They tend to hold the paper until maturity, thus no secondary market exists.

Bottom Fishing   Jargon. Buying of a company's shares by an investor who believes they are not likely to fall much further. Also when a company buys up loss-making competitors or purchases their assets.

Bottom Line   The final or real cost or result. The term derives from companies' profit and loss accounts in which the bottom line shows the extent of the profit or loss after all income and expenses have been accounted for.

Bottom Reversal   An expression used in technical analysis that would be the setting of a new low in a downtrend followed by a higher close than the previous day's closing rate (sometimes the previous two days).

Bottomry Bond   A ship's master can borrow on the security of the ship and cargo via a bottomry bond if funds are needed urgently to complete a voyage. Communication with the owner must not be available and neither must any other means of raising money.

Bought Deal   Commitment from an underwriter or lead manager to purchase the whole issue of a security for resale to the secondary market. This method transfers the risk of being unable to sell a whole issue at the offering price from the issuer to the underwriter.

BPD   See Barrels Per Day.

BPV   See Basis Point Value.

Brady Bonds   In 1989, U.S. Treasury Secretary Nicholas Brady proposed the concept of bonds backed by the U.S. Treasury but with actual repayments being made by a sovereign lesser developed country. If a nation is unable to maintain its current payment schedule then it can reschedule repayments by exchanging its sovereign or bank debt for a Brady bond. This bond is usually guaranteed by U.S. Treasury Zero Coupon bonds which the nation purchases to back the bonds which are in default. See U.S. STRIPS.

Brady Plan   In 1989 U.S. Treasury Secretary Nicholas Brady proposed to the Bretton Woods Committee a plan to use World Bank and International Monetary Fund resources to help reduce the debt burden of Third World nations. Pools of money from existing Bank and IMF resources could be used to reduce debt and to guarantee interest payments of debtors. These pools could be used to collateralise or back bonds issued in exchange for commercial bank debt. The exchange would take place at a significant discount, thus reducing the amount of outstanding debt. Both the institutions could also offer new, additional financial support to collateralise a portion of interest payments for debt or debt service reduction transactions. See Brady Bonds.

Bran   Mostly fibrous material. The outer covering of a kernel. Also called the hull.

Break Forward Option   See Risk Reversal.

Breakeven Point   The level at which an existing position will produce neither a loss nor a gain.

Breakout   Occurs when a price climbs above a resistance level (usually its previous high) or falls below a support level (usually its previous low). Usually breakouts occur from trendlines of formations.

Brent   The Brent System consists of 14 North Sea oil fields linked to the Brent system pipeline which pumps the oil ashore to the Shetland Islands' Sullom Voe oil terminal.

The Brent Field is but one, albeit the largest, in the system and is not to be confused with the pipeline or the whole complex of fields.

At Sullom Voe, Brent system crude is blended with oil from the Ninian pipeline system (four fields - the largest being the Ninian) to create Brent blend crude, the international benchmark blend.

Bretton Woods   An agreement, signed by 44 nations in 1944 at Bretton Woods, New Hampshire, USA, to effect a post-war international monetary system. From this came the creation of the International Monetary Fund and the World Bank. The system was based on fixed exchange rates combined with temporary financing facilities to overcome crises. In 1971 the dollar ceased to be convertible into gold at the then 35 dollars per ounce official price and that element of the Bretton Woods system was superseded by an era of floating currencies.

Bridging   Bridging, or a bridging loan, is made for the short term as an interim aid while awaiting intermediate or long term financing.

Briquette   Sometimes called bricks. Usually of a primary metal recovered in powder form and then made into a briquette. Most common form is of nickel.

British Bankers' Association   Formed in 1919 with membership open to U.K. banks in the U.K. and the Commonwealth. Foreign banks in London were allowed as members in 1972 when U.K. accepting houses also joined. Its work is varied ranging from the development of business and banking law at the European Community level, domestic legislation and regulation, to the fight against fraud and influencing public and political perceptions. It has instituted a code of banking practice.

British Thermal Unit (BTU)   Heat needed to raise one pound of air-free water from 60 degrees Fahrenheit to 61 degrees at a constant pressure of one atmosphere. International unit of heating measure. Standard abbreviation is BTU.

Broadening   A term used in technical analysis. A formation with the appearance of a horizontal triangle with widening trendlines so that the triangle base gets wider. Peaks and troughs get successively higher and lower, showing a market that has lost its way. A significant bear signal is discerned when the fall from the third peak thrusts past the bottom of the second trough. See Peaks / Troughs.

Broken Date   Any trading date which falls outside the standard periods traded in the forward markets. Also known as odd date.

Broker   An individual or company that matches bids and offers in a market and charges a commission or brokerage fee.

Broker-Dealer   Firms involved in both trading and advising clients on equities transactions. Came about as a result of Big Bang's abolition of single capacity in favour of Dual Capacity. See Big Bang.

Brokerage   The commission or fee charged by a broker. In the U.S., it is commonly used to refer to a brokerage firm.

Brokerage House   The broker acting as agent for the buying and selling of listed securities on a stock exchange between the investor and the specialists. Specialists and floor brokers do not trade directly with the public. A commission or Markup/Markdown is charged per transaction.

BSECO   Black Sea Economic Cooperation Organisation. Formed in 1992 to encourage regional trade and cooperation in transport and infrastructure. Members are Albania, Armenia, Azerbaijan, Bulgaria, Georgia, Greece, Moldova, Romania, Russia, Turkey and Ukraine.

BTAN - France   Bons à Taux Annuel Normalisé are French coupon bearing, fixed rate Treasury bills with two and five year maturities. The benchmark is always the most recently issued of the two periods.

BTF - France   Bons à Taux Fixe et intérêts précomptés are French discount Treasury bills with maturities of 13, 26 and 52 weeks. Occasionally four and seven week BTFs are issued outside the calendar and are similar to the U.S. cash management bills.

BTN - France   French Treasury bills are in general called BTNs (Bons du Trésor Négociables) and cover maturities from 13 weeks to five years. Split into two categories: BTFs and BTANs. Issued initially in 1986, both categories are key instruments for short term government debt.

BTP - Italy   Buoni del Tesoro Poliennali are Italian fixed rate Treasury bonds with varying maturities of five and 10 years and now issuing 30 years. Seven year bonds were also issued until July 1992. Most of the liquidity is concentrated in the 10 year maturity. Coupons are paid semi-annually. The share of BTPs in the total government debt market has increased substantially in the last few years by both domestic and foreign investors. This has been greatly helped by the launch of the BTP futures contract on London's LIFFE and Rome's MIF.

BTU   See British Thermal Unit.

Buba See Bundesbank.

Bucket Shop Organisation dealing in stocks or commodities which operates on very low overheads and aims to undercut conventional firms.

Budget Official or governmental statement of actual or projected revenue and expenditure. Such a statement is usually annual and delivered before a country's parliament. Technically any measures therein are usually proposals and subject to parliamentary approval.

Budget Committees U.S. Congressional committees in the House of Representatives and the Senate which are responsible for formulating overall budget resolutions.

Buffer Stock Stock of commodities held by an international organisation to stabilise prices and supplies by buying and selling, using the resources of the stockpile.

Buffer Stock Financing Facility Facility which can be used by member nations of the International Monetary Fund which have balance of payments problems. Nations can draw up to 50 percent of their IMF quota to finance contributions to international buffer stock arrangements.

Building Societies The original purpose of a building society was to finance long term durable consumer expenditure, as in house purchases, and to run retail savings accounts. Since the Building Societies Act of 1986, which formalised the increased competition between banks and building societies, the distinctions between the two have become increasingly blurred. Some building societies now offer current accounts, unit trusts, personal pensions and raise funds through the wholesale money markets.

Bulis Short term money market instruments with a minimum denomination of 500,000 marks. Introduced by the Bundesbank in 1993 as an additional instrument of monetary policy to absorb excess liquidity, following the relaxation of minimum reserve requirements for bank lending.

Bulk Carrier Vessel carrying cargo, such as grain, that is not in the form of separate packages.

Bull A market player who believes prices will rise and would therefore purchase a financial instrument with a view to selling it at a higher price. Opposite to a Bear.

Bull Market Market in which prices are rising or are expected to rise. Opposite to Bear Market.

Bull Market Note A floating rate note which is also known as a reverse yield curve note. Traditional floating rate notes have their coupons adjusted higher or lower, following the direction of interest rates. In contrast, this variety pays a higher coupon when rates fall and a lower coupon when rates rise.

Bull Spread An option strategy combining the purchase and sale of two puts (bull put spread) or two calls (bull call spread) with different strikes on the same underlying.

Bulldog Bond A bond issued in the U.K. by a foreign borrower and denominated in sterling.

Bullet Bond A bond issue which has no early redemption facility and is therefore redeemed fully at maturity. Also known as a straight bond.

Bullion Precious metal in non-coin form such as ingots, bars or wafers.

Bullish Holding a belief that prices will rise. A bullish sentiment in the market will therefore push prices higher. Opposite to Bearish.

Bund (Federal Government) Issuer of German government debt, considered to be part of the second tier of government bond markets in size alongside the U.K., France and Italy, and following the U.S. and Japan.

Bundesbahn The German Federal Railway issues government bonds (Bunds), known as government agency bonds (Agencies) which are backed by the full faith and credit of the German government.

Bundesbank The German central bank based in Frankfurt. Its credit policies are set by its central bank council, which normally meets every second Thursday and consists of board members (directorate) and the heads of its regional arms (landeszentralbanken) which run its operations in Germany's 11 federal states. See Germany - Key Interest Rates.

Bundeskassenobligationen (Kassen) - Germany German federal government notes with maturities between two and six years, also known as Kassen. In 1988 the Kassen were effectively replaced by Schätze and there has been no new issuance for many years.

Bundesobligationen (BOBLs) - Germany Fixed coupon bullet five year special federal government notes issued in tap form, also known as BOBLs. Foreigners are now authorised to invest in these issues which represent 25 percent of outstanding German federal government debt.

Bundespost The German Federal Mail issues government bonds (Bunds) known as government agency bonds (Agencies) which are backed by the full faith and credit of the German government.

Bundesrat Upper house of the German parliament.

Bundesschatzbriefe - Germany German savings bonds. Federal government issues with six to seven year maturities, prohibited to foreigners. Very small and illiquid market.

Bundestag Lower house of the German parliament.

Bunds (Bundesanleihen) - Germany Federal government bonds issued with maturities of up to 30 years (30 year issued beginning 1994). The 10 year bund is, however, the benchmark for German interest rates and is normally issued on a monthly basis.

Bunker Adjustment Factor See BAF.

Bunker C Heavy residual fuel oil used by ships, industry and for large scale heating installations.

Bunker Fuel Any fuel oil or diesel fuel used by ships.

Bunny Bond See Multiplier Bond.

Bushel Measure of volume. In the U.K., it equals eight Imperial gallons or 36.4 litres for corn, fruit, liquids, etc. In the U.S. it equals 35.3 litres. The weight of a bushel varies according to the commodity involved.

Business Risk The risk that the company issuing stock may not produce the sales and earning growth as forecast. In this case, the price of the share will remain depressed. Business risk affects both new and old businesses.

Busted Convertible A convertible issue of little value because the underlying stock has fallen sharply and below the conversion price.

Butane A type of LPG (liquefied petroleum gas).

Butterfly Spread An option strategy involving the simultaneous sale of an At the Money straddle and purchase of an Out of the Money strangle. Potential gains will be seen if the underlying remains stable and at the same time the risk is limited should the underlying move dramatically.

Buy & Hold A strategy of buying high quality stocks with a view to holding them long term. The success of this strategy depends on the long term trend of the stock market, the characteristics of the share and dividend reinvestment plan.

Buy Back Term for a company buying back its own shares with the amount usually defined as a percentage of the shares held by each shareholder. Also used to describe a Repurchase Agreement (repo).

Buyback Price Purchase price an oil company pays to a country for oil which the company produces but which belongs to that country.

Buying the Basis See Cash and Carry Trade.

Buyout The purchase of at least a controlling interest in a company's stock to take over its assets and operations.

C and F Cost and freight. Includes both the cost of the goods and freight charges.

Cabinet Stocks A block of preferred shares which are not traded frequently and are traded in round lots of 10, as opposed to round lots of 100. They tend to be highly priced, hence the trading in smaller amounts.

Cable An informal term for the sterling/U.S. dollar spot exchange rate. Historically a cable was sent to London from New York to advise of the dollar rate in New York against the pound.

Cabotage A key issue for trucking organisations in the European Community - the right to ply for trade in other EC countries. The word cabotage also applies to maritime shipping.

CAC 40 Compagnie des Agents de Change (the National Association of French Stockbrokers to which all Agents de Change must belong). This price weighted index for the Paris bourse consists of 40 shares selected for high market capitalisation, trading volume and key sectoral examples. Stocks in the index represent over 56 percent of bourse capitalisation and some 75 percent of transactions. Calculated every 30 seconds. Futures are traded on the Marché à Terme International de France (MATIF exchange) and options on the Marché des Options Négociables de Paris (MONEP exchange). See SBF 120 Index.

CAF Currency adjustment factor. A charge imposed by shipping conferences to cover currency fluctuations.

Cairns Group Formed in 1986 by major agricultural exporting nations to secure reforms in international agricultural trade. The group accounts for about one third of the world's agricultural output. It favours free trade in such goods and has a strong voice in international trade talks. Member nations are Argentina, Australia, Brazil, Canada, Chile, Colombia, Fiji, Hungary, Indonesia, Malaysia, New Zealand, the Philippines, Thailand and Uruguay. Based in Canberra.

Caisse de Stabilisation In some cocoa and coffee growing countries, notably the Ivory Coast, these organisations exert varying degrees of control on the industries, generally with less direct intervention than marketing boards. Agents can be appointed by a caisse to purchase and export the crops, an export price reference system can be used to stabilise the price received by exporters and timing of export sales is set. They also specify a payments system - the bareme - which fixes the producer price and remuneration for each step in the cocoa marketing chain from farm to export.

Calendar Spread   See Horizontal Spread.

Call Feature   Optional right of the issuer to redeem bonds before their stated maturity (early redemption) at a given price (redemption price) on a given date (call date). The holder of a callable bond is normally compensated with a premium for early redemption. See Put Feature.

Call Money   Refers to interest bearing deposits which are repayable on call, i.e. on demand. This covers both domestic money markets and the Euromarket funds. Also known as day to day money or sight money.

Call Option   A contract giving the buyer or the holder the right but not the obligation to buy the underlying at an agreed price within or at a specified time. The seller or writer has the obligation to sell. See Put Option.

Call Protection   The time during which an issuer cannot redeem or call the bond. The bond is therefore protected from being called.

Call Ratio Backspread   An option strategy where more calls are purchased than sold. All options have the same expiry date.

Call Ratio Spread   An option strategy whereby more calls are sold than purchased. All options have the same expiry date.

Callable Bond   See Call Feature.

Callable Capital   See Paid-Up Capital.

Callable Preferred Stock   A type of preferred stock with a call feature. A company may call back the shares when interest rates are lower than the fixed dividend.

Cambiste   The French term for a foreign exchange dealer.

Canada - Key Interest Rates   The rates to watch are:
Overnight rate - sets the tone for money market rates.
Three month Treasury bill rate - operational target for Bank of Canada money market intervention.
Bank rate - Bank of Canada's minimum lending rate which acts as a benchmark for money market rates.
SPRA rate (rate on special sale and repurchase agreements) - sets the ceiling for money market rates in special circumstances.
SRA rate (rate on sale and repurchase agreements) - sets the floor for money market rates in special circumstances.
The Bank of Canada uses the overnight rate to influence yields on three month Treasury bills.

This, in turn, determines the Bank rate which is set 0.25 of a percentage point above the average tender rate on three month Treasury bills. The Bank rate is set on Tuesdays, the same day as Treasury bill auctions, and is the rate at which the Bank of Canada relieves regular money market shortages.

The intervention rate at which the central bank buys or sells three month Treasury bills compared with the previous three month auction average gives an idea of the next move in Bank rate. Bank of Canada watchers are particularly interested in when the central bank conducts operations and where the when issued three month Treasury bill was trading when the intervention took place.

The first time the Bank intervenes in the money market after Tuesday's Treasury bill auction indicates the maximum amount it wishes the Bank rate to change at the following week's setting. Intervention after that is used to reinforce this policy goal.

The Bank can therefore be expected to regularly intervene by buying/selling Treasury bills at a certain level if it bought/sold them there earlier in the week following the auction unless policy considerations or market conditions change significantly.

Intervention before 1000 is unusual and would therefore be taken as a strong statement.

SPRAs are used by the Bank of Canada to relieve temporarily undesired upward pressure on overnight rates. The rate at which the Bank of Canada chooses to purchase securities under special purchase and resale agreements is generally viewed as a ceiling for money market rates.

SRAs are used to offset undesired downward pressure on overnight rates. The rate at which the Bank of Canada chooses to sell securities under sale and repurchase agreements is generally viewed as a floor for money market rates.

The Bank rate is the minimum rate at which the Bank of Canada lends overnight funds to the directly-clearing members of the Canadian Payments Association (CPA) including chartered banks. The Bank rate applies to the pricing of regular purchase and resale agreements with dealer jobbers. Analysis of money market intervention therefore comes down to how it affects the Bank rate, which is set at 0.25 of a percentage point above the average rate at the weekly Treasury bill auction.

The Bank of Canada sets monetary policy. More precisely, it is set by the governor after consultation with other members of the Bank's management committee. At regular weekly meetings, the Bank's management committee decides an appropriate target range for that week's Bank rate.

While the Bank of Canada is one of the most independent central banks, it is still subject to some restraints. For example, there is a statutory requirement for regular, in practice weekly, meetings between the governor and the finance minister. The minister has the authority to direct the governor, though this has never happened.

Canadian Depository for Securities (CDS)   Canadian clearing house established in 1989 to replace the previous system of physical delivery. Canadian Treasury bonds are now settled and registered via the new book entry system called book based system. International trades can also be cleared through EUROCLEAR.

Canadian Savings Bond   CSB. Type of Canadian government bond which is only available to Canadian residents. Since this bond is not transferable, there is no secondary market.

Cancelling Date   The date agreed between owner and charterer on which the vessel must be ready to load at the latest. If the date is not met then the charterer can choose to cancel the charter party.

Candlestick Chart   A popular technical analysis charting tool that has its origins in Japan. Candlesticks capture the same price information as the bar charts - the open, high, low and close. The thick box (known as the body of the candle) joins the open and close values. The thin lines on either end of the body (known as the shadows), join the high and low prices. If the open value is higher than the close value, the body of the candle is solid or coloured. Conversely, if the close is higher than the open then the body of the candle is clear, white or unshaded.

Various formations show those which suggest a reversal in market direction and those which show a continuation in trend.

Numerous exotic patterns exist on candlestick charts such as:

- three winged crow, consisting of three consecutive daily declines drawn as black candles, a typical bearish continuation pattern.

- hanging men and evening stars, both are bearish reversal patterns.

- frying pan, a rounded, coordinated turnaround, similar to a saucer bottom on a conventional bar chart.

- doji, a single day reversal pattern, a candle with no body where the market opens and closes at the same price.

Canola   Canadian term for Rapeseed or Colza.

CAP   The Common Agricultural Policy by which the European Community aims to guarantee farmers' incomes by bridging the gap between world market prices for major commodities and the normally higher prices set by the EC. It is effected through a complex of price support mechanisms, export restitutions, social and other measures.

Cap   An interest rate option which protects the holder from an increase in interest rates. The holder, by exercising, receives a cash settlement representing the difference between the strike level and the underlying interest rate, should the latter be higher for the set period. Caps have a life of normally between two and five years. The option can be exercised at regular intervals (every six months, for example) during the life of the cap. Originally created by banks to protect issuers of floating rate debt. See Floor.

Capital   In economics, there are three production factors: land, labour and capital. The latter can be factories and machinery or working capital comprising raw materials, components and money.

Also the equity of a company representing net worth in the form of issued stock and shares at book value and retained net earnings.

Can also refer to the basic amount of money that is invested or deposited apart from any interest or reward that is being received.

Capital Account   Comprises, within the balance of payments, long term flows - as used for investment in land and plant - and short term flows such as those stemming from profits from appreciating currencies or high interest rates on deposits. See Current Account, Basic Balance of Payments.

Capital Adequacy   Under an accord of 1988 the central banks of the Group of 10 nations set out convergent capital adequacy standards for the commercial banks they regulate. This was formulated under the auspices of the Bank for International Settlements. Most of the G-10 nations required banks to raise Capital Ratios gradually. The rules determine how much and what type of capital banks can raise in the financial markets and what type of loans they are allowed to make. See Tier One.

Capital Allowances   Allowances which can be set against tax on expenditure for capital equipment.

Capital Base   Issued capital of a company, plus reserves and retained profits.

Capital Controls   Impending capital controls, imposed by governmental regulatory authorities, can cause investors and fund managers to extract money from one country and send it to another. Such controls, which can be short term, would restrict or completely bar sending of capital outside a country. This Flight of Capital can also reflect fears of a currency devaluation or general discontent with a political situation.

Capital Employed Capital used in a business. It may refer to net assets but often includes bank loans and overdrafts.

Capital Equipment Fixed assets such as plant and machinery used in the manufacture of goods. Also known as capital goods.

Capital Expenditure Payment for the acquisition of a long term asset such as land, plant or machinery.

Capital Gain The profit resulting when assets are sold or transferred at a higher price than their initial worth. Inflation and currency movements can affect the real capital gain.

Capital Goods See Capital Equipment.

Capital Intensive Use of a relatively large amount of capital needed to produce goods. This is balanced against the cost and size of the labour force and payments for raw materials and, in the final analysis, whether satisfactory profits can be earned.

Capital Investment Investment in capital equipment such as land, plant or machinery.

Capital Loss The loss resulting when the sale of an asset yields less than the acquisition cost.

Capital Ratios Commercial banks are required to set aside capital equal to eight percent of assets judged to be at risk. Some assets, such as loans to central banks, carry a zero percent risk weighting while, at the other extreme, pure corporate loans are judged as 100 percent risk. See Tier One.

Capital Risk The risk that a company's share price loses its value or becomes worthless which would result in a loss of capital. There are several forms of capital risk: Business Risk, Specific Risk, Liquidity Risk, Systemic Risk, Political Risk and Taxation Risk.

Capitalisation Total market value of a company's issued share capital. It is the number of listed shares multiplied by the price quotation.

Capitalisation Issue An issue of shares - free to the shareholders - which results from a company transferring money from its reserves to its permanent capital. These new shares are then distributed to the existing holders in proportion to their existing holdings. The ratios can be set without limit. Common examples - as in Rights issues - are 1 for 1, 1 for 2, 2 for 1 stretching out to 1 for 9, notably when shares are highly priced. Also known as a free scrip, bonus or scrip issue.

Capitalisation Weighted Index A stock index that weights stocks on the basis of their total capitalisation.

Capped Note A floating rate instrument with an embedded cap which places a maximum coupon rate on the issue.

Car Term used in U.S. commodity trading for a load in a railway freight car. Also known as carload. Colloquially used in U.S. futures to mean one lot of a futures contract.

Carat The purity of gold is described by its fineness or carat as parts of 24. Thus 18 carat (out of 24) is 75 percent gold. Gold is often alloyed with other metals to increase its hardness or change its colour.

Carbon Black Substantially pure form of finely divided carbon based on liquid or gaseous hydrocarbons. Used in making rubber products and inks.

Cargo Heating Some hydrocarbons - bitumen for example - have to be heated while inside a ship's cargo tanks to avoid solidifying. The tanks contain coils which are fed by boiler steam.

Caribbean Council for Europe Formed in 1992 by the Caribbean Association of Industry and Commerce and other regional bodies to represent the interests of the Caribbean private sector in the European Community. Based in London.

CARICOM Caribbean Community and Common Market. Formed in 1973, it replaced the Caribbean Free Trade Association (CARIFTA). Members are Antigua and Barbuda, Bahamas (Community only), Barbados, Belize, British Virgin Islands (Associate), Dominica, Dominican Republic, Grenada, Guyana, Haiti, Jamaica, Montserrat, Saint Christopher and Nevis, Saint Lucia, Saint Vincent and the Grenadines, Trinidad and Tobago, Turks and Caicos Islands (Associate).

Carries London Metal Exchange term for simultaneous matching purchase of one delivery with the sale of another. In other markets, these are termed straddles or switches.

Carrying Charge Usually refers to warehouse charges, insurance, and other incidentals often including interest charge and estimated loss (or gain) in weight. When used in connection with delivery against futures, will include weighing, sampling, taring, checking of weights, repairing and so forth. Also refers to a full carrying charge market which is a situation in the futures market where price differentials between delivery months fully reflect insurance, storage and interest costs.

Carrying Market Situation where the premium of the distant positions over the nearby positions is sufficient to cover the Carrying Charge.

Carryover   Total amount of a commodity left over at the end of the crop year. In the U.S., the total must be broken down between the total in various government programmes, or owned by the government, and the total which is available to the free market.

Cartagena Group   The debtors cartel which began meeting in Cartagena in 1984 formed the eleven strong Latin American group of debtor nations. At a 1985 Montevideo meeting they proposed a sharp reduction in real interest rates, separation of new loans from old and easy terms for old debt against a promise to pay the commercial rate for new loans, an increase in commercial bank lending to keep pace with international inflation and linkage between interest payments and each nation's internal economic growth. Aims to coordinate a common strategy in establishing direct dialogue with the Group of Seven nations to obtain best conditions for renegotiating debt. Members are Argentina, Bolivia, Brazil, Chile, Colombia, Dominican Republic, Ecuador, Mexico, Peru, Uruguay and Venezuela.

Cartel   Group of businesses, organisations or countries who agree, often implicitly, to influence the price or supply of goods. Such a group has less power than a monopoly. In the U.S. sometimes called a trust.

Cash Account   An account held by an investor with his broker which operates much like a bank account, with deposits having to exceed withdrawals to pay for securities purchases. Opposite to Margin Account.

Cash and Carry Trade   An arbitrage position typically comprising a long cash position together with a short position in its respective futures contract whereby the cash price plus the cost of carry of the underlying position is lower than the futures price. Arbitrageurs will therefore buy cash and "carry" to the futures date for delivery into the futures contract. It is assumed that the cash position is financed in the overnight repo market. Also known as basis trading or buying the basis. The short basis trade is the short cash position with the long futures contract and is known as a reverse cash and carry trade.

Cash Commodity   Physical commodity as distinct from a futures contract.

Cash Crop   A crop grown for sale rather than for food.

Cash Dividend   A dividend paid in cash to a company's shareholders. It is distributed from current earnings or accumulated profits.

Cash Equivalent   An asset which is so easily and quickly convertible to cash that holding this asset is equivalent to holding cash. A Treasury bill is considered cash equivalent. Also used to describe the alternative method of liquidating a position, whereby the seller provides the cash equivalent to the buyer rather than the security itself.

Cash Extraction Strategy   A strategy involving transactions where an underlying position is exchanged for a comparable risk equivalent derivative position which allows the purchaser to extract cash.

Cash Flow   Sum of pretax profits and depreciation allowances.

Cash Flow Statement   A summary of the sources and uses of cash by a company over a set period of time.

Cash Management Bills - U.S.   Very short term U.S. Treasury bills with maturities ranging from a few days to six months and issued on a discount basis. They are auctioned in the same way as Treasury bills although not on a regular cycle and can be announced as late as the auction day itself. Non-competitive bidding is not authorised for these bills. Cash management bills are instruments designed to maintain balances until taxes are received.

Cash Market   See Spot Market.

Cash Merchandiser   Firm or person dealing in the buying/selling of a cash commodity. In the U.S., three types exist:
   - Country Merchandiser, located away from the terminal market, buys grain from country elevator operators and sells in terminal markets to grain processors and exporters.
   - Terminal Market Merchandiser, buys grain to be received in a terminal market, such as Chicago.
   - Terminal Elevator Merchandiser, participates in the same merchandising operations as other cash grain merchants but, unlike the others, has storage facilities at terminals and subterminals.

Cash Ratios   Proportion of cash and related assets to liabilities. In the case of a bank, the ratio of cash to total deposit liabilities.

Cash Settled   The process involving the settlement of a cash amount upon expiry or closing out of a futures or options contract as opposed to physical delivery of the underlying. This is the most common method of settling financial futures trades.

Cash Settlement   A trade which settles the same day as the trade date. Also settlement in cash as opposed to physical delivery. See Cash Settled.

Casing   Steel lining which supports the sides of the well and prevents water or gas from entering.

Castorseed Oil   Taken from seeds of the castor plant bean. Used for pharmaceutical purposes, as an industrial lubricant (it has a very low freezing point) and various other industrial uses such as in production of synthetic resins and fibres. Major producers include India, Brazil and China.

Catalytic Converter   Used in the auto industry for exhaust pollution control. The conventional converter uses platinum and rhodium together with palladium to remove carbon monoxide, hydrocarbons and nitrogen oxides simultaneously. Other conventional systems use combinations of platinum and rhodium or rhodium alone. The use of palladium on its own is being investigated on grounds of relative cheapness.

CATS   A Computer Assisted Trading System used for trading securities. It was created by the Toronto Stock Exchange and later used in Paris, Brussels and Madrid.

CATS - U.S.   Certificate of Accrual on Treasury Securities - a Zero Coupon instrument which was created by Salomon Brothers in 1982 as a result of trading note and bond coupons and principal repayments separately. Similar instruments are TIGRs and LYONs. This process is known as coupon stripping. See U.S. STRIPS.

CBOE   The Chicago Board Options Exchange (CBOE) was established in April 1973 and has become the world's largest marketplace for listed options, specialising in the trading of equity options.

CBOT   The Chicago Board of Trade (CBOT) is the world's oldest and largest exchange for financial futures and options, metal futures and options, agricultural futures and options and equity index futures. Founded in 1848 by a group of 82 Chicago businessmen.

CCI   See Commodity Channel Index.

CCT - Italy   Certificati di Credito del Tesoro are floating rate notes with maturities of seven years although there have also been maturities of five and 10 years. The first coupon is fixed and the following coupons are indexed to the six month or one year Treasury bill yields.

CD-Equivalent Yield   See Money Market Equivalent Yield.

CDs   Certificates of deposit are negotiable money market instruments which certify that a time deposit has been made with a bank at a fixed interest rate for a fixed period. The instrument is quoted on an interest bearing face value basis rather than at a discount and interest is paid at maturity. See Fixed Term Deposit, Term CDs,

Variable Rate / Floating Rate CDs, Eurodollar CDs, Sterling CDs.

CDS   See Canadian Depository for Securities.

CEDEL   Centrale de Livraison de Valeurs Mobilières, founded in 1970 and located in Luxembourg, provides clearance/settlements and borrowing/lending of securities and funds through a computerised book entry system.
CEDEL is jointly owned by a co-operative of international banks. See EUROCLEAR.

Centistoke   A measure of viscosity in fuel oil.

Central Bank   Major regulatory bank in a nation's monetary system. Its role normally includes control of the credit system, the note issue, supervision of commercial banks, management of exchange reserves and the national currency's value as well as acting as the government banker.

Central Bank Intervention   The market participation of a central bank to influence monetary conditions. The most common intervention is seen in the currency markets, when the bank or banks may simply be seeking to stabilise exchange rates rather than to steer them to any particular level. See Concerted Intervention, Open Market Operations.

Central Banks   Among major central banks are the following:

Australia	Reserve Bank of Australia
Austria	Oesterreichische National-bank
Belgium	Banque Nationale de Belgique
Canada	Bank of Canada
Denmark	Danmarks Nationalbank
Finland	Suomen Pankki-Finlands Bank
France	Banque de France
Germany	Deutsche Bundesbank
Greece	Bank of Greece
Ireland	Central Bank of Ireland
Italy	Banca d'Italia
Japan	Bank of Japan
Luxembourg	Institut Monétaire Luxem-bourgeois
Netherlands	The Nederlandsche Bank
New Zealand	Reserve Bank of New Zealand
Norway	Norges Bank
Portugal	Banco de Portugal
Singapore	Monetary Authority of Singapore
South Africa	South African Reserve Bank
Spain	Banco de España
Sweden	Sveriges Riksbank
Switzerland	Schweizerische Nationalbank

United Kingdom   Bank of England
United States   U.S. Federal Reserve System

See separate entries such as "Germany - Key Interest Rates" for the Group of Ten nations and Switzerland and "Germany - Money Supply" for the Group of Five nations.

Central Rate   The exchange rate against the European Currency Unit adopted for each currency in the European Monetary System. Central rates are used to tie together member currencies of the Exchange Rate Mechanism.

Cereal Residues   Derived from the milling of cereals (largely wheat) and used as a valuable Animal Feed Ingredient, having a similar nutritive composition to wheat and barley grains. Known variously as brans, middlings, sharps, thirds and pollards.

Cereals   Wheat, oats, barley, rye, rice, maize (corn), millet and sorghum.

Certificate of Indebtedness - U.S.   A certificate similar to a Treasury bill with respect to its maturity but issued with a fixed coupon.

Certificated Stock   Also termed certified stock. Stocks which have been inspected and approved as deliverable quality against futures contracts. In grains, it means stocks in a deliverable position. Such gradings hold good for a specified period or for an indefinite time. Some exchanges list established deterioration schedules.

Certificates of Deposit   See CDs.

CFTC   Commodities Futures Trading Commission, a U.S. government agency that must give permission for any new contract to be created by a U.S. exchange.

CGO   Central Gilt Office, created in 1978 within the Bank of England. It is the book entry clearing system for most gilt trades. If a clearing agent is not a member of the CGO, the trades are settled by physical delivery.

Channel Islands   A self governing U.K. Crown dependency, located offshore France, which comprises five inhabited islands, Jersey, Guernsey, Sark, Herm and Alderney.

Channel Lines   Chart lines connecting highs and lows that run parallel to each other. If either line is broken it may indicate a substantial move in the direction of the breakout.

CHAPS   The Clearing House Automated Payments System (CHAPS), started in 1984, is an electronic method, used in London, of effecting same day value sterling transfers between banks. See CHIPS, SWIFT.

Chapter 11   Under U.S. insolvency laws a debtor who is unable to pay his debts remains in possession of his business and in control of its operations unless a court rules otherwise. The arrangement allows debtors and creditors considerable flexibility in working together to reorganise the business.

Chapter 7   Under U.S. insolvency laws this deals with involuntary liquidation - where creditors petition to have a debtor judged insolvent by a court. Chapter 7 allows a court appointed interim trustee wide powers to generally operate the debtor business in such a way as to prevent loss. The debtor can only regain possession from the trustee by filing an appropriate bond.

Chart Analysis   See Technical Analysis.

Chart Points   Price points or updates on a chart which are connected to form a continuous line. Updates may be random, as and when they occur, or time sampled, i.e. plotted at stipulated times such as every ten minutes.

Chartering Agent   A specialised broker engaged in finding cargo space.

Chartist   An analyst who uses charts and computer generated mathematical indicators to plot historic trends and to project future trends in markets. Chartists use price and rate movements plus a range of technical indicators such as averages to make investment recommendations. One of their main beliefs is that chart patterns recur. See Technical Analysis.

Cheap Money   See Easy Money.

Cheapest to Deliver (CTD)   The security or commodity available in the cash market which can be delivered the most economically against a short futures position.

Chicago Board of Trade   See CBOT.

Chicago Board Options Exchange   See CBOE.

Chicago Mercantile Exchange   See CME.

Chinese Wall   Rules designed to prevent price sensitive information seeping between dealing/fund management/corporate finance operations within the same investment house. For example, it would not be considered appropriate and, in some countries it is actually considered illegal, for a corporate finance team to notify its own in-house market maker of an impending takeover bid.

CHIPS   A New York system, the Clearing House Interbank Payments System (CHIPS), is operated by members of the New York Clearing House Association as an electronic means of settling banking payments. See CHAPS, SWIFT.

Choice Price A firm price where the dealer quotes one price for both bid and ask, i.e. quoting with a zero spread. Also called either way.

Choke Heavy steel valve used to restrict the size of the opening through which oil or gas flows, thus controlling production. The diameter of the choke is an important factor in determining the potential volume from an exploration or appraisal well.

Chooser Option An option which offers the holder the choice between a call or a put option. The choice has to be made by the chooser date, which is a preselected date between the trade date and the expiry date. Once the choice has been made, the option behaves as a standard option.

Christmas Tree Assembly of pipes and valves attached to a production wellhead controlling the flow of oil or gas and stopping a possible blowout.

Churning Excessive buying and selling on a customer's portfolio allowing a broker who controls an account to earn extra commission. This practice can act against the best interests of the customer.

CIF Cost, insurance and freight. A CIF shipping price means that it includes the cost of goods, their insurance and freight to a specified destination.

CIK Caisse Interprofessionnelle de Dépôts et de Virement de Titres (CIK) or the Securities Deposit and Clearing Office of the Financial Sector is the automated clearing system for Belgian bonds organised by the National Bank of Belgium on a delivery versus payment (DVP) basis.

Circling Pre-selling of an issue by taking orders from prospective customers.

City Banks - Japan This term applies to 11 banks which have branches throughout Japan.

Clean (White) Highly refined oil products such as aviation spirit, motor spirit, kerosene, turpentine and some grades of gas oil.

Clean Oil Vessel Ship employed in carrying refined products.

Clean Price Present value of the cash flow of a bond excluding accrued interest. Basically, the quoted price of a bond. See Dirty Price.

Clearing Bank Member bank of a national cheque clearing system. To clear a cheque means to process it through the clearing system so that the payee receives its value. Such systems can also involve clearing financial orders and standardised payment instructions, such as standing orders.

Clearing House The clearing house of a futures exchange becomes the counterparty to both buyer and seller of a futures contract when a trade has been matched, greatly reducing counterparty risk. Clearing houses are sometimes departments within the exchange and sometimes separate entities. Other functions include supervising the deliveries made against futures contracts and maintaining the margin accounts.

Clearing System A system which facilitates the transfer of ownership for securities and arranges custody. See CEDEL, EUROCLEAR.

Cliquet Option An option which allows the holder to lock in gains on the underlying during the life of the option. Also known as a ratchet option.

Close Company U.K. term for a company controlled by five or fewer persons whether directors or otherwise. The U.S. equivalent is the closed company.

Closed End Company Investment company with a fixed capital structure with a fixed number of shares outstanding which are traded in the secondary market. The number of shares cannot be increased and cannot be redeemed by the company. See Mutual Fund, Balanced Fund.

Closed End Fund A fund which, after the Initial Public Offering has taken place, does not typically issue new shares nor redeem old shares. It is therefore closed and thereafter the fund's shares are bought and sold like stock on the stock exchange and over the counter. Also known as a publicly traded fund.

Closed Mortgages Mortgages against which no more bonds may be issued. Opposite to open mortgages.

Club Method of syndicating loans in the Euromarkets which involves general distribution of tasks amongst a group of banks, rather than using the more formal, tiered structure of lead manager, co-manager, and so forth. See Paris Club, London Club.

Cluster Development Fund A one billion Singapore dollar fund set up by the government to help manufacturers keep up with emerging trends in global business. Managed by the Economic Development Board it can be used to attract high technology companies to Singapore, to accelerate development of local manufacturing enterprises and to be used for strategic investments with local and multinational companies.

CME The Chicago Mercantile Exchange (CME) is one of the world's oldest futures and options exchanges. Founded in 1898 as the Butter and Egg Board, the exchange was named the CME in 1919.

Until 1972 the exchange only traded instruments on commodities. When financial products were launched and the International Monetary Market (IMM) became a division of the CME, in 1976, the CME started trading foreign currency contracts. Contracts on short term interest rate products were launched from 1976 to 1981. Options on futures contracts were initiated in the 1980s. In 1993 the CME introduced rolling spot currency futures contracts. Today the CME is the world's leading exchange for short term interest rate and currency products.

CMO Collateralised Mortgage Obligation. A mortgage backed security in which payments by the borrower are passed into a pool from which principal and interest are paid to security holders class by class. Each class has a different coupon, maturity and price. Interest is paid to each class but principal payments are paid to one class at a time in order of maturity. Thus one class is completely paid off before any principal is repaid to the next class.

CMO Residuals The amounts left over from a pool of mortgages once the interest, principal and administration costs have been paid on a CMO. Investors can purchase equity in these residuals.

CNMV In Spain, Comisión Nacional del Mercado de Valores (National Securities Market Commission). Government-run regulatory body for all public issues of shares and bonds on stock exchanges.

Co-Financing Finance jointly provided for a country both by commercial banks and an international financing institution such as the International Monetary Fund, the World Bank or regional development banks. In such cases, the commercial banks become more willing lenders.

Co-Lead Manager See Lead Manager.

Co-Manager See Lead Manager.

Coal (Hydrogenated) Production of artificial mineral oil from coal by combining the carbon in coal with hydrogen to form hydrocarbon.

Coal Equivalent Used in energy consumption statistics as an overall measure.

Coal Gasification Process for producing natural gas by heating coal.

Coarse Grains Maize, barley, sorghum, oats, rye and millet.

COB Commission des Opérations de Bourse, the official French watchdog agency for the stock exchange.

COCERAL Full name is Comité du Commerce des Céréales et des Aliments du Bétail de la CEE (Committee for Trade in Cereals and Animal Feed in the EC). Main cereal lobby in the European Community comprised solely of private grain trade members.

Cocktail Swap A mixture of different types of swaps. Will often be incorporated to spread the risk on a major financing.

Cocoa Crop producing beans which contain 50-57 percent fat called cocoa butter. The manufacturing process includes shelling, roasting and grinding the beans. The fat is largely removed in making powder for drinking while extra cocoa butter is added in making chocolate. Cocoa butter is also used in some cosmetics.

The world's largest producer is the Ivory Coast. Others are Brazil, Cameroon, Colombia, Dominican Republic, Ecuador, Ghana, Indonesia, Malaysia, Mexico, Nigeria, Papua New Guinea, Sierra Leone, Togo and Venezuela.

The European Community consumes about 40 percent of world cocoa output with the Netherlands, Germany and the U.K. the major processors. The U.S. consumes about 12 percent of world output. See Main Crop.

Cocoa Grindings The amount of cocoa beans physically ground by consumer countries represents a standard measure of consumption. Thus they are tallied and issued periodically throughout the year as official data.

Cocoa Producers Alliance This 13 member group produces 87 percent of the world's cocoa. In 1993 it adopted an accord giving producers complete control over their rate of production. This accord - adopted by 44 nations - has to be ratified by at least five producer countries covering 80 percent of world exports and by consumer countries responsible for at least 60 percent of imports. Producers have already agreed to reduce output by an average 74,000 tonnes a year for five years. Based in Lagos.

Cocoa Shipment Declaration An official document confirming to the buyer that his contracted purchase is being shipped. It provides bill of lading details and the number of bags he is to receive.

COCOM Formed in 1949, this Paris based Coordinating Committee for Multilateral Export Controls Group included NATO nations (except Iceland) and Japan. It compiled a list of goods considered to be of strategic importance and therefore not to be sold by the West to East European nations. Since the East European detente much control has been swept away. The 17 nations forming COCOM have taken a decision to scrap the group altogether and to replace it with a new body encompassing former communist states and aiming at controlling the spread of mass destruction arms.

Coconut Oil Lauric vegetable oil extracted from dried kernels of coconut, known as copra. Competes with soybean oil in world markets. Produced in tropical and subtropical regions. Largest producer is the Philippines, followed by Indonesia.

COFACE Compagnie Française pour l'Assurance du Commerce Extérieur. French government funded export credit and insurance agency.

Coffee The two main types of coffee are Arabicas and Robustas with the latter mostly used for instant coffee. The beans are green until they are roasted. Largest producers are Brazil (arabicas, some robustas), Colombia (arabicas), Indonesia (robustas) and Mexico (arabicas). Other producers are Cameroon, Costa Rica, Guatemala, Honduras, India, the Ivory Coast, Kenya, Salvador, Uganda and Zaire. Leading consumers are the U.S., Germany, France and Japan. Coffee production tends to be cyclical with a large crop one year followed by a smaller crop, mainly in Brazil. Drought is the main adverse weather factor. In Brazil, the trees are also vulnerable to frost attacks.

Coffee, Sugar and Cocoa Exchange See CSCE.

COGECA Comité Générale de la Coopération Agricole des Pays de la Communauté (General Committee for Agricultural Cooperation in the EC). A lobby which represents farm cooperatives in the 12 member nations.

Coir The strong fibre of coconut husk, used in making ropes and matting.

Collar Combination of a long cap and a short floor to fix interest payments within a certain range. The premium generated from the sale of the floor may completely or partially finance the premium to be paid for the cap.

Collared FRN Floating rate note which specifies a maximum and minimum interest rate level. See FRN.

Collateral Assets which are guaranteed as security for a loan. High quality collateral reduces the lender's risk and therefore offers a lower rate of interest on the loan.

Collateralised Bond Obligation A security backed by pools of other securities.

Collateralised Mortgage Obligation See CMO.

Colza European name for Rapeseed or Canola.

Combination Option An option comprising at least one call and one put. The components may be exercised or traded separately although they are originally dealt as one. This strategy may be dealt to take advantage of a particular view on the market or to reduce outgoing premium costs. Two common examples of combination options are Strangle and Straddle strategies.

Combo Combined carrier. Vessel able to carry ore, oil or bulk cargoes.

COMECON Council for Mutual Economic Assistance. Formed in 1949 and headquartered in Moscow to coordinate the economic development of member countries. Members were Albania, Bulgaria, Cuba, Czechoslovakia, German Democratic Republic, Hungary, Mongolia, Poland, Romania, USSR and Vietnam. Members agreed in 1991 to dissolve the body but formal disbandment was postponed indefinitely because of asset disposal considerations.

COMEX Commodity Exchange Inc., a New York commodity futures market trading principally in gold, silver and copper. COMEX was formed in 1933 and has become the world's most active precious metals market.

Commercial Banks Profit-earning establishments which operate in wholesale and retail banking and allied markets, the latter including insurance and a wide range of financial services. When in need of very short term funds they are allowed to borrow from their relevant central bank. They have control over their interest rates at which they lend to, and take deposits from, their customers.

Commercial Bill See Bills of Exchange.

Commercial Field Oil/gas field able to generate sufficient income to make development economically viable.

Commercial Paper See CP.

Commerzbank Index Germany's Commerzbank AG publishes an index of 60 leading shares on the Frankfurt bourse. It is calculated once a day, at midsession, not at the close.

Commission des Opérations de Bourse See COB.

Commission House A concern that buys and sells futures contracts for the accounts of customers. Its income is therefore generated by the commission charged for its service.

Commission Merchant One who makes a trade, either for another member of an exchange or for a non-member client but who makes the trade in his own name and becomes liable as principal.

Commissione Nazionale per la Società e la Borsa See CONSOB.

Commitment Fee A fee paid by a borrower for a lender's commitment to make funds available.

Commitments of Traders A monthly report by the Commodity Futures Trading Commission that shows the total of open positions held by large volume traders, speculators, hedgers and small position traders. The report is watched for unusual changes between the categories.

Commodity Channel Index Used in technical analysis. Specially designed for instruments with cyclical or seasonal characteristics. The index shows the difference between the price and simple moving average of the price, divided by the mean deviation of the price. A scale is used to show that the most random variation in price will yield values between -100 and +100. One should be long when the index is greater than +100, short when it is less than -100 and out of the market if the index lies between these values.

Commodity Credit Corporation U.S. government agency set up in 1933 which is responsible for directing and financing major U.S. Department of Agriculture action programmes including price support and production adjustment. Its activities also cover credit sales, barter deals, export payments and foreign food aid.

Commodity Exchange Inc. See COMEX.

Commodity Futures Trading Commission Established by the U.S. Congress to administer the 1974 Commodity Futures Trading Act. It has jurisdiction over all commodities contract markets in the U.S. Comprises five commissioners, one of whom is designated chairman. All are appointed by the U.S. President. They are subject to Senate confirmation and are independent of all government departments.

Commodity Stabilisation Agreements International agreements involving producers and, in some cases, consumers in efforts to stabilise production and/or prices of commodities.

Common Effective Preferential Tariff This CEPT scheme and its progeny CEPTA (Area) is backed by ASEAN, the Association of South East Asian Nations. ASEAN is aiming to set up an ASEAN Free Trade Area (AFTA).

Common Fund Full title is the U.N. Conference on Trade and Development (UNCTAD) Common Fund for Commodities. Negotiated in 1980, the fund was originally conceived as a central pool of finance that could be drawn upon by international commodity agreements to help keep market prices stable through buffer stock operations. Later, UNCTAD put more emphasis on the fund's second window which provides finance for research, development, marketing and diversification. Only international bodies representing both consumers and producers are eligible for second window funds. Based in The Hague.

Common Market A customs union which also has a common system of commercial law allowing freedom of movement of goods, services, capital and labour with domestic parameters. Often used as a reference to the European Community.

Common Stock U.S. equivalent of ordinary shares.

Commonwealth of Independent States Voluntary association of 11 states. Originally established at the time of the collapse of the USSR in 1991 by the Minsk Agreement. Members are Armenia, Azerbaijan, Belarus, Kazakhstan, Kyrgyzstan, Moldova, Russia, Tajikistan, Turkmenistan, Ukraine and Uzbekistan. States currently outside the Commonwealth are Georgia and the Baltic states - Lithuania, Latvia and Estonia.

Commonweatlh See The Commonwealth.

Community Reinvestment Act In the U.S., an act which has a rating system encouraging banks to open branches in inner cities and to provide various financial services. The accent is on adherence to fair lending practices to minorities. With an improved rating, the banks can expand sales of some services into other geographical areas.

Compagnie des Agents de Change See CAC 40.

Compensatory Financing International Monetary Fund facility providing short term finance to compensate for fluctuations in a country's exports caused by circumstances largely outside a country's control.

Competitive Bid Auction Method commonly used for issuing government bonds, with underwriters submitting bids for certain amounts of the issue. The bonds will then be allocated according to the level of demand at rates determined by the level of the bids. See Dutch Auction, English Auction, Non-Competitive Bid Auction.

Completion Process whereby a finished well is either sealed off or prepared for production by fitting a wellhead.

Compound Interest The interest amount paid or earned on the original principal plus the accumulated interest. With interest compounding, the more periods for which interest is calculated, the more rapidly the amount of interest on interest and interest on principal builds.

Compounding annually means that there is only one period annually when interest is calculated. See Simple Interest.

Compound Option An option which grants the holder the right to buy or sell an option at a set price on a predetermined date. If the first option is exercised, the underlying option will then behave as a standard option.

Compulsory Liquidation A court-ordered liquidation, normally after a creditor's petition.

Concentrates Product of a mill or concentrator. The result of the first process in increasing the metal content from the low levels in the mined ore. The eventual outcome will be refined metal.

Concert Party See Acting in Concert.

Concerted Intervention Intervention in foreign exchange markets which is carried out by several central banks simultaneously. Any number can join at the same time in the defence of a currency or several currencies. Intervention can be carried out by a central bank outside its own national borders. See Central Bank Intervention.

Concerted Lending Lending to debtor states to help them meet the repayment and interest obligations on old loans - in effect, rollovers. Such loans are put together by central banks while commercial banks with outstanding loans are asked to participate.

Concession A licence area leased to a company for a given period for exploration and development. Specifications include the area to be explored, time period for the concession and how the area's owner (i.e. a government) is to be compensated if oil/gas is found.

Condensates Mixture of hydrocarbons which occurs as vapour in underground gas reservoirs and condenses to liquid when brought to the surface.

Condenser Equipment which changes a material from a vapour to a liquid state.

Conditionality Conditions imposed when a country draws funds from the International Monetary Fund related to its credit tranches. There are four regular tranches and borrowing under each tranche is subject to specific conditions. Other conditions apply to borrowing beyond regular credit tranches such as the Extended Fund Facility.

Conditioning Improving grain quality by:
- running, which is cooling and aerating of grain to prevent deterioration.
- drying, which is removal of enough excess moisture to allow safe storage.
- cleaning, which is removal of unwanted material from grain by using air blowers and screens.

Condor Spread An option strategy which involves the simultaneous purchase of an Out of the Money Strangle and sale of an even further out of the money strangle or vice versa.

Conduit An agency, i.e. FHLMC or FNMA, or private company that buys mortgages to create pools to be on-sold to investors.

Conduit Finance Funding used by companies in a private enterprise project which has been provided via securities issued by a government unit. Backing for the issue is normally the credit of the company which also, mostly, has to assure the generation of pledged revenues. Industrial development bonds are an example of this financing method.

Confederation A group of sovereign states which share some governmental duties. Members normally have the power of veto. National parliaments usually need to ratify confederal decisions. See Federation.

Conference Lines Association of ship-owning lines which operate on a given route. Standard tariff rates are fixed and a regular service operated for the mutual benefit of the merchant trading and the shipowner.

Conforming Mortgages Mortgages that conform to the agencies' standards for inclusion in a pool. The three standards to which they must conform are a maximum payment to income ratio, a maximum loan to value ratio and a maximum loan amount. See Non-Conforming Mortgages.

Congressional Budget Office A Congressional support agency which works on U.S. budget estimation as well as analyses of broad policy choices.

Conillon Brazilian variety of Robusta coffee.

Conseil National de Crédit See France - Key Interest Rates.

Conseil Politique et Monétaire See France - Key Interest Rates.

Conservation Regulation of oil or gas production from a reservoir so as to prolong its life and thereby recover a larger quantity of oil/gas.

Conservation Reserve Program Programme under which the U.S. government pays farmers to keep cropland fallow or idle for ten years.

CONSOB Commissione Nazionale per la Società e la Borsa. Italy's official body for regulating and supervising companies and stock exchanges.

Consolidated Balance Sheet A report showing the financial position of a company and its subsidiaries. Also known as consolidated account.

Consolidation Phase A sideways move in the market which remains on the same level although experiences minor changes either way. Usually has a low steady volume.

Consols Undated gilt issue, i.e. undefined maturity date, formed by consolidating several small issues to increase liquidity.

Consortium Group of companies formed to promote a common project.

Constant Percent Prepayment A calculation representing a Single Monthly Mortality which is assessed on an annual basis.

Constructive Total Loss Insurance term where the cost of repairing, retrieving and forwarding the goods exceeds their insured value.

Contango The relation between a futures market and a spot price where the futures price is higher than the spot price. Opposite to Backwardation.

Continental Shelf Edge of a continental mass of varying width which lies under the sea in comparatively shallow water - up to 200 metres in depth.

Contingent Option An option for which the holder only pays the premium if the option is exercised. Contingent options are therefore a Zero Cost option strategy, unless exercised.

Continuation Used in technical analysis, these patterns usually indicate that the sideways price action is more likely to be a pause in an underlying trend (possibly to correct an overbought/oversold condition) and that the next move will be in the direction of the main trend. A major difference between continuation patterns and reversal patterns is that reversals usually take much longer to develop and represent major trend changes. Continuation patterns are shorter in duration and can thus be called intermediate patterns.

Contract For Differences An off exchange-traded oil contract for the difference between the price of a crude oil, usually Brent blend, for prompt delivery and the price of a forward traded month. Typically, it is the average difference over a five day working week taken from published sources.

Contract Grades Standard grade for each commodity which must be observed when commodities are delivered against futures contracts. Most contracts have a number of grades or qualities which result in a premium or discount when delivery actually takes place.

Contract Month Month in which delivery is due under a futures contract, i.e. when the contract expires.

Contrarian The theory of contrary opinion holds that when more than 80 percent of analysts are bullish then it can be assumed that they and their followers have taken long positions leaving fewer potential buyers to absorb any selling that develops. The converse is true when 80 percent of analysts are bearish.

Conventional Mortgage Loan A loan that is not insured or guaranteed by a government agency. It is either privately insured or not insured.

Convergence The process by which the futures price moves toward the price of the underlying as expiry approaches. See Basis Risk.

Conversion Arbitrage A strategy combining a long underlying position with the simultaneous purchase of a put and sale of a call. Both options are normally European style with the same strike levels and expiry date. See Reversal Arbitrage.

Conversion Ratio The ratio fixed on the convertibility of a preferred share into a fixed number of common shares, or from a convertible bond into the underlying shares.

Convertible Bond A bond that is convertible into another instrument, sometimes another type of bond but more commonly into company shares at a fixed price which usually represents a premium over the current or average share price. Because of this inducement, the bond can carry a lower coupon at par. The option to convert usually lasts the life of the bond but borrowers often reserve the right to call the bond earlier than the normal call if the share price reaches up to, say, 150 percent of the conversion price, thus protecting them from offering shares at the lower fixed price should the market price suddenly surge.

Convertible Currency One that is freely traded internationally and which can easily be converted into other currencies.

Convertible Preferred Stock A type of preferred stock granting the holder the right to convert preferred shares into common or ordinary shares. The terms and conditions of the conversion and the conversion ratio are stipulated at the time of issue. The ratio to convert one preferred share into a fixed amount of ordinary shares is called parity. Once trading begins, the two prices of the two types of share move and disparity may occur which could lead to arbitrage opportunities.

Convertibles - U.K. Gilts which tend to have a short maturity and the option to be converted into longer maturity gilts. Each convertible gilt has a conversion schedule which indicates the issues into which it can be converted (conversion gilts) with conversion dates and conversion prices.

Convexity Convexity is regarded as the second criterion, after duration, for measuring the price sensitivity of a bond. It can be used to measure the rate at which duration changes in response to a change in interest rates.

For two bonds with identical yield to maturity and duration, the price of the bond with the higher convexity will be more sensitive to a change in yield.

Copey   Dealers' language for the Danish Crown.

Copper   Base metal used widely in the electrical, engineering and building industries. Producing countries include Australia, Canada, Chile, China, the Commonwealth of Independent States, Finland, Mexico, Peru, the Philippines, Poland, South Africa, Zaire, Zambia and the U.S.

The London Metal Exchange (LME) and the Commodity Exchange in New York (COMEX) dominate the world's copper industry. World producers and the European consumers take the LME prices as a reference basis for deals. U.S. producers offer metal on the basis of published COMEX prices. The LME and COMEX copper prices are closely related.

The two common forms of pure copper used in trading are cathodes - a slab - and wirebars, which are elongated ingots used as a starting rod for drawing copper wire. Copper can be recovered as scrap.

Copra   The dried kernel of the coconut, yielding coconut oil. Major producers include the Philippines and Indonesia.

Core   Cylindrical rock sample cut from the well during drilling by means of an annular cutter.

Core Capital   See Tier One.

Corn   U.S. term for Maize.

Corn Refining   A two-stage operation:
- wet milling, which separates the kernel into its principal parts.
- conversion, which transforms starch (the milling product) into syrup, sugar and alcohol.

Corn Starch   Provides a multitude of products, much of it for use in sauces, puddings and brewing of beer. Other forms of corn starch are used in the paper-making and textile industries and for cosmetics and laundry purposes.

Corn Sugar   A refined corn syrup (dextrose) used in making confections, carbonated beverages, ice cream and canned fruit. Highly purified dextrose is used for post-surgical and other medical purposes.

Corn Syrup   Made from corn starch. Used in foods such as canned fruits, jellies, preserves, carbonated beverages and, in industry, in the paper and textile fields.

Corp.   Corp. is the acceptable abbreviation of corporation. A corporation is a legal entity chartered by a U.S. state or by the Federal government. The owners have limited liability and can only lose what they invest. A corporation provides for easy transfer of ownership through the sale of stock and allows shareholders to profit through the growth of the business.

Corporate Dealer   A dealer or group of dealers responsible for advising and dealing with the corporate customers of their bank who have direct access to the trading room. Corporate dealers may quote independently of their own dealers and run their own positions but for larger deals may need to obtain prices from the respective dealers and subsequently hand the positions over.

Corporate Results - Japan   Japanese companies report results on a parent company basis - operating, current (sometimes called recurring by analysts/brokers) and net profits. Group, or consolidated earnings terms, may vary but generally include operating, pretax and net.

- Operating profit is before tax, obtained by subtracting operating expenses from sales and is considered a better indicator of the company's core business activities.

- Current profit is before tax but includes gains and losses made on securities investments and other non-operating activities. Extraordinary profit/loss is listed as a separate category and the cause of the profit/loss will be specified.

- Net profit is obtained by subtracting extraordinary profit from current (this may then be reported as pretax profit) and then further deducting income tax. Sales are referred to as operating revenues by banks and brokers while for non-life insurers they become net premiums. Dividends in Japan are mostly low, often still based on a percentage of the totally unrealistic 50 yen share price, and typically paying five to 10 yen a share. The dividend yield is therefore much lower than in Europe or the U.S. but companies help this along with frequent bonus issues and sharesplits instead of big dividends.

Corporate Settlement   Market standard for settlement and delivery five business days or seven calendar days from the trade date. Also known as regular way settlement.

Correction   A correction in technical analysis refers to a movement in price in the opposite direction of the trend. Corrections can occur on both the up and downside of a trend. It is called a correction because the market ultimately reverts to the overall trend.

Correlation   The degree to which two variables move in the same direction on a line.

Corset   An official measure introduced in the U.K. - and abandoned in 1980 - which aimed at restricting monetary growth. If banks increased their eligible liabilities by more than a fixed amount then they had to make deposits at the Bank of England at a penal (low) interest rate. However, the measure resulted in Eurosterling products being offered in other centres which were outside the jurisdiction of the U.K.

Cost of Carry The difference between the interest generated on a cash instrument and the cost of funds to finance the position. See Positive Carry, Negative Carry.

Cost to Close This method calculates the effect of having to liquidate outstanding contracts at prevailing market rates. Used in forward foreign exchange revaluations.

Cotton The soft, white fibrous hairs which cover the seeds of the cotton plant. Used for making thread, yarn, cloth and piece goods. Has a strong competitor in man-made fibres. Cotton producing nations are consuming domestically larger proportions of their cotton crop as well as exporting cotton as manufactured goods. This is a contributory factor to the static volume in international trade of raw cotton. Products from the plant include cottonseed cake (pellets of compressed cottonseed) cottonseed meal, both used as animal feed and Cottonseed Oil. Main producers are China, the U.S., the Commonwealth of Independent States, India, Pakistan and Brazil.

Cotton Boll The pod of the cotton plant.

Cotton Gin Machine for separating the seeds from the fibre of cotton.

Cottonseed Oil Oil is extracted from cottonseed chemically or by crushing. It is used in salad and cooking oils. The residue is used as cottonseed cake but most becomes cottonseed meal, with both being used as animal feed. Major producers include China, the Commonwealth of Independent States, the U.S., India, Pakistan and Brazil.

Council of Arab Economic Unity Based in Cairo. Seeks to coordinate measures for a customs union. Members are Egypt, Iraq, Jordan, Kuwait, Libya, Mauritania, Palestine Liberation Organisation, Somalia, Sudan, Syria, United Arab Emirates and Yemen.

Council of Europe An institution, based in Strasbourg, which has a parliamentary assembly. Countries which wish to be represented have to have governments founded on wide-ranging democratic principles. The Council drew up the European Convention on Human Rights.

Counter Clockwise Used in technical analysis and is a chart that plots price against volume over the last set number of periods. Analysis helps to determine behaviour when prices rise or fall before there is any volume increase or decrease. Such behaviour tends to create elliptical patterns, typically in a counter clockwise direction. Price/volume patterns can be identified and strategies can be planned, based on pattern repetition.

Counter Cyclical Stock A share whose market value moves against the rise and fall of the economy. Typically, shares of companies producing necessities whose demand remains relatively constant irrespective of economic cycles. Examples would include food retailers.

Counter Trade The exchange of goods or services where no money is paid over. It encompasses simple barter; a counter purchase which is an agreement by a seller to spend all or part of his receipts on purchases from the buyer; and a buy back, a deal under which a company opens a plant abroad and agrees to buy all or part of its output.

Counterparty Risk See Credit Risk.

Countervailing Duty Import duty imposed over and above normal levels when an importing country considers the export price to contain a subsidy.

Country Fund A type of mutual fund which invests in a group of securities from a particular country.

Country Limit The limit deemed advisable, in risk terms, by a lender when making a loan to a country. This can apply to the terms and conditions for the loan he is making and also to the cumulative debt owed by a country and the prospects overall of paying interest and return of capital.

Country Risk Risks associated with lending funds to, or making an investment in, a particular country. Also known as sovereign risk.

Coupon The annual or semi-annual interest paid on a debt security expressed as a percentage of the face value. A coupon is fixed for the life of the security. It also describes the detachable certificate entitling the bearer to payment of the interest. A security which pays interest at predetermined intervals is known as coupon bearing.

Coupon Stripping Detaching the coupons from a bond and trading the principal repayment and coupon amounts separately, thus forming Zero Coupon bonds.

Coupon Swap See IRS.

Covariance The degree to which two variables move in the same direction.

Covered Call Writing An option strategy combining a short call position and a long underlying. By owning the underlying on which the option is written, the call is covered (if assigned).

CP Commercial paper. A money market instrument issued by non-financial and financial institutions as a short term borrowing facility. The U.S. domestic commercial paper market uses a promissory note or draft of a corporation, government agency or bank holding company. This is generally unsecured but backed by unused bank credit lines and issued for short term credit needs. It has a maturity of up to 270 days and can be sold at a discount from face value or pay interest at maturity. Directly placed paper is sold by the issuer to the investor while dealer placed paper is sold to an intermediary who in turn reoffers it to investors. Domestic commercial paper markets now exist in other countries such as the U.K., Germany, France and Japan. See Direct Paper, ECP.

CPR Constant Prepayment Rate. Measure of the percentage of outstanding mortgage balances in a pool expected to prepay in a year.

Crack Spread Calculation showing the theoretical market value of petroleum products that could be obtained from a barrel of crude after the oil is refined or cracked. The crack spread does not represent the refining margin because a barrel of crude yields varying amounts of petroleum products such as heating oil, gasoline, jet fuel and kerosene.

Cracking Production process in the petroleum industry whereby feedstock is subjected to a high temperature for a limited period to boost the output of light products at the expense of heavier types of fuel.

Credit Limit The level considered prudent to which funds in a credit line should be offered. Penal interest rates are often imposed when a credit limit is exceeded and in some cases all the funds extended can be called in at short notice.

Credit Line An agreement in which a bank lends or borrows money up to a specified limit for a set period.

Credit Rating Overall creditworthiness of a borrower. In the U.S. the two main rating agencies are Moody's Investor Service and Standard & Poor's Corporation. A top rating means that there is thought to be almost no risk of the borrower failing to pay interest and principal. As the rating grade falls, the perceived risk grows.

Other rating agencies include: Duff & Phelps, Fitch, IBCA, Japanese Bond Research Institute (JBRI), Japanese Credit Rating (JCR), Mikuni, Nippon Investor Services.

Credit Risk Exposure to a loss resulting from a default on a payment due. Also known as counterparty risk.

Credit Squeeze Occurs when the supply of money is unable to keep up with demand, thus interest rates rise exacerbating the borrowing position. Also, a government-imposed situation to rein in excessive spending in macro-economic terms. In this case, interest rates do not have to rise excessively because the government can, for example, impose higher reserve requirements upon banks and lending institutions.

Credit Watch A credit rating agency makes an announcement that it is putting a company on credit watch, meaning that it expects shortly to issue a lower or higher credit rating.

Creditors' Voluntary Liquidation See Liquidation.

Crop See Main Crop.

Crop Diseases These include witches broom, swollen shoot, black pod (all of which affect cocoa), blossom blight (which affects orange trees), coffee rust (which causes loss of leaves), wilt (which affects cotton), black sigatoka (which affects bananas).

Crop Year Time period from the start of one harvest to the next, varying according to the commodity and country. Examples are U.S. wheat June 1 to May 31, U.S. soybeans September 1 to August 31. The Bangladesh cotton crop year runs from sowing to harvest, i.e. July to February. Also referred to as the season.

Cross In the U.S., where the broker acts for both the buyer and seller of a security in the same deal. Known in the U.K. as a put through.

Cross Border Activities in the financial and economic sector which involve movement of goods or negotiations across national borders.

Cross Currency Interest Rate Swap See Currency Coupon Swap.

Cross Currency Swap A currency swap typically with fixed against fixed interest rate payments.

Cross Default Clauses When a lender declares that a loan made to a borrower is in Default then - according to the terms of the loan - cross default clauses may be activated automatically. This could mean that other loans and borrowing instruments made to the borrower by the lender - and by other lenders - are also in default.

Cross Listing Shares which are officially listed on more than one stock exchange and therefore freely traded away from their domestic centre. They can also appear in cross border stock market indices.

Cross Rate The exchange rate between two currencies neither of which is the U.S. dollar. However, usually calculated from the exchange rate of each currency against the dollar.

Crude Oil Oil produced from a reservoir after any associated gas has been removed.

Crush Soybeans have to be crushed in a processing plant to extract oil and meal. Practically all U.S. soybeans used domestically are crushed.

Crush Margin The price difference between the value of an oilseed such as soybeans and the value of the end products - oil and meal.

Crush Spread A futures deal where a trader buys soybeans and sells the same amount of meal and oil that the beans would produce. The reverse is known as a Reverse Crush. See Putting On the Crush.

CSB See Canadian Savings Bond.

CSCE The Coffee, Sugar and Cocoa Exchange, a New York futures market which trades contracts in these three commodities.

CTD See Cheapest to Deliver.

CTE / BTE - Italy Certificati e Buoni del Tesoro in ECU are Italian fixed rate ECU denominated bonds. BTEs are discount bonds with maturities of one year. CTEs are five year bonds with an annual coupon. Both interest and principal can be redeemed in ECU or the equivalent in Italian lira at the holder's request.

CTO - Italy Certificati del Tesoro con Opzione are Italian fixed rate notes with six year maturities, puttable at par after 3 years. Coupons are paid semi-annually.

Cubic Participation Standard unit of measurement for quantities of gas at atmospheric pressure. One cubic foot equals 0.0283 cubic metres.

Cum Latin for "with", thus used as cum cap, cum div, cum rights. Indicates that a buyer of shares is entitled to a current capitalisation issue, a current dividend or a current rights issue. Also short for cumulative when describing a cumulative preference share. Opposite to Ex.

Cum All Means a buyer of shares is entitled to all the supplementary advantages attached to a share at the time.

Cumulative Method A method of voting rights which allows the ordinary shareholder to cast votes in any combination for a set number of positions being elected. There is no commitment to equally distribute the votes.

Cumulative Preferred Stock A type of preferred share which grants the holder the right to dividend arrears before any payments are made to holders of ordinary shares.

Currency Coupon Swap A combination of a currency and interest rate swap. An exchange of payments in one currency for another with fixed against floating interest rate payments. Also known as a cross currency interest rate swap.

Currency Fixings In some markets a daily meeting is held at which the rates for different currencies are officially fixed by adjusting the buying and selling level to reflect market conditions. The central bank of the relevant country often participates to influence the fix.

Currency Limit The maximum amount a dealer, a group of dealers or a dealing room is allowed to deal per currency.

Currency Risk The potential for losses arising from adverse moves in exchange rates.

Currency Swap An exchange of fixed interest payments in one currency for those in another, coupled with a commitment to exchange the notional principal amount at the end and possibly at the beginning of the swap agreement at a predetermined exchange rate. The exchange of principal increases the credit risk.

Current Account Current account balance of payments comprises imports and exports of merchandise, payments and receipts for services such as shipping, banking and tourism, private transfers like remittances from migrant workers, official transfers such as contributions to international bodies like the European Community. See Capital Account, Basic Balance of Payments.

Current Assets Corporate assets which can be realised easily. These include stock in trade, work in progress, bank balances and marketable securities. In the U.S., the definition can be defined as cash, U.S. government bonds, receivables, monies usually due within one year and inventories.

Current Coupon The prevailing coupon on a floating rate note or other variable rate security.

Current Issue See On the Run Issue.

Current Liabilities Short term working commitments of a company such as trade creditors, sums due to banks, taxation and dividends payable.

Current Market Value The value at today's market prices of an investor's total holdings including instruments sold short or on margin.

Current Maturity The time remaining to maturity, an important factor in bond valuation.

Current Yield A measure of the return to a bondholder calculated as a ratio of the coupon to the market price. It is simply the annual coupon rate divided by the clean price of the bond. See Yield to Maturity (YTM).

CUSIP Numbers Identifying numbers assigned, for a fee, by Standard & Poor's to Treasury, federal, municipal and corporate securities. CUSIP stands for Committee on Uniform Securities Identification Procedures.

Custody Traditionally this term means the storing and safekeeping of securities together with maintaining accurate records of their ownership. As a result of an increase in cross border trading, there is a growing need for custody services in several countries. Rather than have several custody services in several countries, investors may prefer to have one global custody service. The services offered by these bodies are also expanding into areas such as settlement of securities bought and sold, coupon/dividend collection and tax matters.

Custom Smelter A smelter which relies on concentrate bought from independent mines instead of its own captive sources.

Customs Union Has a common external tariff but has no internal customs duties.

Cyclical Stock A share whose market value moves in line with the rise and fall of the economy, for example shares issued by home building and durable goods companies.

Cylinder See Risk Reversal.

Daily Price Limit The maximum amount, fixed by the futures or options exchange, that prices are permitted to rise or fall in one day before trading on a contract is suspended. The daily limit is measured from the previous day's settlement price. See Limit Up / Limit Down.

Daimyo A bond issue placed within Japan but listed in Luxembourg.

Daisy Chain Sequence of deals in which a forward (paper) Brent or Dubai cargo of crude oil is traded ahead of receiving loading dates (known as turning wet). A paper Brent cargo may be traded several months ahead of turning wet. A Brent paper chain may be anything up to or over one hundred deals long with an active market player involved many times on both the buy and sell side. Also known as a paper chain.

Dated Barrels Physical (wet) Brent cargo which has been awarded its loading date. This occurs 15 days ahead of loading - or the nearest to 15 days allowing for weekends, the non-trading days. Also, the published Platt's Dated Brent price is the reference price for all European crudes and crude imports to Europe.

Dated Date Date from which interest begins to accrue on a new issue, frequently the issue date.

Dawn Raid Buying a large block of shares in a short time, usually for the buyer to position himself in a possible or actual takeover situation. The purchase often takes place at the start of a trading day.

DAX Composite A Frankfurt bourse index comprising all 320 shares traded on the exchange and calculated once a minute. Established in April 1993.

DAX Index Deutsche Aktien index. Frankfurt Stock Exchange's capitalisation weighted arithmetic 30 blue chip share index representing over 60 percent of market volume. Calculated every minute. Options and futures on the index are traded on the Deutsche Terminbörse (DTB).

Day to Day Money See Call Money.

Day Traders Traders who acquire and liquidate the same futures position during one trading day. Known as scalpers in the U.S.

Daycount Conventions Every bond market has its own system of determining the number of days in a year and even the number of days between two coupon dates. These different methods are referred to as daycount conventions and are important when calculating accrued interest and present value (when the next coupon is less than a full coupon period away). See ISMA Basis.

Dead Rent In mining leases, rent which is payable whether a mine is worked or not.

Deadweight Weight which a vessel is capable of carrying by way of cargo, bunkers, stores and fresh water when loading to the maximum permitted marks.

Deal Limit The maximum amount which a dealer can trade per transaction.

Dealer An individual or company that trades financial instruments and takes positions for its own account.

Dealers' Language Dealers use various expressions when dealing foreign exchange. Examples are:

Cable	Sterling/dollar spot
Paris	French franc
Swissy	Swiss franc
Kiwi	New Zealand dollar
Aussie	Australian dollar
Stocky	Swedish crown
Copey	Danish crown

Other technical terms used when dealing are:

Yard	one billion (used for yen and lira).

Yours	to sell may be expressed in this way, qualified by an amount.
Mine	to buy may be expressed in this way, qualified by an amount.
Given	mainly heard through a broker's box when the latter's bid has been hit.
Taken	mainly heard through a broker's box when the latter's offer has been lifted.
Figure	in a quotation of 1.6890/00 the dealer may quote "ninety the figure". Similarly in a quotation of 1.6900/10 the dealer may quote "figure ten".
Choice	indicating a choice price where the dealer quotes one price for both bid and ask, i.e. quoting with zero spread. Also called either way.
Your Risk	the quoted price is subject to change. Also called at your risk.
Done	to verbally confirm the deal.
Off	the price quoted has changed.

Dear Money   A term used when the cost of funds produces a constricted borrowing environment. Also known as tight money. Opposite to Easy Money.

Debenture Bond   Debt not secured by a specific property but which gives bondholders the claim of general creditors over all assets which are not specifically pledged elsewhere.

Debit Balance   The balance due to a brokerage firm from an investor who has dealt on margin. Interest is charged on this balance.

Debt for Equity   A debtor country buys back its foreign debt at a discount in line with market conditions for local currency which the creditor can then use to invest in one of that nation's companies. The debtor country is then said to have securitised its debt.

Debt for Nature Swap   A swap whereby the debtor country agrees with a creditor that the local currency used to buy back debt will be spent on an environmental project.

Debt Ratio   A ratio which measures the amount of long term debt of a company. Calculated by dividing the total amount of outstanding bonds by the company's total capitalisation.

Debt Service Ratio   Cost to a country of servicing its foreign debts and in particular debts owed by the public sector and publicly guaranteed debt. The total of interest payments and repayments of principal is expressed as a percentage of export earnings. A level of 20 percent is normally considered an acceptable maximum but establishing the exact figure is often difficult.

Debt Warrants   A right to buy debt instruments (bonds) at a set exercise price. They can be issued either attached to a host bond or can be offered naked, i.e. on their own.

Declaration Date   See Expiry Date.

Decoupling   Concept which argues that payments to farmers be separated from direct effects on production and market prices. Under decoupling, payment would be made to farmers regardless of production, making farm subsidies more of a social programme than an economic one.

Deep in the Money   A term used to describe an option whose strike price is much more advantageous than the current market price of the underlying instrument.

Deep Out of the Money   A term used to describe an option whose strike price is much less advantageous than the current market price of the underlying instrument.

Default   Failure to meet an obligation such as a payment of interest or principal. Technically the borrower does not default. The initiative comes from the lender who declares the borrower is in default. However, a declaration can be made to cover anything from failure to make an interest payment up to an intent never to pay off a debt at all. The borrower may be in breach of certain agreements concerning its overall financial health in which case, and in others, an Event of Default may have occurred. In such instances, bankers may wish to avoid using the word default and instead call the loans substandard, non-performing or value impaired. These terms all have differing precise meanings under various bank supervisory regimes.

In the commodities market, it is the decision by a farmer, under the U.S. farm loan programme, to surrender his crops rather than repay a government loan. Also, failure of a party under a futures contract to fulfil the contract requirements or failure to make or take delivery of the physical commodity in the futures market. See Cross Default Clauses.

Defense Logistics Agency   U.S. government agency that buys and sells metals and other commodities for the U.S. strategic stockpile. Former title was the General Services Administration.

Defensive Stock   Shares with a high yield, low price/earnings ratio and modest prospects for price appreciation. Usually located in economic sectors which are less subject to cyclical fluctuations, for example shares issued by food companies and the pharmaceutical industry.

Deferred Coupon   A bond which delays coupon (interest) payment for the first few years, paying it in a lump sum at maturity. Aimed at investors who want delayed cash flow and who also seek a lower tax bill in early years when their income might be higher than in later years.

Deferred Futures Distant months of a futures contract. In particular, where there are two contracts for the same month in two different years, the near (March) is called near March and the distant (March) is called red (or distant or long) March.

Deferred Strike Option An option which allows the holder to fix the strike price at an agreed date in the future.

Deficiency Payments System of supporting farm product prices used in the U.K. before it joined the European Community. It involved payments to farmers of the difference between average free market prices for certain products and guaranteed prices - usually higher - fixed annually.

Also, in the U.S., deficiency payments are made by the government to farmers who participate in the feedgrain, wheat, rice or cotton programmes. They are based on the difference between a target price and the domestic market price or loan rate, whichever is the less.

Deficit The difference when expenditure is greater than income. Opposite to Surplus.

Deficit Financing Budgetary policy which produces a deficit and a government borrowing requirement. It can be the direct result of positive government action or failure to control spending.

Delayed Pricing Allowing for physical delivery of grain at one time and the pricing of it at another. Price is determined by the market on the day in the future that the seller - the farmer - chooses, plus or minus the day's basis. Ownership goes to the elevator at the time of delivery.

Deliverable Grades See Tenderable Grades.

Delivery Current delivery is during the current month. Nearby delivery is during the nearest active month. Distant delivery is for a month further on.

Delivery Points Locations where stocks of commodities or financial instruments represented by futures contracts may be delivered in fulfilment of contract. The commodity exchanges designate the specific locations.

Delivery Price Settlement price set by a clearing house for deliveries of commodities against futures contracts.

Delivery Versus Payment (DVP) Normal method of settling bond trades whereby delivery of the security is made on the same day as payment is being effected. See Free Delivery.

Delta The measure of change in the value of an option compared with a change in the price of the underlying. The delta can be expressed within a range of 0 to 1.0. The delta factor is also used to keep a risk neutral position. See Gamma, Theta, Vega, Rho.

Delta Hedging A method used by option writers to hedge the risk exposure of their option book by purchasing or selling the underlying in the spot market in proportion to the delta. For example, an option with a delta of 0.5 would imply that half of the amount of the underlying would need to be covered to become delta neutral.

Delta Neutral A position is delta neutral once the delta of the asset position is offset by the delta of the option position. There is therefore no exposure to changes in the price of the underlying.

Dematerialisation The replacing of paper share certificates and records by electronic screen storage.

Demerger A company hives off some of its units into a wholly owned separate concern which may also be listed on a stock exchange. Can occur following a number of acquisitions of a similar nature which may diverge from a company's mainstream operations.

Demurrage Extra charge paid by cargo suppliers, receivers or charterers for delaying a vessel at a port of loading or discharge beyond the scheduled time of departure. Applies also to barges, freight cars and other carriers.

Denatured Wheat Wheat treated under the European Community Common Agricultural Policy to make it unfit for human consumption. The intention is to stop it qualifying for a bread wheat subsidy.

Department of Finance (DOF) - Canada The highest quality securities issued in the Canadian market are direct issues of the government of Canada in the form of Treasury bills and Treasury bonds. Although primarily issued in Canadian dollars only, the government has a Canadian bills programme whereby it regularly issues Canadian Treasury bills in U.S. dollars. The Canadian Treasury market shares many of the characteristics of the U.S. Treasury market.

Depletion Control Restriction on the rate at which oil and gas and other mineral reserves can be used.

Depository Trust Corporation In the U.S., shares which are kept in Street Name or Nominee Account may be deposited in a central depository such as the DTC for safekeeping.

Deposits See Fixed Term Deposit.

Depreciation Accounting term which allows for the loss of value of a company's assets.

Derivatives Instruments derived from existing instruments in the cash market. Comprising a whole range of futures, options and swaps traded on futures/options exchanges and over the counter. These instruments, often used within a portfolio of holdings, allow investors to hedge. They are often complex and therefore customised, in the case of OTC transactions, for the individual investor. Have become increasingly popular due to their off balance sheet status. See Futures, Option, FRAs, IRS.

Derived Fuel Form of energy made from a primary fuel such as coal or oil, e.g. electricity, coke or town gas.

DERV In the U.K., Diesel Engine Road Vehicle fuel derived from gas oil.

Detachable Warrant Issued as part of a bond but then detached and traded separately in the secondary market. The warrant holder has the right to buy new equity or debt.

Detergent Cleansing liquid or solid, normally made from petroleum products.

Deutsche Terminbörse See DTB.

Devaluation Formal downward adjustment of a currency's official par value or central exchange rate. Opposite to Revaluation.

Developing Country Higher up the economic scale than a Lesser (or Less) Developed Country and usually manages better its amount of overseas debt relative to the strength of its economy. The more successful ones aim to become members of the Organisation for Economic Cooperation and Development (OECD).

Development Assistance Committee Comprises 20 of 24 wealthier countries which are members of the Organisation for Economic Cooperation and Development (OECD), under whose aegis it operates to provide aid to poor nations. Such help is termed Official Development Assistance.

Development Phase Period when a proven oil or gas field is brought into production by drilling production wells.

Development Well Well used to produce oil or gas from a proven field.

Deviated Well Well drilled at an angle rather than vertically primarily to allow as large an area as possible to be drained of hydrocarbons from a single production platform.

Dextrose Sugar substitute obtained from corn starch.

Diesel Fuel Light oil fuel used in diesel engines.

Differentials See Allowances.

Digital Option See Binary Option.

Dilution Reduction in per share participation of net earnings through an increase in issued stock. Occurs when a rights or free scrip issue is made. In the U.S., fully diluted earnings per share are earnings after assuming the exercise of warrants and stock options and the conversion of convertible bonds and preferred stock.

Direct Paper Paper, typically Commercial Paper (CP), issued directly by the issuer to the investor, without the intervention of an intermediary. Firms issuing by this method are typically large finance companies and bank holding companies.

Direct Quotation The number of units of domestic currency that can be exchanged for one unit of foreign currency. Also known as a European quotation. See Indirect Quotation.

Directional Movement Index Determines the strength of any upward or downward trends present in a market. It plots four indices. +DM, a measure of a price rising over a period of time, -DM, price falls over a period of time, -DX, the overall index of directional movement up and down, ADX, a smoothing of that overall index. A buy signal can be interpreted when +DM is greater than -DM with the ADX rising. A sell signal is seen when -DM is greater than +DM with the ADX falling.

Dirty (Black) Crude oils, fuel oil and some lower grades of gas oil.

Dirty Bill of Lading Bill of lading which qualifies the goods being carried.

Dirty Cargo A cargo of crude oil carried in tankers.

Dirty Float A system where no official parities for currencies are declared or maintained. In this scenario, a nation's monetary authority intervenes in foreign exchange markets. Also known as a managed float.

Dirty Price Present value of the cash flow of a bond including accrued interest. Also known as gross price. See Clean Price.

Discount An amount paid below the normal price level. In the money markets it is the action of buying financial paper at less than par value. In the foreign exchange markets it is a margin by which the forward rate falls below spot. In the futures market it is referred to as Backwardation. An option can also trade at a discount, meaning that the premium is less than the intrinsic value. Opposite to Premium.

Discount Bond Bond launched at a deep discount to face value, typically with a coupon well below current market levels. See Zero Coupon Bond.

Discount Factor The rate used to derive net present value of a sum of money to be paid at a future date. See Present Value.

Discount House - U.K. Institution acting as an intermediary between the Bank of England and the banking system. In fact, the Bank of England lends to the market via the discount houses by repurchasing U.K. Treasury bills as a form of managing liquidity and implementing monetary policy. Discount houses are known as bill brokers since they specialise in bills. See U.K. - Key Interest Rates.

Discount Rate Interest rate at which a central bank will discount government paper or lend money against government paper collateral. See separate entries such as "Germany - Key Interest Rates" for the Group of 10 nations and Switzerland.

Discount Window The facility set up by central banks who will act as "lender of last resort" to their commercial banks. Central banks lend at their discretion, and not as a right, to commercial banks at the discount rate.

Discount Yield The yield on a security which sells at a discount.

Discounted Cash Flow Establishes the relative worth of a future investment project by discounting the expected cash flows from the project against its net present value, commonly used in valuing companies and as a component of equity valuation.

Discovery Well Exploratory well that finds new reserves of oil/gas.

Discretionary Account An account for which the broker or bank has a discretionary power of attorney from the holder, either completely or within set limits, to manage on his behalf.

Disintermediation Process where borrowers move to borrow directly from investment institutions and bypass banks, typically by issuing securities.

Disinvestment Cutting capital investment by disposing of capital goods such as plant and machinery or by not replacing capital assets.

Disparity Disparity occurs when the total market value of the ordinary shares does not equal the market value of the convertible shares. This happens when the prices on both shares move in opposite directions, providing the investor with an arbitrage opportunity.

Distillates Products resulting from condensation during distillation in a refinery, i.e. gaseous fuels, gas oil and kerosene oils. The refining process separates or purifies liquids by successive vaporisation and condensation.

Distributed Profits Profits distributed to shareholders via dividend payments.

Diversification An investment strategy which involves investing in different securities or industries to reduce the risk associated with investing in too few securities. This risk of "putting all your eggs in one basket" is also known as stock specific risk. By investing in a wider range of companies, a loss in one share could be offset by a gain in another.

Dividend The part of a company's after tax earnings which is distributed to the shareholders. The board of directors of the company decides how much dividend is paid and when. The dividend is neither automatic nor guaranteed for ordinary shareholders. The dividend can be in the form of cash or shares.

Dividend Cover Extent to which a company's dividend and/or interest disbursement is matched or exceeded by its earnings. Expressed as a multiple. The company's rating in the market increases as the multiple rises.

Dividend Discount Model A model of share valuation most readily comparable with bond evaluation, whereby the expected dividend payments on the shares are discounted by an appropriate rate. This assumes a constant rate of performance and a constant discount rate.

Dividend Reinvestment The reinvestment of the cash dividend by buying further shares in the same company.

Dividend Right Certificate A Swiss security, similar to a participation certificate, which does not confer ownership but instead gives a right to a share in a company's profits or any proceeds from its liquidation. Known as Genußschein in German and Bon de Jouissance in French.

Dividend Stripping A term used to describe a speculator's strategy whereby shares are purchased shortly before a dividend payment date, based on the belief that a much higher dividend will be paid than normal. Also practised in Germany where dividend income is taxable but, after six months, price gains are not.

Dividend Yield The return that the annual dividend of a share represents in relation to the current share price. Calculated by dividing the annual per share dividend by the current market price.

Dividends in Specie Particularly applies to South Africa where a company is not giving or receiving a dividend in cash as the dividend is in the form of shares in other companies in which it has a stake. It can retain them or hand them over to shareholders in any stipulated ratio to shares already held.

DIW   Deutsches Institut für Wirtschaftsforschung in Berlin. One of six German research institutes which produce regular individual reports and in spring and autumn a joint report on the state of the economy.

DJIA   See Dow Jones Industrial Average.

Dockage   Waste and foreign material found in grains and oilseeds when grading takes place.

Documentary Credit   Used in financing foreign trade. May be confirmed or unconfirmed, revocable or irrevocable. Provides an exporter with immediate payment and an importer with credit.

DOF   See Department of Finance - Canada.

Dollar Duration   See Basis Point Value.

Domestic Bond   A bond issued in the country in which the borrower is domiciled and issued in the currency of that country. See Foreign Bond.

Done   Dealers' language to verbally confirm a deal.

Double Barrelled Securities   Municipals backed by not only tax revenues but also specific fees and charges.

Double Dated Gilts - U.K.   U.K. Treasury securities with a call feature which may be exercised with three months' notice by the government on any date between the two fixed redemption dates (normally a three year gap). Also known as optional redemption gilts or callable gilts.

Double Top / Bottom   A double top is a reversal pattern that occurs in an uptrending market. The market sets a new high but then declines to a support level. The following rally is unable to break the previous peak on the close and consequently begins to fall again. The double top is confirmed when the price breaks through the previous reaction low. The typical top has two prominent peaks at about the same level. The minimum measuring target is the height of the top projected down from the breakdown point. The process works in reverse for a double bottom. A double top is often called an M and a bottom a W.

Dow Jones Average   A composite index made up of the Dow Jones Industrial, Transport and Utility averages.

Dow Jones Industrial Average (DJIA)   The DJIA is a stock index showing the price weighted arithmetic average of 30 representative industrial blue chips which are actively traded on the New York Stock Exchange. No futures or options are traded on this index. Calculated continuously. It is

actually one segment of a larger index known as the Dow Jones Average.

Dow Theory   Holds that a major stock market trend has to be confirmed by a parallel change in the Dow Jones Industrial Average and the Dow Jones Transportation Average. A trend is perceived as unconfirmed until both indices touch new highs or lows.

Down and In   A trigger option that is activated when the price of the underlying falls to a predetermined level. A type of barrier option.

Down and Out   A knockout option that is cancelled when the price of the underlying falls below a predetermined level. A type of barrier option.

Down Average   The indication in a moving average convergence that shows an overbought situation and, hence, a sell signal. See Moving Average Convergence / Divergence (MACD).

Downgrading   The reduction of credit rating for a borrowing institution or its debt instruments. Opposite to Upgrading.

Downstream   Operations such as refining, transportation and marketing, all of which take place after crude is produced.

Downtrend   See Uptrend / Downtrend.

Dragon Bonds   The Asian Development Bank set up the dragon bond market three years ago in an effort to develop the area's capital markets. Bonds, usually denominated in U.S. dollars, are offered throughout the region but not in Japan. They are usually short-dated, three to five years. Bonds tend to come from companies well known in the U.S., Japan and Europe, who want to expand their range of investors from among Asia's rapidly growing economies.

Draught   Distance between the surface of the water and the keel of a ship. A safe draught allows the vessel to negotiate shallow water.

Drawdown   Drawing down funds made available from financial institutions. It can include credits from the International Monetary Fund, Eurocredits from banks or a corporate use of credit granted by a domestic bank.

Dried Cocoon   Raw material for silk, traded in Maebashi and Toyohashi in Japan.

Drill Bit   Head of a drilling tool which cuts through rock.

Drill Collars   Heavy steel tubing located immediately above the drill bit to maintain pressure on the bit and keep the drill string in tension.

Drill Ship   Vessel with a derrick for drilling in waters which are too deep for a jack-up rig.

Drill Stem Test Test of the formation fluids in a possible oil/gas bearing stratum by letting them flow to the surface through the drill string under strictly controlled conditions.

Drill String Steel piping in approximately 10 metre lengths which connects the bit to the drilling rig. As the hole is drilled, the rotation allows the lubricating mud to circulate. Sometimes called the drill pipe.

Drilling Mud Mix of clays, water and chemicals pumped down the drill string to lubricate the system. It also carries away rock cuttings and maintains pressure at the bit end.

Drilling Platform Platform for drilling offshore, or for inland waterways exploration, or for development wells but without the processing facilities found on a production platform.

Drilling Rig Mobile machinery which has all the equipment needed for drilling a well.

Dry Hole Non-productive well, i.e. no gas or oil in commercial quantities.

Dry Natural Gas Natural gas with few associated liquids and mostly methane.

DTB The Deutsche Terminbörse (DTB) is the German futures and options exchange based in Frankfurt and was the first fully electronic exchange to be introduced in Germany, i.e. totally computer based and no actual trading floor. Contracts include the Notional Government Bond future and option, the DAX Index future and option and standard equity options.

DTC See Depository Trust Corporation.

Dual Capacity U.K. securities firms were allowed from 1986 to undertake both broking (retail) and jobbing (wholesale) activities. See Big Bang.

Dual Currency Bond A bond that pays a coupon in one currency but is redeemed for a fixed amount of another currency, often the dollar. Investors usually get an above market coupon but run the risk that, in this example, the dollar would fall below the exchange rate implied when the amount was fixed. These bonds are attractive to borrowers that operate in the currency of redemption because they have no long term exchange rate risk. For other borrowers the guaranteed exchange rate can be used in a swap, for example, with corporations having liabilities in the currency of issue.

Dual Currency Warrant The holder is able to switch into an issue in a currency different from that of the original bond. Thus he can avoid currency depreciation.

Dual Listing A company which is listed on more than one stock exchange.

Dual Pricing Identical product sold at different prices in different markets or countries.

Dubai Crude A leading benchmark crude oil produced in the United Arab Emirates, used in pricing sour crudes. Used predominantly in pricing Middle East crude exports to Asia.

Dunnage Materials - boards, matting, burlap - used to prevent cargo coming into contact with the ship's metal structure or with other cargo.

Duration A measure of the average maturity of a series of cash flows, i.e. the coupon payments and principal of a bond. Quoted in years and indicates the average exposure to market risk. A five year zero coupon bond will have a duration of five years since coupons are not paid and reinvested. Known as Macaulay Duration.

Dutch Auction An auction where the price is lowered gradually - from a price well above the true value - until a responsive bid is seen. This then becomes the price at which the offering is sold. The U.S. Treasury sells its Treasury bills using a similar basis where the bids are termed tenders.

Dutch Bullet Bonds These bonds have become the most liquid issue since they replaced sinking funds. Although guilders carry maturities from five to 30 years, the most recently issued 10 or 15 year bond is always the benchmark issue.

Dutch Sinking Fund Issues These issues dominated the market until the mid 1980s. Since international investors showed less interest than domestic investors in sinking fund issues, they have been replaced by bullet issues in an effort to internationalise the Dutch government bond market. The outstanding sinking fund issues have therefore become illiquid.

DVP See Delivery Versus Payment.

Dynamic Asian Economies See Newly Industrialising Countries.

Early Redemption The repurchase of a bond before maturity by the issuer.

Earnings Per Share See EPS.

Ease of Movement A method of measuring how easily prices are moving. Its basic definition is percentage price change (trading range midpoint) multiplied by the price range and divided by volume. Range and volume are normalised by making each relative to its moving average which then allows meaningful comparisons of ease of movement between instruments with differing range and volume concepts.

East Asian Economic Caucus A loosely defined consultative forum to discuss trade and economic matters affecting the East Asian region. It has been adopted as an ASEAN initiative.

Easy Money A term used when credit and money are lavishly available, associated with a relaxed monetary policy and often, but not always, accompanied by moderate or low interest rates. Opposite to dear money. Also known as cheap money.

EBRD See European Bank for Reconstruction and Development.

EC Monetary Committee See Monetary Committee of the European Community.

ECGD U.K. government funded Export Credits Guarantee Department.

ECLAC Economic Commission for Latin America and the Caribbean. Based in Chile, it is a United Nations sponsored body which coordinates economic development policies in the region. Has 41 members and seven associates.

ECO Economic Cooperation Organisation. Based in Teheran. Stimulates cooperation in economic and infrastructure projects. Members are Afghanistan, Azerbaijan, Iran, Kyrgyzstan, Pakistan, Tajikistan, Turkey, Turkmenistan and Uzbekistan.

Econometrics Use of statistical and mathematical methods to verify and develop economic theories. Also covers the development of plans and implementation of policies based on economic findings.

Economic and Monetary Union (EMU) Planned by the European Community, involving a single market which allows free movement of people, goods, capital and services; formation of the European Monetary Institute, the precursor to the single EC central bank; and a single EC currency.

Economic and Social Commission for Western Asia Aims to stimulate inter-nation trade among its 13 members which includes the six from the Gulf Cooperation Council.

Economic Indicators Barometers of a nation's growth, with major ones issued usually monthly or quarterly by a government department. Examples are gross domestic product, consumer price index, money supply, trade balance and unemployment.

Economic Recovery Programme - Germany The ERP was set up as one of the primary sources of economic support for Eastern Germany. Only issued two 10 year German government bonds (Bund) which carry the explicit guarantee of the government.

Economic Risk The risk associated with changes in exchange rates or local regulations which could favour services or products of a competitor.

ECOWAS Economic Community of West African States. Based in Nigeria. Promotes trade, cooperation and self reliance and aims to accelerate economic integration. Members are Benin, Burkina Faso, Cape Verde, the Ivory Coast, the Gambia, Ghana, Guinea, Guinea-Bissau, Liberia, Mali, Mauritania, Niger, Nigeria, Senegal, Sierra Leone and Togo.

ECP Commercial paper issued in the Euromarkets and usually placed via a dealer mechanism. The market began in 1986 but has not been without difficulties as it tends to be less well regulated than the domestic markets, with fewer restrictions on the quality of issuers. See CP.

ECU See European Currency Unit.

Edge Act The U.S. federal law of 1919 which gives commercial banks the right to carry out international activities across state lines.

Edge Act Corporation A subsidiary in the U.S. involved with foreign lending activities. It is federal or state chartered. See Edge Act.

EDR See European Depositary Receipt.

EDSP The Exchange Delivery Settlement Price is the official closing price of a futures contract given by the futures exchange at the end of every trading day. This price is used for marking to market purposes and for calculations of actual cash settlement amounts required on the expiry date or on the closing out of a futures position.

EEA See European Economic Area.

Effective Date The date on which some feature of a risk management contract begins or becomes due. In the swap market, it is the date from which the fixed and floating start to accrue and it usually coincides with the settlement date of the swap.

Effective Exchange Rate Composite exchange rate, normally presented as an index intended to reflect the overall performance of a currency against its main trading partners on a trade weighted basis.

EFTA See European Free Trade Association.

EFTPOS Electronic Funds Transfer at Point of Sale such as the use of credit or debit cards at a retail outlet.

EFTS Electronic Funds Transfer System such as automatic teller machines for the customers of banks.

EIB See European Investment Bank.

Either Way See Choice Price.

El Niño Periodic warming, in varying degrees and of varying duration, of the cold water Peru Current. Beyond the immediate effect - a reduced anchovy catch off the Peru coast - El Niño is believed to be the cause of various weather disruptions around the Pacific notably bringing drought in Australia and storms affecting California.

Elevators Storage facility for grains, oilseeds and some by-products. Can be a commercial facility or a storage on a farm. Some elevators are approved by commodity exchanges as delivery points for grain under futures contracts. Public elevators are licensed and regulated by state and federal agencies.
   In the U.S., there are three classes:
   - independent elevators, owned and operated by individuals who provide the capital and share in the profits.
   - cooperative elevators, run by associations of farmers with their own capital structures and with returnable profits.
   - line elevators, chains owned by a grain company and usually near a railroad system.

Eligible Bills A bill is said to be eligible when it can be taken by a central bank at the discount window in return for funds to a bank. See Bills of Exchange.

Elliott Wave Theory A theory which holds that the market follows a repetitive pattern consisting of a five wave rise followed by a three wave fall, with these rises and falls completing the cycle. In the advance, the impulse waves (1, 3 and 5) are rising waves while the corrective waves (2 and 4) move against the uptrend. In the subsequent three wave decline, waves A and C are falling but B moves against the downtrend. Each wave forms part of the wave of the next higher degree. There are many different degrees of trend but the Elliott Wave theory categorises nine different trends (or magnitude) ranging from a Grand Supercycle covering 200 years to a subminuette of only a couple of hours. The eight wave cycle is constant regardless of what degree of trend is being considered.

Eluvial Deposit disclosed by movement of water with the deposit remaining in its original position.

Embargo Temporary action, generally by one country, to halt shipment of goods into or out of another country.

EMCF See European Monetary Cooperation Fund.

Emerging Growth Stock Shares issued by a newly underwritten company with no previous growth record but showing good prospects. Such companies are often financed by venture capital.

EMI See European Monetary Institute.

Employee Stock Option Plan See ESOP.

EMS See European Monetary System.

EMS Realignment The changing of the currencies' central rates within the European Monetary System. This occurs if market pressure is too strong in terms of a currency weakening or strengthening within the system. The moves are then decided in detail, with various options considered, by the Monetary Committee of the European Community.

EMTN See MTN.

EMU See Economic and Monetary Union.

Endosperm That part of a grain kernel that contains the gluten and starch particles.

English Auction An auction where an item goes to the highest bidder providing it is above the seller's reserve price.

Enhanced Scrip Dividend Offers a dividend to shareholders in the form of extra shares which have a market value greater than the value of the dividend. They can usually be sold immediately by the holder.

Enhanced Structural Adjustment Facility Funds lent by the International Monetary Fund at a very low interest rate, currently 0.5 percent, to low income developing nations, mostly in sub-Saharan Africa.

Enlarged Access Method of allowing countries to bend some of the rules in lending by the International Monetary Fund, provided they promise to undertake strong policy measures aimed at redressing payment imbalances.

Enterprise Zone Sites in depressed, mostly inner urban areas, where companies are given favourable taxation treatment and are freed of various planning regulations.

Entrepot A warehouse. Also a major international trading centre to which goods are shipped for re-export.

EOE The European Options Exchange (EOE), located in Amsterdam, opened in April 1978 to establish a regular market in options. Option contracts exist on individual stocks, the Dutch Stock Index, the Major Market Index, the Eurotop 100 Index, Dutch Government bonds, dollar/guilder and gold. The EOE owns 100 percent of the shares of the Financial Futures Market Amsterdam (FTA). Futures contracts are traded at the FTA. See EOE Index.

EOE Index The main Netherlands stock market index is the Amsterdam based European Options Exchange (EOE), price weighted, arithmetic and composed of 24 of the most actively traded Dutch shares. Calculated continuously. Options on the index are traded on the EOE and futures are traded on the Amsterdam Financial Futures Market (FTA). See EOE, FTA.

EPS Earnings per Share. A figure representing the amount of a company's net earnings which is available to each outstanding ordinary share. The number of outstanding ordinary shares does not include treasury stock or any ordinary share equivalents, such as convertible bonds, convertible preferred shares, warrants or stock options. If these are included, the company would report a fully-diluted earnings per share. The EPS is calculated by dividing the net earnings available for distribution to ordinary shareholders by the number of ordinary shares in issue. This figure is a very important indicator of a company's present growth as well as future growth prospects.

Equity Crude A company's share of oil production in a concession and normally given in proportion to its stake in the field.

Equity Fund A type of investment fund investing primarily in ordinary and/or preferred shares.

Equity Income Fund A type of investment fund specialising in investing in high dividend ordinary and preferred shares.

Equity Options Similar to a Warrant, in that the option can allow for future purchase or sale of the individual stocks, indices or baskets of stocks. Also known as stock options.

Equity Security A security which represents ownership in a company and the right to receive a share in the profits of that company. Equity securities are therefore stocks or shares.

Equity Warrant Allows investors to buy company shares over the life of the warrant at a fixed exercise price which usually represents a premium over the current or average share price. It is often attached to a bond but, unlike a convertible issue, the bond itself continues to exist if the investor buys shares. Because of this inducement, the bond can pay a lower coupon at par.

ERA An Exchange Rate Agreement is a SAFE contract (Synthetic Agreement for Forward Exchange) whereby settlement has reference to two forward rates and not to the spot rate. See FXA.

ERM See Exchange Rate Mechanism.

ERP See Economic Recovery Programme - Germany.

ESOP The Employee Stock Option Plan is a retirement plan in which employees receive ordinary shares of the company. The company receives an investment tax credit.

Established Growth Stock Shares issued by established companies and which have been trading steadily for some years with established growth.

ETBE Ethyl Tertiary Butyl Ether. An ethyl based gasoline additive used to boost fuel performance and to cut harmful emissions.

Ethane Colourless odourless gas sometimes extracted from natural gas as feedstock for the chemical industry.

Ethanol An alcohol produced from such materials as corn, wheat, sugar, potatoes.
   In the U.S., it is commonly taken from wet milling of corn while in Brazil it is mostly derived from sugar. See Gasohol.

Eurobond A bond issued in a specific currency outside the currency's domicile. Eurobonds are not subject to witholding tax and fall outside the jurisdiction of any one country. Major Eurobond issuers are large international corporations, governments and their agencies and international institutions.

EUROCLEAR International clearing organisation, founded in 1968 and located in Brussels, which provides clearance/settlement and borrowing/lending of securities and funds through a computerised book entry system. EUROCLEAR is managed by Morgan Guaranty Trust Company. See CEDEL.

Eurocredits / Euroloans Large bank credits usually with maturities of three to 10 years granted by international bank syndicates put together on an ad hoc basis. Lenders are almost exclusively banks and finance companies, thus these credits are not placed with private investors. Interest rates are calculated by adding a margin to interbank offered rates and usually adjusted every three to six months. Funds for the loans are drawn from the Eurodeposit market.

Eurocurrency A currency that is held on deposit outside its country of origin. The most extensively used Eurocurrency is the Eurodollar.

Eurodeposits Deposits placed outside the currency's domicile. For example, Eurodollar deposits are dollars held outside the U.S. and Euromark deposits are German marks held outside Germany.

Eurodollar See Eurocurrency.

Eurodollar CDs Major issuers in London are the major U.S. bank names and the U.K. clearers. Delivery is in New York on the day the certificate of deposit is presented for payment in London. Issues are normally for one million dollars and usually for three and six months. Rates track domestic U.S. CD rates but Eurodollar CDs offer slightly more as they are less liquid. U.K. discount houses began the sterling CD market in 1968. See CDs.

Euroilstock Netherlands based Stichting Euroilstock. A reporting system initiated by the oil industry and the European Commission. Issues monthly data covering the 12 EC member nations, including crude oil and petroleum product primary stocks on land and refinery production figures.

Euromarket - History Euromarkets emerged in the early 1950s when banks throughout the world began to lend and borrow in dollars and have prospered since because they are free from domestic regulatory controls. It is accepted that they began because Eastern European nations wanted their dollar earnings to be held outside the U.S. and because the Federal Reserve enforced relatively low interest rates on domestic banks, mostly via Regulation Q. Euromarkets expanded dramatically from 1974 after the Organisation of Petroleum Exporting Countries (OPEC) raised the price of oil and thus "petro dollars" were deposited short term in the relatively high interest Euromarkets. Banks then lent these to other nations. Later, the market expanded and thus the Asian dollar market came into being. In the early 1980s (IBFs) International Banking Facilities were set up via the U.S. as a type of offshore banking area, this being an extension of Euromarket activities inasmuch as they comprised currencies invested outside their country of origin.

European Bank for Reconstruction and Development The EBRD was formed in 1991 in London with the object of helping private enterprises in Central and East European nations. Nearly all of these are members. Known as the European Bank.

European Banking Federation Based in Brussels, the Federation is recognised by the European Community Commission, the European Council of Ministers and the European Parliament as the representative body for the community's commercial banking sector.

European Community The EC is a group of 12 European nations, centred in Brussels, run by a 17 member Executive Commission which has the sole right to propose EC policies but cannot decide them. Decisions are the prerogative of the 12 member governments meeting as the EC Council of Ministers. However, the Commission enjoys discretionary powers for implementing the EC's policies and is the guardian of EC treaties. Each Commission member has a wide range of special responsibilities. One, for example, will handle economic and financial affairs, credit and investment, statistical office matters (plus

monetary affairs together with the EC president). Another will be responsible for external economic affairs (involving North America, Japan, China, the Commonwealth of Independent States, Europe (including central and eastern Europe) and trade policy. See European Union.

European Currency Unit (ECU) The ECU is a composite currency, based on a basket, with each nation's currency weighted according to each country's share in intra-European Community trade, its percentage share of EC gross national product and the relative importance of each country's foreign exchange reserves. It is calculated daily and is the basis for European Rate Mechanism parities. It is being increasingly used in its own right for trading purposes and to denominate bond issues.

European Depositary Receipt Bearer document allowing trading to take place in U.S., U.K. and Japanese registered company shares on certain European exchanges.

European Economic Area (EEA) The single market group that came into being January 1 1994. Formed from the 12 member European Community and the European Free Trade Association. Five of the seven EFTA members joined the EEA on January 1 while Liechtenstein is renegotiating its customs agreement with Switzerland, whose voters rejected taking part in the EEA market. Switzerland aims for bilateral accords with the EC. Four of the EFTA/EEA members - Austria, Finland, Norway, Sweden - are negotiating to join and fully integrate with the EC.

European Free Trade Association (EFTA) The EFTA group comprises Austria, Finland, Iceland, Norway, Sweden and Switzerland. Liechtenstein is an associate member so the group in effect has seven members. Has had a link to the European Community through a customs union. See European Economic Area (EEA).

European Investment Bank (EIB) The long term financing body of the European Community. Its main aim is to help regional development among the member nations and especially to aid less developed areas on a macro-economic scale. It also provides soft loans to developing countries associated with the EC. Based in Luxembourg.

European Monetary Cooperation Fund (EMCF) Also known by the French abbreviation FECOM. It finances and settles claims by EC central banks on each other resulting from intervention under the European Monetary System.

European Monetary Institute (EMI) Precursor to the European Community Central Bank. Came into being January 1994. Permanent location in Frankfurt. Its task is to coordinate monetary policy among members and to deal with the practical details of a future EC single currency, with an effective date near the end of the century.

European Monetary System (EMS) The EMS which began in 1979 is a monetary system among the member states of the European Community. Chief components are the European Currency Unit (ECU) and the Exchange Rate Mechanism (ERM). All EC nations are members of the EMS but they do not all belong to the ERM. ERM members can, in times of currency upheaval, leave and then later rejoin the ERM. The EMS was preceded by the Snake.

European Option An option which the holder can only exercise on the expiry date. See American Option.

European Options Exchange See EOE.

European Parliament Directly elected assembly for representatives of the European Community member states. On most issues its role is purely consultative. The major exception is the budget where it shares decision making powers with the Council of Ministers, which represents EC governments.

European Quotation See Direct Quotation.

European Union The official all-embracing name for the European Community. This follows the effective date - November 1 1993 - for the Treaty on European Union, commonly known as the Maastricht Treaty. The Treaty formally created a new entity, the European Union, with responsibilities beyond the EC focus on economic and trade issues. The EU also takes in rules governing common foreign and security policy, procedures for cooperation on terrorism, crime, immigration, asylum and other domestic and judicial matters.

EUROSTAT The statistics agency of the European Community. The system of actually collating the data, which concerns trade of the member nations, is INTRASTAT.

Eurotop 100 An index traded at the Amsterdam based European Options Exchange (EOE) and comprising 100 of the most actively traded stocks from nine countries - Belgium, France, Germany, Italy, Netherlands, Spain, Sweden, Switzerland and the U.K. Country weightings are by market capitalisation, company weightings are by volume of turnover. It covers 17 sectors. Calculated continuously. The value of the basket of shares is expressed in ECU.

Options on this index are traded by EOE and by the American Stock Exchange. Futures are traded on the Amsterdam Financial Futures Market (FTA). Both options and futures are traded on the New York Commodity Exchange (COMEX).

Even Lot Commodity trading unit governed by official exchange price quotations.

Event of Default A borrower fails to comply with a covenant within a loan agreement (or bond) thereby bringing the debt into Default.

Event Risk The risk that the credit rating of a borrower and therefore the ability to make payments may depreciate owing to an industrial or natural disaster, regulatory changes, a takeover or a corporate restructuring. In 1989 Standard & Poor's introduced event risk ratings.

Ex Means excluding. Thus ex cap, ex div, ex rights. Indicates that a buyer of shares does not receive a current capitalisation issue, a current dividend or a current rights issue. Opposite to Cum.

Ex All Means a buyer of shares does not receive any of the supplementary benefits attached to a share at the time.

Ex Dividend Date Date on which bondholders are eligible for coupon payments. For a certain period of time before the coupon payment, the bond trades in ex dividend form and has a negative accrued interest. An investor who buys a bond between the ex dividend date and the coupon payment does not receive the coupon and it goes to the previous holder of that bond. The ex dividend date varies from country to country.

Ex Pit Transactions Trades executed outside the exchange trading ring or pit. Mainly used for fixing prices when cash commodities are being bought.

Ex Rights Date The date on which shareholders are eligible for the rights issue. Up until this date, the share trades with the rights (cum rights). During the period from the ex rights date to the end of the subscription period, the share is traded without the rights (ex rights). Similarly applies to dividends and capitalisation issues.

Ex Store Relates to the sale of commodities currently held in a warehouse or other storage facility.

EX-IM Bank of Japan The Export-Import Bank of Japan, a state owned bank that specialises in loans to developing countries. As a government backed institution it can borrow on the Japanese markets at favourable rates.

Exceptional Item An item which is within normal business activities but which is of unusual size. It is usually recorded separately in the profit and loss account. See Extraordinary Item.

Exchange Controls Used to protect and maintain a country's financial position and the value of its

currency. The regulations are aimed at preventing or restricting certain foreign currency transactions, mostly by a country's nationals. The movement of precious metals, particularly gold and silver, can be governed by these controls.

Exchange Delivery Settlement Price   See EDSP.

Exchange for Physical   Occurs where the buyer of a cash commodity transfers to the seller an equivalent amount of long futures contracts or receives from him a corresponding amount of short futures at an agreed price. Also termed exchange for cash, and against actuals. In gold trading, an exchange or swap of a position in the futures market for one of the same size in the physical market.

Exchange Option   An option which grants the holder the right to surrender one asset in exchange for another. These options are useful where no traded cross-market option exists.

Exchange Rate Agreement   See ERA.

Exchange Rate Mechanism (ERM)   A system aimed at limiting short term movements between European Community currencies. Most member currencies were allowed to move by no more than 2.25 percent either side of a fixed bilateral central rate against other member currencies. However, a few currencies were allowed to fluctuate by six percent either side of their central parities for an undetermined initial period. In August 1993 - following turmoil on the foreign exchange markets - member currencies were allowed to move by 15 percent either side of their central rates. However, the German mark and the Dutch guilder retained their 2.25 percent fluctuation limits.

Exchange-Traded Contract   Standard futures and options listed and traded on a recognised exchange. Opposite to Over the Counter (OTC).

Exchangeable Bond - France   Emprunts échangeables issued in France with the option to exchange a fixed rate bond for a floating rate bond or vice versa during a predetermined time period. These bonds have become less liquid since the creation of OATs.

Exchanges   Trades of crude or products between producers or refiners usually carried out for quality reasons or to save transportation costs.

Exercise   To make use of the right possessed by the holder of an option. Upon receipt of notification, the writer of the option is obliged to the holder on the terms already agreed. See Assignment.

Exercise Price   See Strike Price.

Exit Bond   A long term bond with a low interest rate, often issued by a less developed country, that gives the buyer the right of exemption from taking part in any subsequent rescheduling. Thus an exit bond allows an investor to convert his existing loans and offers a way out of sovereign lending when the bond is resold or when it matures.

Exotic Currencies   Currencies known as exotics are not traded very often and are thus not considered to be part of the recognised international foreign exchange market.

Exotic Options   Options with a more complicated structure than a standard call and put, incorporating special elements or restrictions.

Expiry Date   The date on which delivery takes place on a futures contract. In options trading, it is the date on which a European option can be exercised. Also known as declaration date and expiration date.

Exploration Drilling   Drilling carried out to establish whether hydrocarbons are present in a particular area or structure.

Exponential Moving Average   Unlike other moving averages, the exponential moving average maintains all price data in its calculation. However, each observation factor is made progressively less significant via the use of smoothing factors. As an indicator, the exponential moving average works in the same way as the simple moving average. See Modified Exponential Moving Average.

Export Enhancement Program   U.S. programme, established in 1985, which allows exporters to receive a subsidy to sell U.S. products to foreign customers at world market prices. The U.S. Department of Agriculture subsidises the difference in the world price and the higher domestic price - which exporters have to pay for the product - in the form of commodities from the Commodity Credit Corporation inventory or cash. The programme is targeted to countries benefiting from subsidised imports from non-U.S. exporters.

Export Quota   Quota set under an international commodity agreement whereby exporting countries of a particular commodity accept limits on their exports.

   Also a bilateral or multilateral agreement between countries governing exports of industrial or other goods.

Export Refunds   Refunds or restitutions made under the European Community Common Agricultural Policy on exports of sugar, grain, beef, skimmed milk powder and so forth. Refunds are intended to help exports by offsetting the difference between the internal EC price and lower world price.

Export-Import Bank   In the U.S., this is a government export credit agency which provides insurance and export guarantees for exports from the U.S. and advances credit to non-U.S. borrowers to buy American goods. It is an independent entity which can borrow from the U.S. Treasury.

Exposure   The total amount of credit committed to a borrower or a country. Banks can set rules to prevent over exposure to any single borrower. In trading operations, it is the potential for running a profit or loss from fluctuations in market prices.

Extendable Bond - France   Emprunts prorogeables issued in France with the option to extend the maturity to a predetermined date. These bonds have become less liquid since the creation of OATs.

Extended Fund Facility   Assistance given to International Monetary Fund member nations with economies suffering from serious balance of payments difficulties due to structural imbalances in production, trade and prices or economies characterised by slow growth and an inherently weak balance of payments position. Drawings can be made over a period of three years under conditions similar to IMF standby drawings.

Extendible Bond   A bond on which terms are reset for a further period beyond the initial maturity date. However, both the borrower and the investor will typically have the right to redeem the bonds at these refixings.

Extraction Industry   Industry involved in extracting raw materials from the land, sea or air.

Extraction Rate   Proportion by weight of a processed product to its raw material.

Extraordinary General Meeting   A meeting of shareholders called in addition to the AGM to discuss a particular situation affecting the shareholders and their holdings.

Extraordinary Item   A non-recurring item which shows gains or losses outside normal business activities that is shown in the profit and loss account and affects the balance sheet. It can be, for example, the sale of property or loss from selling part of the company. See Exceptional Item.

Extrapolation   The process of determining a rate (or other variable) that lies beyond the range of known rates. See Interpolation.

Extrusion   Heating metal to a plastic condition and pushing it through a die thus allowing fast and economical production of long lengths of complicated sections.

Fabricator   Company which makes semi-fabricated products from refined metal and sometimes from scrap.

Face Value   Apparent worth. The nominal value which appears on the face of the document recording an entitlement, generally a certificate or a bond. For debt instruments, the amount to be repaid at maturity. Known as par value or nominal value.

Facility Fee   Payment made by a borrower to a lender for arranging a loan.

Factor   A seven digit decimal number which represents the balance of the principal outstanding in a mortgage pool.

Factoring   A credit collection service. A company sells its receivables to a factor - sometimes a bank subsidiary - at a discount. This firm then collects the funds owed and earns its profit via the discount. The company gains from an improved cash flow. A factor can also offer short term finance.

Failure Swing   A term used in technical analysis with specific reference to the RSI. Failure swings occur at either end of the parameters as set by the user - usually above 70 or below 30. A top failure swing occurs if the market is in an uptrend and the RSI is over 70 but the next peak fails to exceed the previous peak. Similarly, a bottom failure swing occurs if the market is in a downtrend and the RSI is below 30 but the next peak fails to fall below the previous peak. See Relative Strength Index (RSI).

Fair Value   A term used in the futures market which would represent the cash price plus the net cost of carry. In the options market it is the value derived from the mathematical equation used.

Fallen Angels   Bonds which were originally above investment grade but have subsequently fallen in credit quality.

Fannie Mae   Federal National Mortgage Association. A stockholder owned corporation, sponsored by the U.S. government, that provides funds to the mortgage market primarily by buying mortgages from mortgage originators. These are held in an investment portfolio or pooled for FNMA members. Purchases are financed by sale of corporate obligations to private investors.

FAO   Food and Agriculture Organisation, a United Nations body based in Rome. Established in 1945 to improve world agriculture, fishing and forestry. Provides technical assistance, food aid and issues forecasts and statistics on the world agricultural outlook.

FAQ   Fair Average Quality. Used in the sale of agricultural commodities, i.e. average grade based on samples rather than on a specific grade.

Farm In   A term used when one company acquires an interest in an oil exploration or production licence by paying some of the past or future costs of another company which is relinquishing part of its interest.

Farm Out   A term used when a company relinquishes part of its interest in an exploration or production licence to another company in return for part payment of its costs.

Farmer Owned Reserve   In the U.S., a long term price support programme for wheat and feedgrains which allows farmers to use their crops as collateral for government loans of up to three years.

FAS   Free Alongside Ship. A charterer's responsibility for delivering goods on quay within reach of ship's cranes and so forth.

FASB   In the U.S., the Financial Accounting Standards Board which governs accounting rules.

Fast Stochastics   This is a more sensitive analysis than the slow stochastics method. The proximity of the current market close to the high for a given period is shown by the %K line, on a scale of 0-100, where the period high is 100 and the period low is 0. A second line, the %D is a special moving average of the %K taken over in periods.

   A buy signal can be interpreted by a combination of a low %D and an even lower %K (usually less than 20). A sell signal by a high %D and an even higher %K (usually higher than 80).

   As with other momentum indicators, divergences between prices and the stochastic in the overbought (above 70-80) and oversold (below 20-30) regions can signify trend reversals. See Stochastics, Slow Stochastics.

Fats   Tallow, lard, grease and butter. The group usually includes fish oil. Fats are used for cooking oil and therefore compete with vegetable oils.

FAZ Performance Index   A stock market index, weighted according to nominal share capital, for 167 shares on the Frankfurt bourse. It incorporates the 100 shares used for the FAZ Share Index. Takes account of dividend payments as well as share price changes. Calculated once a day on the official closing prices.

FAZ Share Index   A capitalisation weighted arithmetic index of 100 leading shares which are quoted on the Frankfurt bourse. Accounts for 75 percent of the capitalisation of the German market. Calculated from official fixing prices by Germany's daily newspaper, the Frankfurter Allgemeine Zeitung.

FCOJ   Frozen Concentrated Orange Juice. The New York Cotton Exchange lists FCOJ futures and options. Contracts are used for normal pricing and hedging purposes. Florida produces the bulk of the U.S. orange crop with the rest coming from California. Additional supplies are imported, mainly from Brazil as well as from other areas including Israel.

FDIC   See Federal Deposit Insurance Corporation.

FECOM   See European Monetary Cooperation Fund (EMCF).

Fed   See Federal Reserve System - U.S.

Federal Bond Syndicate (Konsortium)   This underwriting syndicate is made up of a large number of financial institutions (German and foreign) located in Germany which are allocated a specified quota of all bond issues. This fixed quota system ensures a more global distribution of bond issues for subsequent reoffering to the public. Foreign banks in Germany were only admitted to this syndicate in July 1986.

Federal Deposit Insurance Corporation   U.S. federal agency that provides limited guarantees for funds on deposit with member banks. It also takes action to help banks merge or avoid failure.

Federal Farm Credit System   Comprises a dozen districts in the U.S. each of which has a Bank for Cooperatives, a Federal Intermediate Credit Bank and a Federal Land Bank. These exist to offer credit services to farm related enterprises and farmers. The system is capitalised by the sale of short term notes (up to 270 days) through dealers.

   A financing unit - the Federal Farm Credit Bank - sets rates while dealers run a secondary market. Six and nine month bonds are likewise available.

Federal Funds - U.S.   Reserve balances of U.S. depository institutions which exceed the level required by the Federal Reserve Bank. These excess funds can be lent out to those institutions with a shortage at the federal funds rate. See U.S. - Key Interest Rates.

Federal Home Loan Mortgage Corporation   See Freddie Mac.

Federal National Mortgage Association   See Fannie Mae.

Federal Open Market Committee   See FOMC - U.S.

Federal Reserve System - U.S.   Known as the Fed, this is the central bank system of the U.S. comprising 12 Federal Reserve Banks controlling 12 districts under the Federal Reserve Board in Washington. The 12 Fed banks are based in Atlanta, Boston, Chicago, Cleveland, Dallas, Kansas City, Minneapolis, New York, Philadelphia, Richmond, San

Francisco and St. Louis. Decisions regarding short term monetary policy are taken by the FOMC (Federal Open Market Committee).

Federal Wire - U.S. The U.S. Federal Reserve's electronic communications system linking Federal Reserve Offices, the Board, depository institutions, the Treasury and other government agencies. Used for transferring the reserve account balances of depository institutions and government securities.

Federation The central power, or national parliament, has law making and executive authority in certain areas while the federation members rule in other areas. See Confederation.

Federation of Oils Seeds and Fats Associations See FOSFA.

Feed Concentrates Term covering maize (corn), sorghum, barley, oats, wheat, rye and oilseed meal. All used in the production of animal feeds.

Feed Grains Cereals used for animal fodder such as maize (corn), sorghum, barley and oats, rye, millet and low grade wheat. Basically the same as coarse grains.

Feed Ratios Relationship between the cost of feeding animals and their market price expressed as a ratio.

Feeder Cattle Young cattle that are ready to be fattened for slaughter.

Feeds Classified by the livestock for which they are designed. i.e. poultry, hog, dairy, cattle/sheep, speciality and small animal. A further breakdown may be made such as starter feed, growing feed, finishing feed, breeder feed.

Feeds can be in the form of:
- meal, comprised of ingredients ground or processed into small particles.
- pellets, which are meal formed into small chunks.
- crumbles, which are reground or cracked pellets.

Feedstock Crude oil product, natural gas liquids or natural gas delivered to a refinery or petrochemical plant for processing. Also, the supply of an intermediate petrochemical.

FELABAN Federación Latinoamericana de Bancos (Latin American Banking Federation). Based in Bogota. Seeks to accelerate economic development. Members are 19 Latin American national banking associations.

FELIN - France Fonds d'Etat libres d'Intérêt Nominal are French zero coupon bonds formed as a result of the coupon and redemption values being traded separately. These have only been issued once and have now become illiquid. Since 1991

the French Treasury allows the SVTs (Spécialistes en Valeurs du Trésor) to strip the long bond. As from June 1993 they were also authorised to strip the new 10 year bond.

FEOP Far East Oil Price Index. Oil price index based on contributions from oil dealers. The index includes Asian price assessments for naphtha, gasoline, jet fuel, gas oil (diesel and heating oil), heavy fuel oil, regional crude oils.

FERC Federal Energy Regulatory Commission. An agency within the U.S. Department of Energy that oversees regulation of interstate natural gas pipelines and gas prices.

FHA Federal Housing Administration. U.S. federal agency which operates a variety of loan insurance and subsidy programmes to help stabilise the U.S. domestic home mortgage market, improve housing construction standards and facilitate sound financing. It is not a lender or builder.

FHA Loan A mortgage or mobile home or property improvement loan made by a private lender and insured by the Federal Housing Administration.

FHLMC See Freddie Mac.

Fibonacci Numbers / Time Targets A number sequence discovered by a 13th century Italian mathematician Leonardo Fibonacci in which the sum of any two consecutive numbers equals the next highest number. The sequence is 1,1,2,3,5,8,13,21,34,55 and so forth. The ratio of any number to its next highest number approaches 0.618 after the first four numbers. For example, 1/1 is 1.00, 1/2 is 0.50, 2/3 is 0.67, 3/5 is 0.625, 13/21 is 0.619 and so forth. These numbers are used to determine price objectives from percentage retracements.

The time targets are found by counting forward from significant tops and bottoms. On a daily chart, a trader would count forward the number of trading days from a key turning point with the expectation that future tops or bottoms are likely to occur on days which are Fibonacci numbers themselves such as the 8th, 13th, 21st and so forth. The same technique can be used on weekly, monthly, or yearly charts.

FIBOR / FIBID / FIMEAN The Frankfurt Interbank Offered Rate (FIBOR) is the rate at which banks are prepared to lend to each other for specified maturities within the Frankfurt market. FIBOR is also fixed daily for reference purposes and is a key interest rate level used for setting rates for loans and floating rate notes and for calculating cash settlements of certain interest rate derivative instruments. FIBID is the Frankfurt Interbank Bid price, the rate at which banks take deposits from each other. FIMEAN is the Frankfurt Interbank Mean price.

Fiduciary Money   Money held in trust and invested on behalf of the beneficiary.

Fifth Generation   A concept introduced in Japan to describe computer architecture using parallel processing instead of the sequential systems used previously. First generation computers were very large machines using valves. The invention of the transistor in 1947 led to the second generation while integrated circuits brought about the third generation in the early 1960s. The fourth generation came with large scale integration of at least 100 logic circuits on a single chip. The embryo sixth generation has the aim of using Neural Network architecture to resemble the working of the human brain - which uses billions of neurons to process information piece by piece at the same time instead of sequentially - and to endeavour to give computers artificial intelligence, basically the ability to solve problems and learn.

Figure   Dealers' language. In a quotation of 1.6890/00 the dealer may quote "ninety the figure". Similarly in a quotation of 1.6900/10 the dealer may quote "figure ten".

Figuring the Tail   Assessing the yield at which a future money market instrument is bought - available at some time in the future - when that instrument is formed by purchasing an existing instrument and funding the initial part with a term repurchase agreement.

Fill or Kill (FOK)   A limit order to buy or sell which must be cancelled if not carried out immediately.

FIMEAN   See FIBOR / FIBID / FIMEAN.

Final Dividend   Dividend paid by a company at the end of its financial year and authorised by shareholders at the annual general meeting.

Financial Accounting Standards Board   See FASB.

Financial Centre   A key location in a nation, often its capital, for international and domestic financial transactions, both commercial and between governmental institutions. For example, Tokyo, Paris, Brussels. In London, the financial centre is often referred to as "The City" or "The Square Mile". Among non-capital cities are New York, Chicago, Frankfurt, Milan, Hong Kong and Osaka.

Financial Futures Market Amsterdam   See FTA.

Financial Profile   An assessment of an investor's assets, liabilities, investment goals and the inclination to bear risk which is carried out by brokerage firms and portfolio managers.

Financial Reporting Standard 3   In the U.K., a company balance sheet accounting standard. Companies reporting results for financial periods ending on or after June 22, 1993 have been virtually barred from showing Below the Line any items which would previously have been described as an Extraordinary Item. The effect is to make the reported earnings figure far more volatile. See Exceptional Item.

Financial Year   The year used for a company's accounting purposes. It can be calendar or cover a different period. In both cases it can be termed the company's fiscal year.

Finanzierungsschätze - Germany   Treasury Financing Notes. German government issues with one to two year maturities, prohibited to foreigners. Very small and illiquid market.

Finanzministerium   Federal Ministry of Finance. Issuer of German government debt, considered to be part of the second tier of government bond markets in size alongside the U.K., France and Italy, and following the U.S. and Japan.

Fine Grains   Wheat and rice.

Fine Ounce   A Troy Ounce of gold that is accepted as 995 parts per thousand pure unless stated otherwise. See Good Delivery - Gold.

Fine Tuning   Flexible fiscal and monetary policies aimed at achieving precise desired short term patterns of economic performance.

Firm (FT)   Firm Transportation. Natural gas sold on a firm uninterruptable basis, usually to domestic users. Typically carries a higher price than gas sold on interruptable contracts.

Firm Order   An order to buy or sell which can be executed without further reference.

First Coupon   The date on which the initial interest payment is due on a bond.

First Notice Day   The first date on which notices of intention to deliver actual financial instruments or physical commodities against futures contracts are authorised.

Fiscal Drag   A drag on demand in the economy which occurs when incomes rise but bring an adverse effect on consumer demand because of the higher tax burden. Governments can adjust allowances and thresholds in line with inflation to reduce this fiscal drag but since, generally speaking, the chance to do this occurs only in an annual budget then a government gains from the benefit of fiscal drag.

Fiscal Policy   Means by which a government influences the economy through its budget by changes in tax and welfare payments and/or government spending. See Monetary Policy.

Fishmeal Fish processed into meal and used for livestock and poultry feed after extracting fish oil.

Five O'Clocking Term applied to a situation whereby a participant in the 15 day Brent market is unable to roll over his paper position by a 1700 deadline and is thereby forced to take possession of a physical cargo. This is normally considered a bearish signal to the market since it indicates lack of prompt demand. See Paper Barrel.

Five Wise Men The name generally given to the Council of Economic Experts in Germany. It is independent of the government and comprises five university professors who have a team of about eight economists working for them in Wiesbaden. The council produces a three part annual report - a general economic review and forecasts, both generally from the economists and a long section on economic policy from the professors. The Council's full name is Sachver-ständigenrat zur Begutachtung der gesamtwirt-schaftlichen Entwicklung.

Fixed / Floating Bonds Bonds which pay both fixed and floating rate interest at different periods during their life.

Fixed Assets Land, buildings, plant, equipment and other assets acquired for carrying on the business of the company with a life exceeding one year.

Fixed Capital Similar to fixed assets except purchased out of paid up capital.

Fixed Exchange Rate A system in which currencies have exchange values with fixed parities, or central rate relationships with Special Drawing Rights, gold, the U.S. dollar or other currencies.

Fixed for Floating Swap See IRS.

Fixed Price Re-Offer The fixed price stipulated by the Lead Manager at which the syndicate members are obliged to sell the newly-issued bond issue to the secondary market, so long as the syndicate remains in effect. Once the syndicate is dissolved, the bond is traded freely in the secondary market, at the re-offer price.

Fixed Term Deposit Deposits placed in the money markets with commercial banks for fixed periods. These deposits are non-negotiable. Maturities extend out to one year and can be as short as overnight. See CDs.

Flag of Convenience Registering a vessel in another country, i.e. changing nationality, to save costs and to benefit from more lax regulations regarding working conditions and labour laws.

Flags / Pennants These patterns, used in technical analysis, represent brief pauses after a sharp advance or decline which has gone ahead of itself. The market trades in a tight range for a while before running off in the direction of the main trend. Flags and pennants are among the most reliable continuation patterns and rarely produce a trend reversal. The flag is like a rectangle constructed with two parallel trendlines that tend to slope against the trend so that in a downtrend it would have a slight slope upwards. The pennant has two converging trendlines and is like a small symmetrical triangle. Both patterns are completed on the penetration of the upper trend-line in an uptrend and vice versa and should take place on heavier volume. Generally the move, after the trend has resumed, will mirror either the size of the flagpole or the size of the move just before the formation of the pattern.

Flaring Burning off gas which results from oil extrac-tion and which cannot be stored, reinjected or shipped ashore.

Flash Point Lowest temperature at which vapour from oil will ignite when briefly exposed to a source of ignition.

Flat Position A position where purchases and sales are equal, bringing the balance to zero, and possibly indicating no further interest to deal. Also known as a square position.

Flaxseed Plant with two main varieties - one for seed (also known as Linseed) that is used for industrial oils and protein meal, and another variety for fibre for linen. Major producers are Argentina, Canada, India, the U.S. and the Commonwealth of Independent States.

Flexible Option Product launched by the Chicago Board Options Exchange (CBOE) for institutional over the counter customers allowing them to select any strike price and expiry out to five years. Initially applied to the CBOE's Standard & Poor's 100 and 500 stock index baskets. The trades have ten million dollars' underlying value - much larger than the CBOE's standard index option contracts.

Flight of Capital See Capital Controls.

Flight to Quality A movement by investors to purchase higher quality securities, typically Treas-uries, which normally occurs if investors are expecting political instability or a deterioration in economic activity.

Floating Debt Debt with a floating interest rate as opposed to fixed.

Floating Exchange Rates A system whereby currencies have no fixed parities and movements are determined by supply and demand.

Floating Rate Bond A bond with a variable interest rate as opposed to a fixed.

Floating Rate Note See FRN.

Floating-Floating Swap See Basis Swap.

Floor An interest rate option which protects the holder from a decrease in interest rates. The holder, by exercising, receives a cash settlement representing the difference between the strike level and the underlying interest rate, should the latter be lower for the set period. Floors have a life of normally between two and five years. The option can be exercised at regular intervals (every six months, for example) during the life of the floor. See Cap.

Floor Broker The person responsible for accepting orders from stockbrokers and submitting them to the specialist at the trading post.

Flotel Floating accommodation rig or barge used as quarters for offshore personnel.

Fluid Catalytic Cracking Refining process that breaks down heavy hydrocarbon molecules into lighter molecules by passing them over a suitable catalyst. Maintained in fluidised state by oil vapours. See Cracking.

FNMA See Fannie Mae.

FOB Free on Board. Means freight and insurance costs are borne by the charterer. Also, it is applied in balance of payments accounts to mean valuation of goods at point of embarkation, thus making imports more directly comparable with exports.

FOK See Fill or Kill.

FOMC - U.S. The Federal Open Market Committee is the 12 member policy committee of the U.S. Federal Reserve which meets periodically to set Federal Reserve guidelines. Market action is taken by the Fed's operating arm, the Federal Reserve Bank of New York which uses its open market desk to buy and sell government securities in the open market as a means of influencing the volume and cost of bank credit and money. The FOMC also establishes policy relating to operations in the foreign exchange markets. See U.S. - Key Interest Rates.

Food Balance Overall availability of food supplies compared with the population to be fed.

FOOTSIE See FT-SE 100.

For Indication Quotations which are not firm and intended as an indication only.

Force Majeure An occurrence outside the control of the contracting parties allows a force majeure clause to be invoked which then exempts the parties from their obligations under the contract. The clause would usually be brought into play by a company supplying goods or services. Events could include an earthquake, hurricane or a serious labour dispute where delivery of goods or services was interrupted.

Foreign Acceptances Similar to domestic bankers acceptances, they are denominated in U.S. dollars and backed by the credit of foreign banks or agencies domiciled in the U.S. They usually trade at a yield premium over normal bankers acceptances.

Foreign Bond A bond issued on the domestic capital market by a foreign borrower and denominated in the domestic currency. These bonds have names such as Bulldog Bond, Matador Bond, Samurai Bond and Yankee Bond. See Domestic Bond.

Foreign Exchange Claims to foreign currency payable abroad, including bank deposits, bills, cheques. Foreign exchange rates refer to the number of units of one currency needed to buy another. Currency markets exist in the form of spot, forward, futures and options.

Foreign Exchange Swap See FX Swap.

Foreign Trade Zone See Free Trade Zone.

Forex Widely used term referring to foreign exchange.

Forex Club Umbrella title for the forex organisations which have been formed in various countries and are groups of foreign exchange dealers linked by affiliation to the Association Cambiste Internationale (ACI). Each national organisation is fully autonomous within the framework of the ACI charter and bye-laws.

Forfaiting The act of raising money when a company sells its invoices (or receivables) to a factor. See Factoring.

Forms - U.S. Form 8-K. Known as the current report as it is used to record any material events or corporate changes which are of importance to investors or security holders and which have not previously been reported by the registrant. Must be filed within 15 days of any event specified. Such events could be resignations or appointment of top executives, dismissal or appointment of corporate auditors.

Form 10-K. A detailed corporate annual reporting form required by the Securities and Exchange Commission. Similar but supplementary to the annual report.

Form 13-D. Disclosures of beneficial ownership of registered equity securities. Any person of group of persons or companies who acquire beneficial ownership of more than five percent of a class of registered equity securities of certain issuers must file within 10 days after such acquisition.

Form 14D-1. Used by any person or corporation or groups making a tender offer for certain equity securities whose offer, if accepted, would cause the filing party to own over five percent of that class of securities. This form additionally has to be sent to other parties such as the target company and any competing bidders.

Form 14D-9. Filed by a company or an interested party (usually a large shareholder or their representatives) responding to a tender offer. The filer may either make a solicitation or recommendation to shareholders regarding the offer.

Form 20-F. An integrated form used both as a registration statement for purposes of registering securities of qualified foreign registrants or as an annual report as required by the U.S. 1934 Securities Act.

Form F-1. Basic registration for certain foreign private issuers. The equivalent of Form S-1.

Form F-2. Optional form that may be used by certain foreign private issuers which are deemed world class, i.e. those with equity float of at least 300 million dollars world-wide or which are registering non-convertible investment grade debt securities, or which have reported under the U.S. 1934 Securities Act for at least three years.

Form F-3. A form which may be used only by certain private issuers which are both world class and have reported under the U.S. 1934 Securities Act for a minimum of three years.

Form F-4. For securities in connection with business combinations involving foreign private registrants.

Form N1-A. Used to register open end management investment companies or mutual funds.

Form N-2. For closed end management investment companies.

Form S-1. A statement registering equity securities to be offered, usually through initial public offerings. May also be used to register secondary offerings, i.e. shares to be sold by shareholders, not by the issuer or the company.

Form S-2. A simplified, optional registration that may be made by companies which have reported under the U.S. 1934 Securities Act for a minimum of three years and have filed in good time all required reports during the preceding 12 calendar months.

Form S-3. The most simplified registration by companies for debt and equity offerings. Only companies which have reported under the U.S. 1934 Securities Act for at least three years and meet timely S-2 reporting requirements may use this form. The offering and issuer must meet stringent qualitative tests under this filing.

Form S-4. Used to register securities in connection with business combinations or transactions that include mergers or exchange offers.

Form S-11. Used to register securities of certain real estate companies, including real estate investment trusts and mortgage banks.

Form S-18. Optional form for small issuers to register securities to be sold for cash of 7.5 million dollars or less. Usually filed by so-called penny stock companies. Less disclosure is required than Form S-1.

Form SB-2. A form used by small businesses or companies with small capitalisation to register securities for the first time under the U.S. 1934 Securities Act.

Forms 3, 4 and 5. Known as the insider filings. These involve every director, officer or owner of more than 10 percent of a publicly traded company's equity securities. The initial filing is made on Form 3 and changes are reported on Form 4. The annual statement of beneficial ownership of securities is made on Form 5.

Fortified Foods Foods to which vitamins, minerals, protein and so forth have been added to improve their nutritional qualities.

Forward / Forward Similar to an FX swap except the first leg shows a value date in the future and not spot. Also, a future loan or deposit. Unlike the FRA, which applies to a notional transaction, the forward/forward is an on balance sheet obligation, derived from current money market rates. See FX Swap, FRAs.

Forward Cap A form of interest rate cap which has a deferred date for commencing.

Forward Commitment A definite promise to take action at a future time or within a specified period, such as to make a loan or purchase mortgages.

Forward Contracting Cash transaction under which the buyer and seller agree on the delivery of a specified quality and quantity of a commodity or other goods at a specified future date. Price may be set beforehand or at delivery.

Forward Exchange Agreement See FXA.

Forward Gold Sales The forward sale is a commitment by the seller (a producer) to sell gold at a predetermined price and date. In this transaction, the seller receives a premium to the current gold price. This contango is based on the difference between the cost of leasing gold and current interest rates. Forward contracts add to current gold supply by accelerating future production into current supply since the buyer (a bullion dealer) borrows gold, normally from a central bank, and deposits the proceeds to earn interest in order to pay the producer on delivery of the gold. See Spot Deferred Gold Sales.

Forward Margin   Discount or premium between the spot and forward rates for a forward foreign exchange transaction which represents the interest rate differential between the two currencies traded. See Discount, Premium.

Forward Market   A market which delivers and settles on a date other than spot. The value date can be the same day as transaction date, tomorrow or from three days following the transaction date. Deals for value up to one month are known as short dates. The standard forward dates are counted from the spot value date.

Forward Outright   The purchase or sale in the foreign exchange market for delivery on any date other than spot, dealt on the Over the Counter market.

Forward Points   The points added to, or subtracted from, the spot price to create a forward price. Forward points represent the interest rate differential between the two currencies traded and are quoted as a premium or a discount. Also referred to as forward pips.

Forward Price   A price composed of the spot price plus or minus an adjustment in forward points.

Forward Rate Agreement   See FRAs.

Forward Shipment   Agreement for the shipment of cash commodities at a set future date.

Forward Start Swap   An interest rate swap with no exchange of payments before an agreed date in the future.

Forward Yield Curve   A yield curve often derived from the zero coupon yield curve and indicating each point as the implied forward interest rate. Used frequently to price interest rate derivatives, such as FRAs, Caps, Floors and Swaps. The forward rate allows the trader to ascertain the current market rate.

FOSFA   Federation of Oils Seeds and Fats Associations. Issues standard cash contracts and keeps them current. Has more than 40 published contracts which cover an estimated 85 percent of international trade in all fats and oilseeds. Based in London.

FOTRA Bonds - U.K.   These bonds are Free Of Tax to Residents Abroad (i.e. no witholding tax). Issued in the U.K. Also known as tax exempts.

FOX   See LCE.

FOX Index   Capitalisation weighted index comprising the 25 most liquid stocks traded on the Helsinki Stock Exchange in terms of their median daily average value. The shares account for over 60 percent of turnover and market capitalisation on the exchange. Futures and options are traded on the Finnish Options Market. Calculated real time, i.e. every time a constituent share price changes.

FRABBA Terms   The terms and conditions recommended for use in the FRA market by the British Bankers' Association.

Fractional Column   Tower in which fractional distillation takes place and which produces different distillates.

Fractional Distillation   Separation of crude oil or one of its components into liquids of different boiling ranges (fractions) by distillation. This is the basic process occurring in an oil refinery.

Fractions   Liquid hydrocarbons with a given boiling range. Produced during the fractional distillation process.

Franc Zone   Comprises the Communauté financière africaine (CFA) in the West African area. Also the Coopération financière en Afrique centrale (CFA) in the Central African area. Members are Benin, Burkina Faso, Cameroon, Central African Republic, Chad, Congo, Equatorial Guinea, Gabon, the Ivory Coast, Mali, Niger, Senegal and Togo.

Also in the franc zone is the Comptoirs français du Pacifique (CFP). Used in New Caledonia, French Polynesia and the Wallis and Futuna Islands.

The Comoros has a special relationship within the franc zone.

The three groups in the franc zone - the CFA franc, CFP franc and the Comoros franc - are linked to the French franc at different fixed rates of exchange. They hold their reserves mostly in French francs.

The ordinary French franc exchange rate applies in Metropolitan France, in the Overseas Departments of Guadeloupe, French Guyana, Martinique, Reunion and in the Overseas Collectivités Territoriales of Mayotte and St. Pierre and Miquelon.

France - Key Interest Rates   The rates to watch are:
Intervention rate - sets the floor for money market rates.
Five to 10 day lending rate - sets the ceiling for money market rates.
The intervention rate at which the Bank of France allocates funds on securities repurchase agreements usually acts as the floor for short term

money market rates while the five to 10 day emergency facility rate sets the ceiling. The intervention rate is generally seen as the most powerfully symbolic of the bank's rates. The five to 10 day lending rate is typically about 75 to 100 basis points above the intervention rate.

The use of repurchase agreements is the main way the Bank of France influences money market liquidity and, hence, is the key monetary policy instrument.

The Bank of France became an autonomous body on January 1 1994 with a nine member Conseil Politique et Monétaire (Monetary Policy Council) that has the power to set interest rate levels, regulate money supply and determine monetary policy objectives. The council consists of the Bank governor, his two deputies and six independent economic experts. Previously, a Conseil National de Crédit was led by the finance minister or the Bank governor. Decisions on policy were, in effect, decided by a number of working groups and committees each of which had limited powers regarding decisions on monetary policy.

France - Money Supply   There are four main monetary aggregates. M1 is notes and coins in circulation plus sight (demand) deposits held by non-financial residents only. M2 is M1 plus various time deposits. M3 is M2 plus money market instruments. M4 is M3 plus negotiable Treasury bills held by non-financial residents only and commercial paper issued by corporates and held by non-financial residents only. The financial markets focus on the seasonally adjusted monthly and year on year change in M3. Three wider measures, P1, P2 and P3, in declining order of liquidity, are used to track total financing of the economy and total financial holdings of non-financial agents.

Franked Income   Income received by an investor which has already borne tax. Hence the investor is not liable to pay more tax. Particularly applies to institutions which are investors, whereby they receive franked investment income.

FRAs   A Forward Rate Agreement (FRA) is an interest rate derivative allowing investors and borrowers to set the interest rate on a short term investment or loan in advance for a predetermined period. The agreement is effected on a notional principal and is settled at the beginning of the period by a discounted cash payment which reflects the difference between the agreed FRA rate and the FRA settlement rate, which is governed by the FRABBA terms and conditions and based on the LIBOR fixing for the period and currency concerned. A buyer of an FRA is

protecting against an increase in rates. A seller of an FRA is protecting against a decrease in rates.

Freddie Mac   Federal Home Loan Mortgage Corporation. Various U.S. savings institutions own the stock of this corporation which purchases residential mortgages from lenders, forms bundles of securities backed by the pools of mortgages and then offers the securities to the public.

Free Delivery   Method of settlement in which the securities are delivered before payment is effected.

Free Port   In its simplest form, a port which allows cargo to be unloaded free of any import tariff or some taxes. Can be part of a Free Trade Zone.

Free Scrip Issue   See Capitalisation Issue.

Free Shares   Shares which have unrestricted ownership. In Scandinavia and other countries such as Japan, free shares means that foreigners are allowed to buy. However, distinctions between free and restricted shares are being eliminated.

Free Supply   Commodity stocks available for sale as opposed to government owned or controlled stocks.

Free to Trade   See When Issued (W/I).

Free Trade Area   Members fix their own tariffs on trade with the rest of the world but there are no internal tariffs.

Free Trade Zone   An extra-territorial area, within a country, designated by the government and having manufacturing facilities free of government hindrance, customs duties or currency restrictions. There is usually a tax free profits element for a set period. Also known as a free trade processing zone and a foreign trade zone.

Freeboard   Distance between the waterline and the ship's main deck.

French National Statistics Institute   See INSEE.

French Treasury   See Trésor Français.

FRN   A floating rate note with a coupon whose rate is periodically changed in line with a specific short term interest rate index, e.g. LIBOR. This may come with either a margin over or below the comparable base rate. It is a negotiable instrument listed on a stock exchange with interest paid free of any withholding tax.

Front End Fees   Lead and co-lead managers for a loan receive front end fees from a borrower for arranging a loan and fees for servicing the loan - arranging interest payments and principal repayments.

Front End Load Occurs with some savings or funds schemes when fund running expenses and the commission earned by a salesman are deducted from the investor's initial contributions.

Front Office Term used to describe the front-line dealing staff of a bank's money market operation. See Back Office, Middle Office.

Frontrunning Activity by an operator on one market based on knowledge of impending trades in another market. In the U.S. this means a broker trading for his own account before buying or selling a large order for his customer.

Frozen Assets Assets, balances or credits temporarily blocked or frozen due to political circumstances such as war or legal action.

Frozen Concentrated Orange Juice See FCOJ.

Frozen Taiga Bonds Exotic name used in trading by banks in Moscow for the dollar denominated bonds issued by Vnesheconombank to pay firms whose funds were frozen in early 1992. Taiga means the Siberian forest.

Fruit Waste A key commodity in this category is citrus waste which is a dry carbohydrate concentrate made from the peel, pith and seed of fresh fruits after juice extraction or the canning of fruit hearts. Its value as an Animal Feed Ingredient is due primarily to the large amount of nitrogen-free extract (soluble carbohydrates) which makes it an attractive energy source.

FT Actuaries All Share Index An arithmetic weighted index based on market capitalisation. It comprises some 650 shares listed on the London Stock Exchange, accounting for more than 90 percent of the total market value of shares traded. Calculated once a day. This index is, additionally, divided into eight equity sections with various sub-groups.

FT Industrial Ordinary Share Index An equally weighted geometric index comprising 30 leading U.K. industrial and commercial shares. The shares account for some 30 percent of the market value of shares traded on the London Stock Exchange. Calculated each time a share price changes.

FT-SE 100 The Financial Times Stock Exchange Index is known world-wide, officially, as the FOOTSIE. It comprises 100 leading U.K. shares quoted in London, representing over 70 percent of the total market capitalisation of U.K. domestic issues listed on the London Stock Exchange. This is an arithmetic capitalisation weighted index, calculated each minute, which takes account of changes in constituents, capital, scrip and rights issues. Futures and options are traded on the Chicago Mercantile Exchange (CME) and the London International Financial Futures and Options Exchange (LIFFE). The Chicago Board Options Exchange (CBOE) trades options.

FT-SE Eurotrack 100 This Financial Times Stock Exchange market value weighted arithmetic index is for 100 non-U.K. shares chosen from European stock markets on the basis of the largest companies by market capitalisation. Calculated each minute.

FT-SE Eurotrack 200 This Financial Times Stock Exchange index is based on a combination of the 100 U.K. shares in the FT-SE 100 share index and the 100 European non-U.K. shares in the FT-SE Eurotrack 100 index. Calculated in real time, i.e. changes every time a constituent share in the index has a price change.

FTA The Financial Futures Market Amsterdam (FTA) was set up in 1987 to establish a regular market in financial futures. Fully owned by the EOE. Futures contracts exist on the Dutch Stock Index, the Eurotop 100 Index and dollar/guilder. Option contracts are traded at the EOE, also located in Amsterdam.

Fuel Oil Heavy distillates from the oil refining process. Used as fuel for power stations, industry and marine boilers.

Fully-Diluted EPS An Earnings per Share figure calculated by dividing earnings by a larger amount of outstanding shares, having assumed full dilution of all convertibles, options, warrants and convertible preferred shares. This leads to a greater dilution of the EPS figure.

Fund Manager An institution, or individual, involved in investing funds, either on own account or on behalf of others.

Fundamental Analysis Like technical analysis, fundamental analysis is also concerned with the task of estimating the future direction of prices. Fundamentalists, however, are more concerned with the details of what causes the markets to move. They capture the economic environment on a domestic and international level. They are concerned with such things as annual reports, budgets of companies as well as financial statements.

Fundamental Disequilibrium Refers to a basic, serious imbalance in a country's balance of payments thus justifying a devaluation or revaluation in a currency by the relevant government.

Funds A term used in European trading for the one day settlement of the U.S. dollar against the Canadian dollar exchange rate which, in North America, is regarded as normal spot trading settlement.

Fungible Bond A new bond issue which is attached to an existing issue in the sense that it has the same specifications, other than price. If a bond is fungible, it can be exchanged for an existing bond with the same characteristics.

In France, this is the basic principle of the government bond market with a view to limiting the total number of bonds quoted and thereby increasing the liquidity of its issues.

Future Value Determines the value, for a set date in the future, of a sum of money invested now at a specific rate of interest until that date.

Futures Exchange-traded contracts which are firm agreements to deliver or take delivery of a standardised amount of an underlying financial instrument or commodity at a standardised date in the future at a predetermined price. Futures exist in currencies, money market deposits, bonds, shares and commodities. The Chicago Board of Trade (CBOT) Treasury bond future is the world's most actively traded derivative contract in terms of volume. The Chicago Mercantile (CME) Eurodollar contract has the world's largest open interest.

Futures Commission Merchant Individual or legal entity registered with the Commodity Futures Trading Commission in the U.S. who solicits business from others for execution on a listed commodity exchange.

Futures Exchange A physical location for the trading of futures and options on futures contracts. Opposite to Over the Counter (OTC) market.

Futures Market - Precious Metals Futures contracts on precious metals are traded on various exchanges. The most important exchange for the trading of gold and silver contracts is the New York Commodity Exchange (COMEX). The most important exchanges for platinum and palladium contracts are both the Tokyo Commodity Exchange (TOCOM) and the New York Mercantile Exchange (NYMEX).

Futures Pit Area on the floor of an exchange where trading takes place by way of open outcry.

FX Swap A foreign exchange swap is a simultaneous purchase and sale, or vice versa, of identical amounts of one currency for another with two different value dates (normally spot to forward). The price of a swap is quoted in forward points. See Forward / Forward.

FXA A Forward Exchange Agreement is a SAFE contract (Synthetic Agreement for Forward Exchange) whereby settlement is based on the difference between the forward rate on the start date of the contract and the spot rate at settlement. See ERA.

GAAP In the U.S., Generally Accepted Accounting Principles. Procedures and rules that define accounting practice.

GAFTA Grain and Feed Trade Association. Has devised approximately 80 grain and feed cash contracts which cover some half of world trade in grain and feed ingredients. Based in London.

Gamma The measure of change in the delta of an option compared with a price change in the underlying. If an option has a delta of 35 and a gamma of 5, this indicates that the new delta will be at 30 or 40 on specific moves in the value of the underlying. See Delta, Theta, Vega. See Rho.

Gann Angles Trendlines drawn to the right from prominent market price tops or bottoms at certain specific angles. The most important angle is the 45 degree line based on a one to one relationship between units of time and price which means prices rise or fall at the rate one price unit (box on the chart) per time unit (say, a week). Breaking of the 45 degree line usually indicates a major trend reversal. Channel lines can also be drawn, using 45 degree angles, from prominent highs and lows that are parallel to the basic trendline. Steeper or flatter geometric trendlines can be drawn combining time and price units by a factor of two. A 1 x 1 line is the 45 degree line, a 2 x 1 line the next flatter. They can be continued up to 1 x 8. In an uptrend, Gann lines offer support and, in a downtrend, resistance. If prices break support during an uptrend they would be expected to drop to the next lower line and there is a similar expectation for a resistance breakthrough in a downtrend.

GANs See Municipal Notes.

Gap A mismatch between a bank's assets and liabilities.

Gapping The process of intentionally mismatching the maturities of assets and liabilities by borrowing short and lending long.

Gaps Price gaps result from such events as prices opening above the previous day's high, thus leaving a space on the chart that is not filled during the day or where the day's high is below the previous day's low.

Different types of gaps exist. Upside gaps portray market strength and downside gaps show the reverse. Most analysts ignore common gaps which occur in thinly traded markets or in the middle of horizontal trading ranges. The breakaway gap appears at the completion of key price patterns and often signals the start of a significant move. The runaway or measuring gap is seen around the middle of the price move when prices leap forward in a phase where the market is moving effortlessly on modest volume. It is a sign of market strength in an uptrend and weakness in a downtrend and is often called a measuring gap because it appears halfway through a trend. An exhaustion gap shows near the end of a move. When all objectives have been achieved and the other types of gap have been detected, this gap should be expected. Near the end of an uptrend, prices surge ahead in a last rally which quickly fades when prices turn lower within a couple of days or a week. When prices close under that last rally, it usually confirms the existence of an exhaustion gap.

Garman Kohlhagen Model   A currency option pricing formula similar to Black & Scholes but with separate conditions for domestic and foreign interest rates. Becoming the market standard for the pricing of currency options. See Black & Scholes Model.

Gas Cap   Layer of natural gas above the oil in an oil reservoir.

Gas Injection   Process of pumping separated associated gas back into a reservoir for conservation purposes or to maintain the reservoir pressure.

Gas Oil   Petroleum distillates from the oil refining process. Intermediate between light and lubricating oils and kerosene. Used to produce diesel fuel and for burning in certain central heating systems. In the U.S., known as heating oil.

Gas to Oil Ratio   Number of cubic feet of gas per barrel of oil at atmospheric pressure or as the volume of gas to volume of oil.

Gasification   Manufacture of gaseous fuel from a solid or liquid fuel.

Gasohol   Unleaded, high octane gasoline which contains 10 percent ethanol as an octane ingredient. See Ethanol.

Gasoline   Light petroleum distillate used in spark ignition combustion engines. Equivalent to motor spirit or petrol.

GATT   General Agreement on Tariffs and Trade, a world-wide group of nations each of which accepts rules laid down to benefit a multilateral trading system which also aims to protect each country's domestic markets. See World Trade Organisation, Uruguay Round.

Gearing   Shows the ratio of a company's senior debt to ordinary capital. Expressed either as a percentage or a ratio in terms of nominal or market value. High gearing means senior debt outweighs ordinary capital, low gearing the reverse. Investors take this into account when buying or selling the company's shares. Financial fundamental analysts look at this as a measure of

company risk. In the derivatives market, it is the measure of the amount of cash spent purchasing an option or a futures contract, compared to the actual value of the underlying position.

Geisha Bond   A bond privately placed in Japan, with a non-yen currency, by a non-Japanese borrower.

GEMS-U.K.   Gilt Edged Market Makers are dealers approved by the Bank of England to provide liquidity in the secondary U.K. gilt market. They were established in 1986 as market makers or primary dealers. One GEM can deal anonymously with another GEM on a trading screen via an inter-dealer broker.

General Accounting Office   Audits U.S. government departments as well as making broader programme evaluation. Headed by the Comptroller-General.

General Arrangements to Borrow   Set up in 1962, involving Group of 10 nations and Switzerland. Countries concerned agreed to provide special credits to the International Monetary Fund in their own currencies for G-10 member nations. The GAB needs the collective agreement of its members to be activated. Credits are separate from the IMF's normal resources and are only for use by a GAB member facing currency or payments difficulties.

General Obligation Bonds   Type of municipal securities issued by states, counties, special districts, cities, towns and schools.

General Services Administration   See Defense Logistics Agency.

Generalised Social Contribution   In France, a broad based income tax.

Generic Commodity Certificates   Issued by the U.S. Department of Agriculture and expressed in dollar value. They can be redeemed for Commodity Credit Corporation commodities or, in some cases, for cash. Can also be sold for cash to other producers or commercial interests.

Gensaki Market   Japanese market for medium term bond financing and is referred to as a repo market. Securities acting as collateral in these operations are both long term bonds (bond gensaki) and Treasury bills. The repo operations hold maturities ranging from three days to three months. There are two types of repo operations: uri-gensaki (repo) and kai-gensaki (reverse repo).

Geometric Weighted Index   A stock index that weights certain components more heavily than others on the basis of a cubic function. A cubic function is a type of curve that approximates and is similar to the exponential function.

GEPLACEA Grupo de Países Latinoamericanos y del Caribe Exportadores de Azúcar (Latin American and Caribbean Sugar Exporting Nations). Created in 1974 and based in Mexico City. Its members produce about 30 percent of world sugar. Undertakes basic research, produces statistical information on production and exports. Has 22 members including Argentina, Barbados, Brazil, Bolivia, Colombia, Costa Rica, Cuba, Republica Dominica, Ecuador, El Salvador, Guatemala, Guyana, Haiti, Honduras, Jamaica, Mexico, Nicaragua, Panama, Peru, Trinidad and Tobago, Uruguay and Venezuela.

German Unity Fund The German Unity Fund was set up mid-1990 to channel funds to the new Eastern states. It issues German government bonds (Bunds) known as Unities or Einheitsanleihen which carry the express guarantee of the government. The fund has a fixed borrowing ceiling until the end of 1994, after which the fund will cease to exist.

Germany - Key Interest Rates The rates to watch are:
Repo rate - sets the tone for money market rates.
Discount rate - sets the floor for money market rates.
Lombard rate - sets the ceiling for money market rates.

The repo rate is now the main tool for guiding the overnight money market rate. Repos enable the Bundesbank to adjust monetary policy without changing its headline rates. A change from a fixed to a variable rate repo (or vice versa) may indicate a policy change. But while higher rates at a variable rate repo reflect higher bids for funds by banks, they do not necessarily point to tighter policy in the short term (and vice versa).

The discount rate normally sets the floor for money market rates while the lombard rate usually sets the ceiling. Thus, the discount rate is more important when interest rates are falling while the lombard rate is the key rate when interest rates are rising.

The Bundesbank's main instruments are either designed for long run major policy changes or to fine tune the money market.

The Bundesbank sets monetary policy and is the most independent of the Group of Seven central banks. It has a legal obligation to protect the external value of the mark. Without prejudice to the performance of its functions, the Bundesbank is required to support the general economic policy of the federal government. In using its powers under the Bundesbank Act, the central bank is independent of instructions from the federal government.

Germany - Money Supply There are two main monetary aggregates. M3 is the broad measure of the money supply targeted by the Bundesbank, the central bank. It comprises notes and coins in circulation (excluding the banks' cash balances), sight deposits (payable on demand and for less than one month), time deposits of less than four years and savings deposits at statutory notice all held with domestic banks by domestic non-banks (thus not including deposits held by banks with each other). Extended M3 is a wider monetary measure which also takes account of Euromark deposits. The financial markets focus on the seasonally adjusted annualised percentage change in pan-German M3 compared with the fourth quarter of the previous year. The Bundesbank began reporting pan-German M3 data (following the unification of the former East and West Germany) for the first time in March 1991 when the January 1991 money supply was published.

Gilts - U.K. Treasury securities issued by the U.K. Treasury are all known as gilts or gilt edged stocks. They are recognised by their different names, depending on which government department issued the stock.

Gilt names include: Exchequer, Treasury, Conversion, Funding, Redemption, Transport, Gas, Consols and War Loan.

However, in recent times most gilt issues have been named either Treasury or Exchequer although the difference is only in the name. Some gilts are callable (double dated gilts) although the majority are Bullet issues.

Only one outstanding gilt issue to date has a sinking fund. It is common practice to see gilts issued in partly paid form. There is no official benchmark gilt.

Conventional gilts can be classified into three types according to their maturities - short-dated gilts (maturity up to five years), medium-dated gilts (maturity between five and 15 years), long-dated gilts (maturity over 15 years, maximum to date 25 years).

Ginnie Mae Government National Mortgage Association. A wholly owned corporate unit of the U.S. government. Operated by the Department of Housing and Urban Development (HUD). Chief function is to guarantee securities backed by pools of federally insured or guaranteed mortgages to aid secondary market liquidity. Its guarantees are known as GNMA pass through certificates.

Given Dealers' language mainly heard through a broker's box when the bid has been hit.

Glamour Stock Stocks, listed on U.S. stock exchanges, which are highly fashionable and which produce rising sales and earnings. Some can quickly become unfashionable. Price performance of the share is as much an investor consideration as financial performance of the company.

Glass-Steagall Act This act was passed by the U.S. Congress in 1933 forbidding commercial banks to own, underwrite or deal in corporate stocks and bonds. Banks have been challenging this act since the 1980s by offering a range of investment services including discount brokerage and money market funds.

Global Environment Facility Funding project administered by the World Bank and some specialised United Nations agencies to provide money for projects that bring global environment gains.

Global Fund A type of investment fund which invests in the ordinary shares of foreign and domestic companies with strong international presence.

Gluten Protein content of flour.

GmbH German company title, meaning Gesellschaft mit beschränkter Haftung, a limited liability company.

GNMA See Ginnie Mae.

Going Public Term for a privately owned company which seeks a listing on a stock exchange and issues shares for the general public. A similar term is "the company is being floated".

Gold A precious metal produced by South Africa, the U.S., Canada, Australia and the Commonwealth of Independent States. Gold, along with silver, is one of the world's oldest traded investment commodities. Gold is traded mainly in bars but is both traded and used in coinage. Used extensively in jewellery, dentistry and electronics. Central banks hold, in total, massive gold reserves. Gold is often seen as a safe haven for investment funds in times of world political and economic turmoil. Gold has been mined for 6,000 years but only some 110,000 metric tonnes have ever been produced.

Gold Assayer See Gold Melter and Assayer.

Gold Bars The main trading unit of gold. A standard gold bar in the spot market is 400 troy ounces or 12.5 kilogrammes. See Gold Price Quotation.

Gold Bullion Standard In this historical standard, money in circulation was either entirely or partly paper with gold acting just as a reserve asset. Gold was freely exchangeable for paper money at the bank of issue. See Gold Standard.

Gold Certificates A document certifying the ownership of gold held at an authorised or recognised depositary, mainly in the U.S.

Gold Coinage Gold coins are traded throughout the world on a daily basis with Zurich an important centre. These comprise those of numismatic value, minted before 1810, where the prices have no direct relation to the price of the metal; and current coins, issued since that date, which are traded on a market basis with varying premiums over gold according to their age. The nominal value on the face of the coin is not to be confused with the value of the gold contained in the coin. One of the best selling bullion coins is the South African Krugerrand.

Gold Delivery A simple spot quotation for gold, which can be used throughout the world, is for "loco London". This means the metal is for delivery in London and avoids complications of freight cost and insurance in the price formula equation. Among other similar centres are Zurich, New York and Tokyo.

Gold Deposit Forward Rate Agreement (GODFRA) A hedging instrument for central banks which nowadays lend to the market.

Gold Fix See Precious Metals Fixings.

Gold Forward Rate Agreement (GOFRA) Producers use this hedging contract when they have drawn down gold loans and want to lock in forward gold interest rate exposure. Settlement is in U.S. dollars.

Gold Institute A world-wide Washington based organisation representing the interests of the gold industry overall. Members include most facets of the industry.

Gold Lease Forward Rate Agreement (GOLDFRA) Similar to a Gold Forward Rate Agreement (GOFRA) but settlement is in gold.

Gold Leasing Central banks can get some return on their gold holdings by leasing the metal out, usually to mining companies, albeit at very low interest rates. Mines can sell the gold on the spot market and then invest the proceeds at a much higher rate of interest at the London interbank offered rate for dollars. The mines repay the loan with gold from future output. They can also use the borrowed gold for more complex hedging strategies. See Gold Loans.

Gold Loans Gold loans are used in part to finance the expansion of some countries' gold mining industries. These loans also add to current supply since producers borrow the gold, sell it in the spot market, and bank the proceeds which are then used to build a new mine. The loan is usually repaid in a series of quarterly or semi-annual payments from future production. The attraction of the gold loan for the producer is the very low gold leasing rates and the fact that a producer can repay the loan in ounces from production, thereby avoiding gold price and currency risk. See Gold Leasing.

Gold Melter and Assayer   Melter and assayer imprints are stamped on gold bars, showing respectively who cast the bar and who analysed the fineness.

Gold Options   Put options are used by the producers to fix a floor price. The purchase of a put is often financed by the producer's sale of a call option. See Put Option, Call Option.

Gold Premium   The amount by which the market value of a gold coin exceeds the actual value of gold content.

Gold Price Quotation   The gold price, when quoted against U.S. dollars, is for one ounce. One ounce is 31.1035 grammes. When quoted against Swiss francs, it is for one kilogramme. One kilogramme is 32.1507425 ounces.

Gold Specie Standard   Gold had a dual function under this historical standard, being the internationally recognised method of payment for international settlement of credits and debts while at the same time gold coins were the accepted means of exchange and payment in the domestic market. See Gold Standard.

Gold Standard   A monetary system of fixed exchange rates whose parities were set in relation to gold. It ran from approximately 1880 to 1914 and consisted of two chief components, the Gold Specie Standard and the Gold Bullion Standard.

Gold Swap   A swap transaction for gold against foreign currency. A country, short of foreign currency, may swap gold by using its gold reserves as collateral to borrow foreign currency at a lower interest rate than it could otherwise obtain.

Gold Wafer   A thin gold bar comprising a small amount of gold such as one, five or ten grammes.

Golden Handcuffs   An inducement offered to an executive by a company which seeks to retain his services, usually a manoeuvre which is spread over a number of years.

Golden Parachute   An inducement offered to an executive by a company which only becomes effective at an agreed departure point. This is primarily if the company is taken over and the executive leaves the company. Can also apply to some cases of retirement.

Golden Share   Exists in various forms but is basically about retaining power if the company is deemed threatened. This is typically achieved by vesting the golden share with sufficient voting rights to maintain control and thus fend off potential predators.

Good Delivery   Delivery of an instrument, in good time, in which all relevant matters - title, endorsement, legal papers and so forth - are in order.

Good Delivery - Gold   Good delivery specifications for gold include a minimum bar gold content of 350 fine ounces and a maximum of 430 fine ounces, a minimum fineness of 995 parts per 1,000 fine gold plus a serial number and stamp of an accepted melter and assayer. Gold stated to be 1,000 fine is marked down to 999.9 fine - gold is in fact made to 999.99 purity but purely for the electronics industry. Swiss banks, in addition to the large good delivery bars, also produce small bars and wafers.

Good Delivery - Silver   Good delivery specifications for silver include a minimum bar weight of 500 ounces and a maximum of 1250 ounces, a minimum fineness of 999 parts per 1000 fine silver, a serial number and stamp of an accepted refiner and assayer.

Good Till Cancelled (GTC)   Limit order which remains valid until ("till") the order is executed or cancelled.

Government Agency Bonds (Agencies) - Germany   These bonds, although issued by the Bundesbahn and the Bundespost, are backed by the full faith and credit of the Federal government. Referred to as "agencies", "bahns" and "posts".

Government Agency Bonds - Japan   Thirty five government agencies in Japan issue bonds whose principal and interest payments are guaranteed by the government. The largest issuer is the Japan Finance Corporation for Municipal Enterprises (JFC) which issues bonds with 10 year maturities.

Government Bonds - Japan   The basic principle in Japan's Finance Law prohibits the issue of government bonds because a massive flow before World War Two sparked sharp inflation. However, construction bonds are offered, aimed at raising funds to finance public works, and deficit financing bonds to finance ordinary expenses or to fill a gap in government revenues as well as stop-gap bonds which are relatively short term securities issued only to fill a gap in tax revenue. Government thinking is that stop-gap bonds are different from deficit financing bonds because the government must secure in advance a source of funds to redeem them. Stop-gap bonds issued in 1990 to finance Japan's Gulf War contribution were financed mainly through corporate taxes and increased petroleum taxes and also by reducing defence spending. The government must pass special legislation if it wants to issue deficit financing or stop-gap bonds.

Government National Mortgage Association See Ginnie Mae.

Government Selling Price The price which an oil producing government announces as its GSP. It will not necessarily actually sell at that price. GSPs have become a formality since producers started to sell their oil at prices linked to spot market quotations in discount competition in the late 1980s. Also known as the OSP (Official Selling Price).

Grace Period The period agreed by the lender whereby the borrower does not start to repay the principal for a number of years although interest payments are made.

Grades Standards set for judging the quality of a commodity.

Graduated Payment Mortgage Monthly payments which increase periodically at a predetermined rate during the early years of a loan.

Grain Reserve U.S. government operated stockpile of grain designed to keep surplus supplies off the market until prices reach relatively higher levels and allow for release of the grain.

Grains Wheat, corn (maize), oats, barley, sorghum, rye and millet. See Coarse Grains, Fine Grains, Heavy Grains, Light Grains.

Gramm-Rudman-Hollings Act A U.S. law, signed by President Reagan in 1985, to seek an end to the federal deficit. To achieve gradual elimination of the national debt, the law requires cuts in many programmes if Congress fails to agree to reductions in the deficit. The law, which marked a radical revision of the budgeting procedures, was sponsored by Representative Phil Gramm and Senators Warren B. Rudman and Ernest F. Hollings.

Grant Anticipation Notes See Municipal Notes.

Green Rates Green currency rates set by the European Commission to translate European Community guaranteed farm prices into national currencies. Large fluctuations in exchange rates can radically affect the relevance of the green rate's basic calculations and, in such instances, the EC can devalue or revalue the green rate.

Greenmail In the U.S., payments by the target of a takeover attempt to the bidder, usually to buy back acquired shares at a premium, with the aim of dissuading the predator from pursuing the bid effort.

Grey Market Unofficial market, not subject to official controls, when a new security is traded before its formal offering on a fully termed when, as and if issued basis. See When Issued (W/I).

Gross Domestic Product Similar to Gross National Product but does not include income from abroad.

Gross National Product Total value of goods and services produced within a period of time by an economy including government and private spending, fixed capital investment, net inventory change and net exports. Real GNP growth describes the increase in national output after subtracting inflation. See Gross Domestic Product.

Gross National Product Deflator A U.S. method to establish the actual growth of goods and services by eliminating growth due to price increases. Normally expressed as a percentage and based on an index figure.

Gross Price See Dirty Price.

Gross Processing Margin Determines profitability in the U.S. domestic processing of soybeans. Measures the cost of soybeans relative to the sales return on processed soybean oil and meal. The GPM should return the processor's manufacturing costs plus a profit.

Gross Profit Total profit before deduction of tax and expenses.

Gross Registered Tonnage Total enclosed capacity in a ship in units of 100 cubic feet, less certain exempted spaces.

Grossing Up An accounting practice calculating the amount of tax needed, in the case of an investment which is subject to tax, to equal the income from an investment which is not subject to tax.

Groundnuts Used to produce vegetable oil and meal for animal feed. Also known as (the edible) peanuts. Grown mainly in tropical and sub-tropical regions. Major producers are China, India, the U.S., Senegal and Sudan.

Group of 10 (G-10) An economic grouping of industrialised nations that aims to coordinate monetary and fiscal policies to form a more stable world economic system. Consists of 11 members - Belgium, Canada, France, Germany, Italy, Japan, the Netherlands, Sweden, the U.K., the U.S. and Switzerland - although still called G-10.

Group of 15 (G-15) Inaugurated in Caracas in 1991, this group seeks international South-South liaison in economic and political North-South representations. Member nations are Algeria, Argentina, Brazil, Egypt, India, Indonesia, Jamaica, Mexico,

Nigeria, Peru, Malaysia, Senegal, Venezuela, former Yugoslavia and Zimbabwe.

Group of 24 (G-24)   An informal grouping of developing nations known as the G-24.

Group of 30 (G-30)   The G-30 is a group of industry leaders, bankers, central bankers and academics world-wide which discusses possible improvements in the economic and financial spheres and undertakes studies, for instance, on capital adequacy and on the trading of swaps, futures and options. Based in Washington.

Group of 77 (G-77)   Comprises more than 125 nations although originally established with 77 countries. It helps promote the views of developing nations on international trade and development in UNCTAD.

Group of Five (G-5)   An economic grouping of industrialised nations that aims to coordinate monetary and fiscal policies to form a more stable world economic system. Consists of France, Germany, Japan, the U.K. and the U.S.

Group of Seven (G-7)   An economic grouping of industrialised nations that aims to coordinate monetary and fiscal policies to form a more stable world economic system. Consists of France, Germany, Japan, the U.K. and the U.S. - the Group of Five nations - plus Canada and Italy.

Growing Equity Mortgage   The principal and interest payment on a mortgage loan increase each year by a set percentage of the previous year's payments. Such mortgages are insured by the Federal Housing Administration, are backed by the Government National Mortgage Association and run for 15 years instead of a standard 30. The aim is to allow the borrower to build up his equity in the home and to obtain earlier maturity.

Growth Fund   A type of investment fund which often specialises in investing in new emerging companies. In the short term, this fund provides no income but offers longer term prospects, such as greater capital appreciation and increasing dividend payments.

Growth Stock   A company with faster than average share price appreciation, reflecting a fast growth rate in the company's activities and an optimistic outlook on both counts. The market considers two kinds of growth stock - the established growth stock and the emerging growth stock.

Growths   Types of coffee, cocoa, cotton and so forth according to area or country in which it is produced. Also used widely to describe type and location of grapes in wine making.

GTC   See Good Till Cancelled.

Guaranteed Bonds   Securities which carry an explicit guarantee by a third party such as a government, parent company and so forth.

Guaranteed Exchange Rate Option   An option on one currency asset denominated in a second currency with the exchange rate fixed at the beginning of the option. Similar to a Quanto Option.

Gulf Cooperation Council   Full title is Cooperation Council for the Arab States of the Gulf. Encourages integration in economic and social affairs. Members are Bahrain, Kuwait, Oman, Qatar, Saudi Arabia and the United Arab Emirates. Based in Riyadh.

Gusher   Flowing oil well, possibly not under control.

Hagberg Number   The Hagberg Number, often called the Hagberg falling number, measures protein and protein quality in grains in percentage terms. The higher the number, the better the quality.

Haircut   The difference between the actual market value and the value ascribed to the collateral used in a repo transaction. See Repurchase Agreement.

Handle   See Big Figure.

Hard Currency   A currency in which there is a general wide-ranging confidence, accepted as one issued by an economically and politically stable nation.

Hard ECU   A U.K. idea for a parallel currency which would bridge the gap between national currencies and the scheduled new single currency for the European Community. Hard ECU would circulate in parallel with national currencies and would be freely convertible.

Harmless Warrants   These are attached to a callable bond. The harmless feature allows the borrower to phase out the original, often more expensive borrowing, and to replace it with the bonds bought through the warrants. See Income Warrant.

Head and Shoulders   Used in technical analysis. Considered to be one of the most reliable of all major reversal patterns. The pattern consists of a final rally (the head) separating two smaller, though not necessarily identical, rallies (the shoulders). The first shoulder is the second last advance of a bull phase and the second shoulder is the first bear phase rally. A neckline can be drawn connecting the bottom of the two shoulders and confirmation is normally accepted on a decisive close below that neckline. A recovery back to the neckline without penetration also confirms the pattern. The price objective is based on the vertical distance from the head to the neckline which should then be projected down from where the neckline is broken. The head and shoulders bottom, or inverse head and shoulders, is a mirror image of the head and shoulders. A head and shoulders variation is the complex head and shoulders which has two heads and double left and right shoulders.

Heating Oil   See Gas Oil.

Heaven and Hell Bond   A bond whose redemption value is linked at maturity time to the spot exchange rate of another currency against the denominated currency of the bond. Proceeds from the redemption can take any value between five and 200 percent of the face value. See Purgatory and Hell Bond.

Heavy Crude Oil   Thick viscous crudes with a high specific gravity but a low API gravity of 20 degrees or less. Extraction of heavy crudes needs special costly techniques such as steam injection.

Heavy Grains   Wheat, maize (corn) and rye.

Hectare   Land measurement used outside the U.S. and the U.K. One hectare equals 2.471 acres. There are 259 hectares per square mile.

Hedge   A strategy used to offset market risk, whereby one position protects another. See Long Hedge, Short Hedge.

Hedge Funds   Highly leveraged, aggressively managed investment funds, typically backed by a small number of wealthy individual investors and, often, private investment partnerships and exempt from disclosure. The funds make large investments in markets aimed at maximising returns from short term movements and also make full use of market derivatives. These funds take long and short positions and, where they are heavily exposed to a sector in which prices move against them, they might exit quickly. This often accelerates price trends and affects market sentiment.

Hermes   Hermes Kreditversicherungs Ag. German state export insurance agency.

HEX Index   The main share price index including all companies traded on the Helsinki Stock Exchange. Capitalisation weighted and arithmetic. Calculated every two minutes.

HIBOR / HIBID / HIMEAN   The Hong Kong Interbank Offered Rate (HIBOR) is the rate at which banks are prepared to lend to each other for specified maturities within the Hong Kong market. HIBOR is also fixed daily for reference purposes and is a key interest rate level used for setting rates for loans and floating rate notes and for calculating cash settlements of certain interest rate derivative instruments. HIBID is the Hong Kong Interbank Bid rate, the rate at which banks take

deposits from each other. HIMEAN is the Hong Kong Interbank Mean rate.

High / Low / Open / Close   These represent the different types of price information available on the markets and captured by various charts. Technical analysts maintain that in order to understand the market, these prices are the only four pieces of information you really need.

High Fructose Corn Syrup   A U.S. term. These corn syrups are sweeter than sucrose (table sugar) and less costly and have thus taken a significant share of the sucrose market. They are most frequently found in foods using a liquid sweetener. A major use is in carbonated beverages and fruit juices. See Isoglucose.

High Tech Stock   Companies in high technology fields such as computers, biotechnology and electronics.

Highs and Lows   The high and low for the traded price of a financial instrument over a period which can cover one complete trading day or any other desired period. Sometimes abbreviated to hi/lo. Often referred to as the trading range.

HIMEAN   See HIBOR / HIBID / HIMEAN.

Historic Cost   The original cost of a company's assets as distinct from replacement cost.

Historical Volatility   A measure of the Volatility of the underlying instrument in terms of the movements of its price, rate or return over a past period (e.g. 10 day, 50 day, 100 day).

Holder of Record   The name of the owner of a security as recorded in the issuing company's records.

Holding Company   A company which has control of one or more other companies, often by having a majority of the shares in each subsidiary. Control is usually over areas such as marketing and financial and not investment.

Home Heating Oil   A light gas oil that is similar to diesel fuel and often used for domestic heating. Most widely used type is Number 2 heating oil.

Horizontal Drilling   A well where the direction of drilling is deviated from the vertical to the horizontal.

Horizontal Spread   An option strategy which involves buying and selling contracts with the same strike price but different maturities, in view of expected moves in volatility. Also known as a calendar spread.

Hot Stock   A share whose price activity suddenly leaps into prominence regardless of volume.

House Ways and Means Committee Key U.S. House committee which is responsible for tax and other revenue bills.

HWWA Institut für Wirtschaftsforschung in Hamburg. One of six German research institutes which produce regular individual reports and in spring and autumn a joint report on the state of the economy.

Hydrocarbons Compounds of hydrogen and carbon. Can be found as solids, liquids or gas. Used as a synonym for petroleum.

Hydrocracking Refining technique for converting residual petroleum liquids into high octane gasoline, jet fuels and fuel oils.

Hyperinflation Galloping, self fuelling inflation which may bring an economic collapse.

IACO Inter-African Coffee Organization. Producer group of African coffee countries which acts as a consultative and lobby body to the International Coffee Organization. Committed to the export Retention Scheme of the Association of Coffee Producing Countries. Based in Abidjan.

IBEX 35 Index A market value weighted arithmetic index comprising the 35 most liquid shares on the Madrid stock exchange. The shares account for more than 70 percent of total market capitalisation and nearly 80 percent of the turnover value of all stocks traded. Calculated each time a share price changes.

IBFs International Banking Facilities are shell branches that U.S. banks in various states may institute at their headquarters so they can undertake some form of Euro-business.

ICCH See LCH.

ICCO The International Cocoa Organization whose official acronym is the ICCO (ICO is the International Coffee Organization). Includes both producers and consumers. It set up an economic pact in 1986 but its buffer stock reached capacity in 1988 and it then became largely an administrative agreement. However, a new agreement in 1993 allows for the collection of statistics and a forum for discussion on the cocoa market between producers and consumers. It also has policies for regulating production but it does not have the power to intervene directly in the market in the way similar to its predecessor agreement.

ICO The International Coffee Organization was set up in 1962 with the U.S. wanting to help Latin America. Export quotas were introduced in 1963 but suspended ten years later after a prices dispute. A new pact was negotiated in 1976 but Brazil's frosts in 1975 kept supplies short and prices high. Brazil's drought of 1985 pushed prices up again and quotas -reactivated in 1980 - were suspended in 1986. Various events led to the collapse of talks on a new pact in 1989 when quotas were suspended. The ICO pact is now purely administrative. Comprises importing and exporting nations. The U.S. is no longer a member.

The Non-ICO Market is a parallel market of nations with prices often lower than accepted market levels. See ICCO.

ICSA International Councils of Securities Associations. A forum for non-governmental regulatory organisation. Objective is to assist and encourage growth in the international securities markets.

ICUMSA International Commission for Uniform Methods of Sugar Analysis. Aims to further the elaboration and recommendation of uniform methods of analysis of sugar industry products, including an international colour standard.

IDA International Development Association. Created in 1960, this is the affiliate of the World Bank which finances development projects and programmes on concessional terms in the poorest countries. IDA funds are obtained mainly through periodic replenishments. Contributions come from the richer members of the World Bank, usually led by the U.S. but assistance can come from the wealthier developing nations.

IDB Inter-Dealer Broker, brokers serving the U.K. gilts market.

IEA International Energy Agency, based in Paris. Set up by the Organisation for Economic Cooperation and Development. Formed after the 1973 oil crisis and includes the 23 leading Western oil consuming nations. Intended to prevent another oil crisis by monitoring supply and demand and supervising consumer levels of oil stocks. See Arab Oil Embargo.

IFC International Finance Corporation. An affiliate of the World Bank which helps private enterprises in developing nations and mobilises domestic and foreign capital including its own for this purpose.

IFO Institut für Wirtschaftsforschung in Munich. One of six German research institutes which produce regular individual reports and in spring and autumn a joint report on the state of the economy.

IMC International Monetary Conference, a key annual event organised by the American Bankers Association. It centres on financial and monetary topics and attendees have to be the chairman or chief executive of the member bank.

IMF A specialised agency of the United Nations which provides funds to member countries with balance of payments problems under certain conditions of need and strict policy commitments. The IMF has a wide-ranging brief to oversee the international monetary system. It was established by the Bretton Woods agreement on a system of differential quota subscriptions representing drawing rights and voting powers. Subscriptions come from its member countries.

IMM Located in Chicago, the International Monetary Market (IMM), which was created in 1972, became a division of the Chicago Mercantile Exchange in 1976. See CME.

IMM Dates Standardised dates dealt on IMM exchange-traded futures and options contracts indicating the expiry date, which falls on the Monday preceding the third Wednesday of the third month of the year, i.e. March, June, September and December.

Implied Repo Rate The funding cost implied in futures prices which reflects the difference between the cash price of the underlying and the price of its futures contract.

Implied Volatility The Volatility implied in the price of an option. The calculation is made by using the options market price (premium) as the fair value in an option model and then assessing the volatility level consistent with that option price.

It is a measure of how much the market thinks prices will move given a known option price but does not indicate the direction of the movement expected. Volatility is expressed as an annualised percentage.

Implied Yield A forecast based on present yields and using a theory that the yield curve on one set day gives an indication of its future trend.

Import Deposits Method of import restrictions requiring importers to deposit a percentage of the value of their imports for a set time before it is repaid. Falling into disuse with the growing world-wide practice of free trade.

In Arrears Swap An interest rate swap with a floating rate which is set at the end of the reset period and paid in arrears. Also known as arrears reset swap.

In Strike The designated point when a trigger option, such as a Down and In or an Up and In, turns into a conventional option.

In the Money A term used to describe an option whose strike price is more advantageous than the current market price of the underlying instrument. The option becomes more expensive as the advantage increases because its intrinsic value is greater. See Out of the Money, At the Money.

Inc. Incorporation is the process by which a company receives a U.S. state charter and is allowed to operate as a corporation. This process must be recognised in the legal name, i.e. Inc.

Income / Growth Fund A type of investment fund investing in a combination of high dividend stock with established growth.

Income Statement See Profit and Loss Statement.

Income Stock See Blue Chip Stock.

Income Warrant Pays income, or interest, up to the exercise date, based on the issue price of the warrant. It is often added to a Harmless Warrant to make it more attractive.

Incomes Policy Broad term covering various direct forms of inflation control by a government. Can include a freeze or limitation on increases in prices, wages, dividends, investment income, rents.

Independent A non-integrated oil company usually active in only one or two sectors of the industry. An independent marketer buys a product from major or independent refiners and resells it under its own brand name. There are also independents which are active either in refining or crude and gas production exclusively.

Independent Petroleum Exporting Countries See IPEC.

Index Linked Bond Bond with coupon payments linked to the national consumer price index.

Index Linked Gilts - U.K. First issued in 1981, these gilts have a fixed maturity but a semi-annual coupon linked to the U.K. retail price index. Their redemption value is also protected against inflation, although only at maturity.

Index Tracking A process whereby a fund manager aims to reproduce the performance of a stock market index. Simply, a manager buys the shares which make up the index in the relevant proportions in which they are represented in the index.

Indirect Quotation The number of units of foreign currency that can be exchanged for one unit of domestic currency. The most common example of an indirect quotation outside the U.S. is the sterling/dollar rate. U.S. banks use indirect quotations in their international dealings but use Direct Quotations for domestic purposes.

Individual Retirement Account See IRA.

Inert Gas System Tanks filled with inert (non-combustible) gas which is used to prevent explosions on oil tankers.

Infill Drilling Development of an oil or gas field by drilling additional wells between existing ones.

Inflation Persistent upward movement in the general price level together with a related drop in purchasing power.

The nominal rate of return on an investment should be distinguished from its real rate of return, i.e. the net yield after deduction of inflation.

Inflation Risk The risk associated with the return from an investment not being offset by the loss in purchasing power as a result of inflation.

Initial Margin The downpayment paid to the clearing house of the futures exchange or to a brokerage firm by both the buyer and the seller of a futures contract once a deal is struck. The amount of the downpayment is determined by the maximum movement permitted on a futures contract before trading is suspended. The balance on the margin account will fluctuate daily as a result of marking to market by the clearing house. See Mark to Market, Maintenance Margin, Variation Margin, Margin Call.

Initial Public Offering The primary market of the stock market, i.e. the very first offering of shares being made to the public by a company. If the same company issues more shares to the public, these are referred to as new issue shares. Proceeds from the IPO go to the issuer. The issuer normally offers to the public through an underwriter who sets the price and promotes the offering. Initial public offerings can take place in the over the counter market or, if the company has met the listing requirements, on a stock exchange.

Injection Well Used to inject gas or water into the reservoir to maintain pressure during secondary recovery for conservation purposes.

INMARSAT International Maritime Satellite Organisation. Operates a satellite system which provides telephone, telex, data and facsimile as well as distress and safety communications services to the shipping and offshore industries.

INRO International Natural Rubber Organization. Group of producing and consuming nations which participate in the International Natural Rubber Agreement, a pact which seeks to stabilise prices through the operation of a buffer stock.

INSEE Institut National de la Statistique et des Etudes Economiques (French National Statistics Institute). Collates and issues a number of government economic indicators.

Insider Trading Exploitation of inside or privileged information for profit in market transactions.

Insolvency A company is insolvent when it is unable to pay its debts as and when they fall due. Arises when, for instance, judgement debts remain unsatisfied or cheques are returned unpaid by the company's bankers. A company is also insolvent when its liabilities, including contingent and prospective liabilities, exceed the value of the assets.

Insolvency - Japan Japan's Corporate Reorganisation and Rehabilitation Act provides for joint stock companies to apply for protection from creditors. The court can refuse the petition, in which case the firm would be declared insolvent. If the court accepts the petition it will appoint a receiver who draws up plans for the future.

Institute of Petroleum U.K. petroleum industry organisation which provides a discussion forum. Also deals with the standardisation of test methods for petroleum.

Institutional Investors Refers to organisations such as pensions funds, investment trusts and insurance companies, which are investors in the market.

Institutional Shareholder Services An independent Washington based U.S. group which advises large investors on corporate governance issues.

Intangibles See Assets / Liabilities.

Integrated Oil Company One that undertakes all principal oil industry functions - exploration, production, transportation, refining and marketing.

Integrated Producer A producer which owns mines, smelters and refineries and, in some cases, fabricating plants.

Inter-African Coffee Organization See IACO.

Inter-American Development Bank Promotes economic and social projects in developing countries by financial, via loans, and technical assistance. Set up in 1959.

Interbank Market The professional market between banks. The interbank money market is used to borrow and lend for short periods and to aid asset and liability management at the end of a day's trading.

Interbank Rates See LIBOR / LIBID / LIMEAN.

INTERCARGO International Association of Dry Cargo Shipowners.

Interest Bearing Term used to describe instruments which pay a given rate of interest on the principal amount, either in one payment, typically at maturity, or as a series of payments over the life. Also referred to as coupon bearing.

Interest Equalisation Tax A U.S. tax - introduced in 1963, ended in 1974 - on interest income paid on securities issued by foreign borrowers in U.S. capital markets. This tax was a significant factor in the development of the Eurobond market.

Interest Rate   The cost, often annual, paid by a borrower to a lender over a period of time. It is intended to compensate a lender for the sacrifice of losing immediate use of money and for the inflationary erosion of its buying power over the life of the loan and for the risk involved in lending the money. Interest rates are sensitively responsive to the supply and demand factors of credit and to inflationary expectations.

Interest Rate Differential   The difference in yield between two comparable instruments denominated in different currencies. Used in forward foreign exchange pricing.

Interest Rate Guarantee   See IRG.

Interest Rate Risk   The potential for losses or reduced income arising from adverse moves in interest rates.

Interest Rate Swap   See IRS.

Interim Committee   Ministerial group in the International Monetary Fund that deals with proposals to reform the international monetary system. Its membership mirrors that of the IMF Board.

Interim Dividend   Dividend paid by a company in a trading period, usually half yearly but can be quarterly. Authorised solely by the board of directors.

International Accounting Standards Committee   Based in London. Formulates and publishes accounting standards. Members comprise 110 accounting bodies in 82 countries.

International Bank for Reconstruction and Development   See World Bank.

International Banking Facilities   See IBFs.

International Chamber of Commerce   Based in Paris, this groups chambers of commerce, business and banking associations from around the world. It has an arbitration court used for settling international business disputes.

International Cocoa Organization   See ICCO.

International Coffee Organization   See ICO.

International Commodities Clearing House   See LCH.

International Councils of Securities Associations   See ICSA.

International Development Association   See IDA.

International Energy Agency   See IEA.

International Finance Corporation   See IFC.

International Lead and Zinc Study Group   Brings together producing/consuming countries and industry representatives. Handles statistics.

International Monetary Conference   See IMC.

International Monetary Fund   See IMF.

International Monetary Market   See IMM.

International Natural Rubber Organization   See INRO.

International Organization of Securities Commissions   See IOSCO.

International Petroleum Exchange   See IPE.

International Rubber Study Group   Intergovernmental organisation mainly representing synthetic and natural rubber producers. Collects statistics, undertakes economic studies and provides a forum for discussion of rubber supply and demand.

International Securities Market Association.   See ISMA.

International Share Offering   Occurs when shares of a domestic company are sold internationally via a syndicate of underwriters. They can be either new shares or a secondary offering. International share offerings often give a wider distribution to shares and thus limit any depressive impact of an additional supply on the domestic market. However, the normally liquid domestic market is where shares from an international offering might be sold later. This could create a substantial flowback if large scale selling materialised.

International Sugar Organization   Group of sugar importing and exporting countries which formed the International Sugar Agreement. However, this pact is now purely administrative and has no market regulatory or economic clauses.

International Swap Dealers Association   See ISDA.

International Tin Council   See ITC.

International Wheat Council   Group of wheat producing and consuming countries which cooperate under the International Wheat Agreement. This pact has no market regulatory or economic clauses but provides for the collection of statistics on world wheat and coarse grain production.

International Wrought Copper Council   Industry group consisting of European, Japanese and Australian consumers which handles statistics on the world copper market.

Interpolation   The process of determining a rate (or other variable) that lies between a series of known rates. Three types of interpolation exist: linear, logarithmic and cubic. See Extrapolation.

Interruptable (IT)   Natural gas sold on an interruptable basis, meaning delivery can be cut off over short periods if the demand exceeds supply. Typically used in gas sales to industry and carries a lower price than gas sold on a firm basis.

INTERTANKO   International Association of Independent Tanker Owners. Acts as a lobby group.

Intraday Refers to within the day and is thus any point at which a price or rate is noted in market trading between the opening and the close with particular reference to a high or low during trading. Common intraday intervals include tick, five minute, half-hourly and hourly.

Intraday Limit Limit allowed on a dealer's position in each and all currencies during the course of the trading day.

INTRASTAT The system used to collate trade data of the member nations of the European Community. It is run under the aegis of EUROSTAT, the EC statistical agency.

Intrinsic Value The value of an option. The intrinsic value indicates how much an option is In the Money. Calculated by taking the difference between the forward market value of the underlying instrument and the strike price of the option. Out of and At the Money options have zero intrinsic value. See Time Value.

Introduction Method of share issuance requiring only an abridged announcement in the national press, and typically used only when existing shares are widely held, or when seeking a listing on a second stock exchange.

Investment Bank A bank acting as an underwriter for new issues of stocks or bonds and which, as part of a syndicate, redistributes the issue to investors. In the U.S., an investment bank should not be described as a bank but rather as a financial institution.

Investment Grade Bonds which are rated BBB or above by the credit rating agencies and are considered to be safe investments, in that the agencies do not anticipate that the issuers are likely to default at the time the rating is issued.

Investment Services Directive A proposed directive of the European Commission allowing share dealers a single licence to operate throughout the European Community. Proposed effective date is January 1996. Broadly, the Commission is seeking to reinforce supervision of the banking, insurance and securities activities of member nations and to lay down the minimum capital requirements needed for securities trading.

Invisible Supply Stocks - notably commodities - outside commercial channels whose exact quantity cannot be identified but which in theory are available to the market.

Invisibles Export and import of services as opposed to trade in physical goods or merchandise. They form part of the current account balance of payments and include funds arising from shipping, tourism, insurance, banking and commodity services. Such items can comprise a significant amount of a nation's current account.

IOSCO International Organization of Securities Commissions. An organisation comprising the securities administrations from more than 50 countries. Seeks to develop securities markets and observance of securities regulations. Based in Montreal.

IPE The International Petroleum Exchange was established in November 1980 in London. Trades gas oil, crude and gasoline futures and options contracts. The IPE is Europe's leading exchange in the energy derivatives market.

IPEC The Independent Petroleum Exporting Countries. An informal group of oil exporters who do not belong to the Organisation of Petroleum Exporting Countries. Usually coordinated by Oman. Participants have included Angola, China, Egypt, Malaysia, Mexico and Russia while Norway, Alberta and Texas have sent observers.

IRA In the U.S., an Individual Retirement Account where an individual gains tax advantages with a personal pension plan.

IRG Interest Rate Guarantee. An option to buy or sell a Forward Rate Agreement on a future date. See Borrower's Option, Lender's Option.

Iridium A precious metal produced as a co-product of platinum and palladium.

IRS Interest Rate Swap. An exchange of a fixed rate of interest on a notional principal amount for one on a floating basis against the same notional amount and in the same currency. Also known as a coupon swap or fixed for floating swap.

ISDA The International Swap Dealers' Association set up in the mid 1980s to promote activities in the swap market. Based in New York.

ISEQ Index A capitalisation weighted arithmetic index for the Irish Stock Exchange, Dublin, comprising all Irish stocks officially listed. Futures are traded on the Irish Futures and Options Exchange. Calculated four times each day.

Islamic Development Bank Based in Saudi Arabia. Encourages economic and social development of 46 member nations and of Muslim communities in non-member countries following Islamic law.

Island Reversal See Reversal Day.

Isle of Man A self governing British crown dependency, part of Great Britain but not of the United Kingdom. It is not a European Community member but does observe some of the trade rules.

ISMA International Securities Market Association. Incorporates the Association of International

Bond Dealers whose members comprised organisations in 40 nations and which acted as a forum for questions concerning international securities markets and issued and enforced rules governing operations. Responsibilities are now widened out from purely bond dealers to encompass Euromarket bond dealers and managers in the international securities market. The Association changed its name from Association of International Bond Dealers (AIBD) to International Securities Market Association (ISMA) in January 1992. Based in Zurich.

ISMA Basis A method of calculating accrued interest using a 360 day year made up of 30 day months. Known as 30/360 or 360/360 bases. Used in the Eurobond market. See Daycount Conventions.

Isoglucose A sweetener known in the U.S. as High Fructose Corn Syrup. Derived from corn (maize) and used in soft drinks and manufactured products.

Issue Date See Dated Date.

Issue Price Price at which securities are sold on issue. This can be at face value or par, at a discount or at a premium.

Issued Shares Authorised shares which have been distributed and which may now trade in the market. Also known as outstanding shares.

Itaku Gensaki A Gensaki trade between two clients of a Japanese securities house with the house acting as an intermediary.

Italy - Key Interest Rates The rates to watch are:
Fixed term advances rate - usually sets the ceiling for money market rates.
Repo rates - sets the tone for money market rates.
Discount rate - a strong signal of the general interest rate trend.
The two most important Bank of Italy interest rates are the fixed term advances rate (similar to Germany's lombard rate except that the amount advanced is at the central bank's discretion) and the repo rate. The fixed term advances rate usually sets the ceiling for repo rates. However, repos are now the main short term liquidity management tool. They are conducted in both lira and foreign currency. The discount rate still has a strong symbolic value and indicates where the Bank of Italy feels interest rates should be. Money market rates are usually kept above the discount rate.
Clues on the direction of monetary policy can be picked up from the amount allocated at repos and the average and marginal rates set. Also important is any change in the spread of the fixed term advances rate over the discount rate.

There are five main ways in which the Bank of Italy can provide liquidity to the market. They are: rediscounting, ordinary advances, fixed term advances, repos and outright operations in Treasury securities.
Since the early 1980s the Bank of Italy has been steadily distancing itself from the Treasury and now has an independence similar to that of the Bundesbank. No government representatives take part in the Bank's decisions on monetary policy and those decisions do not require government approval. The governor of the Bank of Italy is chosen by the board of the Bank of Italy and the appointment has subsequently to be confirmed by the president of the Republic. The term of office is indefinite.

ITC The International Tin Council is an organisation grouping tin consumer and producer nations which previously regulated the tin market through its buffer stock operations. These operations collapsed in 1985 after surplus tin had been bought up at a floor price well above the value at which the buffer stock would otherwise have held the metal. Buffer stock funds ran out and tin prices went into free fall. Lengthy proceedings ensued - on an abortive rescue package involving governments, banks and brokers and in court hearings. The ITC is now defunct.

IWH Institut für Wirtschaftsforschung in Halle, eastern Germany. One of six German research institutes which produce regular individual reports and in spring and autumn a joint report on the state of the economy.

J Curve A U.K. expression to describe the reaction of the balance of trade following a devaluation. The trade balance deteriorates as import costs rise, then recovers to surplus as exports expand in volume due to cheaper exchange costs.

Jack-Up Rig Mobile offshore drilling platform with extendable legs on which the platform rests on the sea bed when in use.

Jacket The steel legs and sub-structure resting on the seabed and supporting the decks of an offshore platform. Kept in position by steel piles driven into the sea bed.

Japan - Key Interest Rates The rates to watch are:
Uncollateralised (unsecured) overnight call rate - sets the tone for money market rates.
Official discount rate (ODR) - lagging rate of psychological significance.
Japan is nearing the end of a decade long period in which most interest rates have been deregulated. These changes mean the Bank of Japan (BOJ) now sets only its official discount rate, at which it lends to commercial banks, and

the liquidity deposit rate. Other interest rates are set in the open market and the BOJ aims to influence them, indirectly, through its market operations.

The most important short term interbank money market rate is the uncollateralised overnight call rate. The BOJ closely monitors call rate movements and puts most emphasis on them when managing the market. The BOJ appears to have an unpublished target zone for the call rate but the market usually gets an idea of the BOJ's target range and credit stance by interpreting the signals in its daily operations. For the past several years, the market has focused more on the amount and timing of BOJ operations. Rates set by the BOJ have rarely ruffled any market feathers, as they have been largely in line with prevailing market rates. The weekly average call rate, and its level at intervention time, can provide signals on the BOJ's policy stance.

Since the BOJ prefers to signal monetary policy changes through the uncollateralised overnight call rate, the official discount rate (ODR) is now typically a lagging indicator of monetary policy. Nevertheless, the ODR still has an impact. The ODR applies to the rediscounting of commercial bills and official loans secured with Japanese government bonds (JGBs), specially designed securities and bills corresponding to commercial bills as collateral.

If the ODR is increased, financial institutions find that the cost of raising funds is affected directly, via the higher cost of acquiring discount window loans from the BOJ and, indirectly, through the increased money market rates that usually precede, and often trigger, an ODR change. The opposite is true for a reduction in the ODR.

Under the Bank of Japan Law (1942) the Bank's policy board has the authority to formulate, direct and carry out monetary policy. While ultimate control of monetary policy rests with the Ministry of Finance, the Bank of Japan Law gives the central bank sole responsibility for changing the official discount rate. There is no hard and fast rule.

There are seven members of the policy board, four of whom are appointed by the cabinet and approved by both houses of the Diet (Japanese Parliament). There are four representatives from private industry, one from the Bank of Japan and two from the government. The government members, taken from the Ministry of Finance and the Economic Planning Agency, do not have voting rights.

Japan - Money Supply The chief monetary aggregate is M2 + certificates of deposit (CDs). This includes currency in circulation, demand deposits and time deposits (savings deposits which include certificates of deposit). The data is seasonally adjusted. Financial markets focus on the seasonally adjusted year on year percentage change in M2 + certificates of deposits each month. Also watched is broad liquidity, a wider measure of the money supply which emphasises the need to monitor the total financial system. Broad liquidity is M2 + CDs plus the deposits of post offices and other non-banks (including agricultural cooperatives, fishery cooperatives, credit cooperatives and labour credit associations), gensaki, bank debentures, government and foreign bonds held outside the banking system (external bonds), bonds with repurchase agreements, government bonds, and money (or investment) trusts and loan trusts of all banks (excluding inter-financial institution deposits, trust accounts and cheques and bills held by financial institutions).

Jebel Ali Free Zone Authority An industrial free trade zone in Dubai set up in 1985.

Jiko Gensaki A regular Japanese Gensaki trade with a securities house as the counterparty.

Jobbers A term for market maker, derived from the London Stock Exchange.

Jobbers - Canada A group of investment dealers and banks who are active in the Treasury bill repo market directly with the Bank of Canada. Jobbers also ensure liquidity in the Treasury bond market by providing two-way prices in all issues. There are fewer jobbers than primary distributors, although banks or dealers with both functions exist.

Junk Bonds High yield bonds rated below Investment Grade.

Junked Term used to describe a well where equipment has been lost down and cannot be retrieved economically. The well is therefore plugged and abandoned.

Jute Plant fibre used for sacking, mats and cord. Second to cotton in world fibre consumption. Major producers are Pakistan, India and China.

Kairi In technical analysis, this charts the percentage difference between the current closing value and its simple moving average. Can be used either as a trend indicator or as an overbought/oversold signal. In a volatile market, the kairi moving to a high value indicates a breakout and the beginning of a new trend. In a flat market, it shows an overbought position when it reaches a high value.

Kampo The Postal Insurance Bureau of the Japanese Posts and Telecommunications Ministry. It is one of the major Japanese institutional investors in foreign bonds and foreign exchange markets.

Kassen See Bundeskassenobligationen - Germany.

Kassenverein (KV) The Central Depository Bank for Securities. The clearing agent of the German stock exchanges.

KCSPI Index Capitalisation weighted index comprising all 686 companies listed on the Korea stock exchange.

Keidanren In Japan, a forum that comprises leading industry and business figures.

Keiretsu Japanese corporate groupings centred around a trading house, bank or manufacturing firm which are linked by intertwined management, cross shareholdings and long term supplier/user relationships.

Kelly Bushing The rotating table on the drill room floor that drives the drill string. Significant because the depth of many wells is measured from the kelly bushing.

Kerb Trading Trading that takes place outside official market hours. The expression comes from trading literally taking place on the kerb outside the stock exchange.

Kern River A very heavy crude oil with an API rating of 13. Produced in California.`

Kerosene Medium light distillate used for lighting and heating and to provide fuel for jet and turbo-prop aircraft engines. Also spelt kerosine. In the U.K., called paraffin or paraffin oil.

Key Interest Rates See separate entries such as "Germany - Key Interest Rates" for the Group of 10 nations and Switzerland.

Key Reversal Day See Reversal Day.

Keynesian Economics Theories developed by the U.K.'s John Maynard Keynes based on a cause and effect analysis of variations in aggregate spending and income. These thoughts opposed the free market philosophy and believed that economic performance could be improved by government intervention. They held sway in the 1960s and 1970s in the Western world.

KFX Index Capitalisation weighted arithmetic index of 20 high volume companies on the Copenhagen stock exchange. Futures and options are traded on the Guarantee Fund for Danish Options and Futures Exchange. Calculated continuously.

Kicker An added feature of a debt obligation designed to enhance marketability.

Kiel Institute Institut für Weltwirtschaft in Kiel. One of six German research institutes which produce

regular individual reports and twice a year a joint report on the state of the economy.

Killing a Well Overcoming the tendency of an oil well to flow naturally by filling the well bore with drilling mud or similar substance.

Kingdom of Sweden Issuer of government debt in the form of Treasury bonds (Statsobligationslan). Issuance resumed in 1991 due to the reappearance of a budget deficit. Methods to improve market liquidity have effectively reduced the number of issues outstanding and increased the average size of issues. The authorities permit older issues to be converted into benchmark issues. There are several benchmark issues which remain very liquid.

Kiwi Dealers' language for the New Zealand dollar.

KLSE Composite Index Capitalisation weighted arithmetic index of 83 companies listed on the Kuala Lumpur stock exchange.

Knockout Option A type of barrier option. See Down and Out, Up and Out.

Knockout Warrant Can be in the form of knockout put and call warrants. If, during the life of the call warrant, the index closes higher or equal to a set knockout level or if, during the life of the put warrant, the index closes lower or equal to a set knockout level, then the warrant is automatically exercised and payment is made to the investor. The warrant then ceases to exist.

Knot Measurement of speed. One nautical mile equals 6,080 feet per hour.

Kommunalobligation Bonds offered by German banks to finance public sector loans. Collateral for such bonds comes from a pool of public sector loans.

Konsortium See Federal Bond Syndicate.

L/C See Letter of Credit.

Ladder Option An option on which the strike price can be moved to a more favourable level when the original strike price is reached or overtaken by the spot rate.

Lagged Moving Average The value of a moving average in a previous set period. The chart of a lagged moving average is the chart of the moving average shifted to the right by determined periods.

Lakehead Ports of Duluth, Superior and Thunder Bay on the North American Great Lakes.

Lambda The measurement of the leverage of an option, showing the relationship between a percentage change in the price of the underlying and a percentage change in the option premium.

Landed Price   Total cost of oil to a refiner after accounting for all costs from point of production, or purchase, to the refinery.

Länder   Regional states in Germany, of which there are 16, following unification of East and West Germany.

Last Notice Day   Final day for the issuing of notices of intent to deliver against a futures contract.

Last Trading Day   Last day for trading in the current delivery month. Futures contracts outstanding at the end of the last trading day must be settled by delivery of underlying physical commodities or financial instruments, or by agreement for cash settlement, if the former is impossible.

Late Night Trading   Trading on the London Metal Exchange in the period from the close of the afternoon kerb to the close of the comparable U.S. markets. The contracts are registered in the next day's business.

Latex   Rubber trees produce a milky white fluid which comprises 30 percent latex and 70 percent water. See Rubber.

Laundering   The covert action of passing money through channels secretively or via a chain of financial transactions, often using offshore facilities, to evade detection.

Laurics   Oilseed market term for palm and coconut products.

Lay Barge   Barge built for laying submarine pipelines.

LCE   The London Commodity Exchange is recognised as Europe's primary centre for the trading of soft commodity futures and options contracts including cocoa, coffee, sugar, wheat, barley, potatoes and the (Baltic International Freight Futures Exchange - BIFFEX) dry cargo freight futures. Originally formed in 1954. It merged the major soft commodity futures market associations to form a single Recognised Investment Exchange under the U.K. 1986 Financial Services Act.

   The present exchange stems from the London Commercial Sale Rooms which were built in 1811 as a centre for selling a variety of soft commodities by auction. These sale rooms continued through until 1941. The LCE came into being after the Second World War. In 1987, its name became the London FOX, the Futures and Options Exchange, but in 1993 the title was again changed, going back to its original name of the London Commodity Exchange. See Baltic Futures Exchange.

LCH   Owned by U.K. clearing banks, the London Clearing House registers, guarantees and clears all trades for the London Commodity Exchange (LCE), London International Financial Futures and Options Exchange (LIFFE), London Metal Exchange (LME), International Petroleum Exchange (IPE), Baltic International Freight Futures Exchange (BIFFEX) and all agricultural futures and options. LCH is the operating arm while the holding company is the International Commodities Clearing House (ICCH).

LDC   Lesser (or Less) Developed Country. Seen as lower down the general economic scale than a developing country and usually taken as a nation which is not a member of the Organisation for Economic Cooperation and Development (OECD). However, the term is not precise. One rough measure is the amount of overseas debt relative to the strength of the economy.

   Also means Least Developed Country for which one definition is a nation where annual per capita income is less than 400 dollars. Another adds where illiteracy rate is more than 20 percent and where industry contributes less than 10 percent of gross national product.

LDC (Local Distribution Company)   The local or regional gas distributor or utility.

Lead   Base metal. Its main use is in storage batteries. Other markets for lead are much smaller, such as semi-manufactured goods, chemicals, tetraethyl lead (compounds of which are used in petrol) and cable sheathing. However, lead has met competition in these sectors while environmental concerns are an inhibiting factor. Lead can be recovered as scrap. Producers include Australia, Belgium, Bulgaria, Canada, China, the Commonwealth of Independent States, France, Germany, Japan, Mexico, Peru, Spain, the U.K., the U.S. and former Yugoslavia.

Lead Manager   The institution awarded the mandate by a borrower to raise money via a bond or loan agreement. The lead manager guarantees the liquidity of the deal, arranges the syndication of the issue and undertakes a major underwriting and distribution commitment. The lead manager forms a syndicate of co-lead managers, co-managers and underwriters. See Mandate.

Leads and Lags   Accelerated and decelerated foreign trade payments and receipts, usually associated with exchange rate speculation. In anticipation of a devaluation, payments for exports are delayed while an importer accelerates his payments.

LEAPS   Long term Equity Anticipation Securities (LEAPS) are long term options on individual stocks with an expiry date of up to two years. LEAPS trade in contracts of 100 shares of well-known companies with large capitalisation.

Least Developed Country   See LDC.

Legumes Plants such as soybeans which produce pods containing seeds that are eaten or crushed. They also aid nitrogen enrichment of the soil.

Lender of Last Resort The lender of last resort in a country is the central bank.

Lender's Option An option to sell an FRA on a predetermined date in the future. Opposite to Borrower's Option. Also known as an Interest Rate Guarantee (IRG).

Lending London Metal Exchange term for the sale of a nearby delivery date coupled with the simultaneous purchase of a more distant date.

Lending Margin The fixed spread which borrowers agree to pay above an agreed base of interest.

Lesser (or Less) Developed Country See LDC.

Letter of Credit If a company wants to finance some sort of international trade on credit it can ask a bank to issue a letter of credit in favour of its supplier. By this, the bank guarantees to make payment on a specific date as long as certain qualifications have been met such as providing satisfactory shipping documents. When the bank accepts the bill it writes "accepted" above the signature. The supplier can either hold the bill to maturity - whereupon the company pays the supplier - or discount the accepted bill with another bank which will either hold it as an investment or trade it on the secondary market.

Letter Stock A type of ordinary share in the U.S. which has been issued privately and therefore not registered with the Securities and Exchange Commission (SEC). These shares are not easy to transfer.

Leverage In options trading this measures the percentage change in the premium for a given percentage fluctuation in the price of the underlying.

Leveraged Buyout Funds are raised to take over a company and that company's assets are used as collateral (or as leverage) for the borrowing. The purchaser then repays the loans out of the acquired company's cash flow, or by selling its assets.

Liabilities See Assets / Liabilities.

Liability Management See Assets / Liabilities.

LIBOR / LIBID / LIMEAN The London Interbank Offered Rate (LIBOR) is the rate at which banks are prepared to lend to each other for specified maturities within the London market. LIBOR is also fixed daily for reference purposes and is a key interest rate level used for setting rates for loans and floating rate notes and for calculating cash settlements of certain interest rate derivative instruments. LIBID is the London Interbank Bid rate, the rate at which banks take deposits from each other. LIMEAN is the London Interbank Mean Price.

Licence Block Continental Shelf section in a particular national sector typically bounded by latitude and longitude lines at one degree intervals. Usually sub-divided into smaller quantities than an oil company contracted for.

Licensed Warehouse Warehouse approved by an exchange from which a commodity may be delivered under a futures contract.

Lien The right to take assets to cover an unpaid debt. See Prior Lien.

LIFFE The London International Financial Futures and Options Exchange (LIFFE), opened in September 1982, provides a market within the European time zone for financial futures and, since 1985, for financial options. In 1992 LIFFE merged with the LTOM (London Traded Options Market). Contracts include futures and options on government bonds, short term interest rates and the FT-SE 100 Index.

Lifting Oil companies lift crude or products when their tankers or barges take on cargoes at export terminals or trans-shipment points. Underlifting means to load smaller quantities than a company contracted for.

Light Crude Low specific gravity crude with high API gravity.

Light Ends The more volatile products of petroleum refining such as butane, propane, gasoline and naphtha.

Light Grains Barley and oats.

Lighter Vessel, usually flat bottomed, used for loading and unloading ships not brought to wharf.

Lighterage Fees paid for loading /unloading ships by lighters or barges.

LIMEAN See LIBOR / LIBID / LIMEAN.

Limit Order An instruction to act in a market. An order stipulating that the deal should be executed at a certain level and under certain specified conditions.

Examples are: Normal Order (N/O), Stop Loss (S/L), One Cancels the Other (OCO), Buy after Sell (B/S), Sell after Buy (S/B), Fill or Kill (FOK), All or None and Alternative Order.

Limit orders are normally valid until a certain time specified by the counterparty or Good Till Cancelled (GTC) and can be passed on to other financial centres for possible execution in other time zones.

Limit Up / Limit Down The maximum advance and decline from a previous day's settlement price allowed in one trading session are known as limit up and limit down. Some markets do not trade again during the session after a limit up/down move unless prices fall (or rise). Other markets suspend trading temporarily when limits are hit and then reopen with expanded limit levels. See Daily Price Limit.

Limited Liability A restriction of the owner's loss in the business to the amount of capital invested.

Line Chart Used in technical analysis. A plain record of a price charted against time with the changes marked as dots and conjoined in a determining line.

Liner Conference Voluntary organisation in which a number of shipowners - often from different nations - offer regular services to a series of ports on a given sea route on conditions agreed by the members.

Liner Service Service provided by a shipping company whereby cargo-carrying ships are operated between ports on a regular basis.

Linseed Variety of Flaxseed used to produce linseed oil (also known as linoil) and protein meal for animal feed. Linoil is used in paints and varnishes and also in linoleum, the floor covering. Major producers are Argentina, Canada, India, the U.S. and the Commonwealth of Independent States.

Liquefied Natural Gas See LNG.

Liquefied Petroleum Gas See LPG.

Liquidation Occurs - in the U.K. - where a limited company's assets are realised and the company dissolved. Statutory term is winding up. There are three main types of liquidation:

　　1) Members' voluntary (or solvent) liquidation in which all debts are paid in full and shareholders receive a return on the capital they have subscribed. The directors make a formal declaration of solvency.

　　2) Creditors' voluntary liquidation in which the shareholders and the creditors of an insolvent company appoint a liquidator.

　　3) Winding up by the court following an application to the court by an affected party.

　　Liquidation also refers to a process whereby a market transaction reduces or closes out a long or short position, although more often the trade uses it to refer only to a long position.

Liquidity The depth of the market and its ability to absorb sudden shifts in supply and demand without price distortions.

Liquidity Diversification Using a portfolio to invest in various maturities and types of issues to lessen the risk of illiquidity. Also, investors can sometimes show a willingness to surrender return in order to gain entry to more liquid issues.

Liquidity Margin A liquidity margin is a good faith performance guarantee. Lenders, in repurchase agreements, often seek such a margin from borrowers perhaps by receiving securities in excess of the money borrowed.

Liquidity Risk The risk a dealer has of not being able to unwind a position or enter into a position at a desired point of time.

Listed Stock A security which has been admitted to the listing of a stock exchange and can therefore be traded in the stock market.

Listing Requirements Required by a stock exchange before a share is listed on the stock exchange and ready to trade. Each stock exchange sets its own listing requirements and criteria include considerations such as number of publicly held shares, number of shareholders, price and trade volume of that particular share and the company's aggregate before tax earnings. If companies do not meet these requirements, shares may be traded in the Over the Counter market.

Lists Closed A list of applications to subscribe for a securities issue is closed on a set date and time by those organising the issue. Also known as the closing date of the issue.

Live Cattle See Beef.

Live Hogs See Pork Bellies.

Lloyd's Register Published in London, this is an annual world-wide alphabetical list of commercial vessels of more than 100 tons classified according to seaworthiness. Lloyd's formulates rules for the building of vessels and assigns classes to them when its rules have been followed.

LME Established in 1877, the London Metal Exchange now acts as an international barometer of supply and demand for metals world-wide and its official prices are used by producers and consumers for their long term contracts. These prices can be hedged on the LME through a variety of futures and options contracts.

　　Dealings take place in minimum quantities of 25 tonnes for copper, lead, zinc and aluminium while nickel is traded in lots of six tonnes and tin in lots of five tonnes. All sales due for delivery are backed by warehouse warrants. Stocks are held in warehouses listed by the LME in locations throughout the U.K. and Europe as well as Singapore, Japan (for aluminium storage only) and the U.S.

　　Both floor and inter-office trading are covered by the terminal network indicative quotation system used by the LME. This allows effectively a 24 hour market.

Floor trading takes place in two sessions per day with each broken down into two rings made up of five minutes trading in each contract. Each session is followed by a short period of open outcry dealing in all metals simultaneously known as kerb trading. After the second ring of the first session the official prices for the day are announced. These prices are used as benchmark prices by the international metals trade.

LME traded options contracts are also available. LME brokers offer their clients the facility to trade in many leading currencies. See Late Night Trading.

LNG   Liquefied Natural Gas. Natural gas that has been liquefied by refrigeration or pressure to facilitate storage or transport. Generally consists of methane.

Loan Loss Provisions   Funds set aside to cover anticipated loan losses which appear on a bank's income statement as an operating expense. See Non-Performing Loan.

Loan Rate   The price per unit - such as bushel, bale or pound weight - at which the U.S. government makes loans to farmers, enabling them to hold their crops for later sale. The loan rate has served as a floor to the market because farmers can default if the market falls below the loan rate, forfeiting their grain to the Commodity Credit Corporation rather than paying back the loan and selling their crops on the open market.

Loan Selling   Involves taking large bought deal Multi-Option syndications into major money centre banks and then on-selling to smaller banks. This means the commercial syndicated loan is being turned into a money market instrument very close to commercial paper and negotiable certificates of deposit, especially as a secondary market develops. Commercial banks thus use loan selling to recapture ground they lost to the securities houses in the boom of debt securitisation which began in the early 1970s. It also allows these major money centre banks to use their capital more efficiently with the paper passing down to the smaller regional banks. See Bought Deal.

Loan Signing   The official signing of a loan by all parties which acknowledges that all monies have been committed and that all terms have been agreed.

LOC Paper   Paper issued with the additional backing of a bank line of credit (LOC), which commits the bank to repaying the borrower's debt should they default.

Local Authorities   In the U.K., local authorities venture into the money market for short term funds - up to 364 days- but obtain long term funding - one year or longer - generally from the Public Works Loan Board. Most popular borrowing by local authorities is for two or seven days notice. The deposits and loans of these U.K. municipal governing bodies comprise an important secondary money market.

Local Traders   Individual traders operating on futures or options exchanges purely for their own account.

Locked in   An investor is locked in when he finds a potential profit is reduced if he disposes of the security, e.g. through imposition of a tax measure. Also where he cannot establish or unwind a position due to a limit move. See Limit Up / Limit Down.

Loco   The cost of goods where they lie. In gold trading the price is quoted for delivery to a certain location. Delivery of most gold is quoted loco London. See Gold Delivery.

Lodging   Describes the condition of grain crops when bent over and broken, e.g. by wind or rain and thus making the crop difficult to harvest.

Loi Monory   French measure which offers tax relief for investments via the French investment funds known as SICAV (Société d'Investissement à Capital Variable).

Lombard Rate   The rate charged by central banks for commercial banks to borrow overnight against collateral. See separate entries such as "Germany - Key Interest Rates" for the Group of 10 nations and Switzerland.

Lomé Convention   An economic treaty between the European Community and the African, Caribbean and Pacific group of developing countries (ACP). It offers duty free access to the EC by some 70 ACP nations. It also provides programmes for financing export shortfalls, mining products and financial aid.

London Bullion Market Association   Members are actively engaged in trading, refining, melting, assaying, transporting and vaulting gold or silver. The Association maintains close links with the Bank of England and acts formally on behalf of its members with the authorities.

London Clearing House   See LCH.

London Club   An informal group of commercial banks which holds discussions in London on an ad hoc basis on loan problems with a particular debtor nation. Sometimes referred to under the umbrella heading of the London Club but meetings are not necessarily held in London. See Paris Club.

London Commodity Exchange   See LCE.

London International Financial Futures and Options Exchange   See LIFFE.

London Metal Exchange   See LME.

London Traded Options Market   See LIFFE.

Long Bond   Commonly used name for the 30 year U.S. Treasury bond.

Long Hedge   The purchase of a futures or option position to protect against an increase in price in the corresponding cash market. Opposite to Short Hedge. See Hedge.

Long Position   A position showing a purchase or an excess of purchases over sales in anticipation of a rise in prices. A long position can be closed out through the sale of an equivalent amount. See Short Position.

Long Straddle   An option strategy combining a long call and a long put with the same strike and same expiry in expectation of a strong move in the underlying although the direction is uncertain.

Long Strangle   An option strategy combining a long call and a long put with the same expiry but different strike prices in anticipation of a strong move in the underlying although the direction is uncertain. The different strike levels (Out of the Money) reduce premium costs.

Long Term Banks - Japan   Three banks which mostly raise funds through five year bank debentures. They cannot take deposits from individuals. They can issue debentures worth up to 30 times as much as their capital and reserves.

Long Term Treasury Bonds - Japan   Semi-annual coupon bearing instruments issued monthly in Japan with maturities up to 10 years. The 10 year bond is the most liquid and holds benchmark status. These bonds are non-callable, although the government is able to buy them back in the secondary market. Each issue is given a serial number. In fact, the issues are standardised in such a way that they are identified solely by this number and not by coupon and maturity.

Long Ton   A ton of 2,240 pounds weight, equal to 1.016 metric tonnes.

Long-Dated Forwards   Forward foreign exchange contracts with value dates in excess of 12 months.

Long-Dated Gilts - U.K.   U.K. Treasury securities with a maturity of over 15 years. The market has not, so far, seen maturities of more than 25 years.

Lookback Option   An option which grants the holder the retroactive right to set the strike at the lowest price (on a call) or at the highest price (on a put) reached by the underlying within the lookback period.

Lookforward Option   An option granting the buyer the right to the difference between the spot level at the beginning of a period and the high (for a call) or low (for a put) over the same period.

LOOP   Louisiana Offshore Oil Port. The only U.S. deepwater port able to offload giant tankers. LOOP is situated in the Gulf of Mexico, near New Orleans, and can offload up to 1.4 million barrels per day.

Loss Limit   The maximum loss permitted on a position before the dealer is required to cut losses and square or reduce the position. See S/L.

Lot   See Round Lot Trade.

Louisiana Offshore Oil Port   See LOOP.

Louvre Accord   An agreement on currency stability reached in Paris in February 1987 by the finance ministers of the Group of Five nations and Canada following the prolonged fall in the U.S. dollar after the Plaza Agreement.

LPG   Liquefied Petroleum Gas. Light hydrocarbons from oil-bearing strata which are gaseous at normal temperatures but which are liquefied by refrigeration or pressure to facilitate storage or transport. Mainly propane and butane.

LSWR   Low Sulphur Waxy Residue. A type of fuel oil. Sometimes used for power generation.

LTD   U.K. company title, meaning Limited. Generally replaced by Public Limited Company or PLC. Still used for quoted companies in Australia, Canada and New Zealand.

LTOM   See LIFFE.

Lubricant   Generally based on heavy liquid hydrocarbons, lubricants are used to reduce friction in an engine or machine.

Lumber   About 50 percent of U.S. wood production is in the form of sawlogs which yield stud (split) lumber and plywood. These account for 80 percent of lumber in construction usage. Other uses of wood include paper (22 percent), fuelwood (16 percent) and veneers (4 percent). The Chicago Mercantile Exchange (CME) lists futures and options on lumber. Contracts are used for normal pricing and hedging purposes. Delivery is for 100,000 board feet of construction grade stud lumber. Delivery is at on-track locations in California, Idaho, Montana, Nevada, Oregon and Washington, the main logging states. In 1994 the Chicago Board of Trade began trading a Structural Panel Index futures contract based on an independent index of three-ply (layer) plywood values.

LYONs - U.S. Liquid Yield Options Notes were created in 1982 by Lehman Brothers and are zero coupon instruments similar to TIGRs and CATS. See U.S. STRIPS.

Maastricht Treaty An accord agreed by the 12 member nations of the European Community. It created a new entity, the European Union, with political and social responsibilities beyond the EC focus on economic and trade issues. It set the timetable and criteria for Economic and Monetary Union, leading to the creation of a single EC currency. Also known as the Treaty on European Union. Came into force November 1, 1993.

Macaulay Duration See Duration.

Macro-Economics Study of human activity in large groupings as indicated by economic aggregates such as total employment, national income, investment, consumption, prices, wages, costs.

Magnetometer Survey Geological survey identifying sedimentary basins by measuring the magnetic properties of the underlying igneous rock.

Main Crop In most cocoa growing countries there are two crops a year. The main is the larger while the smaller crop is known as mid-crop or the light. In Brazil the two crops are termed main and the temporao but both are of a similar size.

Maintenance Call See Margin Call.

Maintenance Margin The lowest balance of funds which a clearing house of the futures exchange or brokerage firm will allow a counterparty when trading on margin. Should an unrealised loss be reported, the counterparty is required to bring the account back to the maintenance margin level or the initial margin level. This demand is known as a maintenance or margin call.

Maize Also known as corn. Widely cultivated cereal plant which is a major world feed grain for animals. Used to yield edible vegetable oil, alcohol, high fructose corn syrup, corn gluten feed for animals and products for human consumption such as corn meal and corn flour. The U.S. accounts for about 45 percent of world corn output and some 75 percent of world trade. Corn is the largest U.S. crop in terms of both area planted and total production. Major producers are the U.S., China, Brazil, the European Community and the Commonwealth of Independent States.

Maize Gluten (Corn Gluten) By-product of the maize starch extraction process. Once the starch and protein are separated, the protein is dried as a gluten feed. Has relatively high protein content

and is widely used in dairy and beef cattle feeds. See Animal Feed Ingredients.

Majority Interest A major equity interest comprising more than half the shares in a company. Opposite to Minority Interest.

Majority Rule In technical analysis, calculates the percentage of the last specified periods during which an instrument had rising values. This analysis may be used either as a trend following device or as an overbought/oversold indicator.

Majors Multinational oil companies which by virtue of size, age and/or degree of integration are among the pre-eminent firms in the international petroleum industry.

Make Up Day Day when bank figures must be compiled for reporting to the central bank.

Man-Made Fibres Industrially produced fibres such as nylon and rayon as opposed to natural fibres such as cotton and wool.

Managed Float See Dirty Float.

Management Buyout Purchase by the managers of a company of part or all of its shares in order to set it up as an independent concern. The managers act as principals and usually do not provide all the financing.

Management Group Group of financial institutions which coordinates closely with the lead manager in the distribution and pricing of an issue.

Mandate The authority from a borrower to the Lead Manager to proceed with a loan or bond issue on the terms agreed.

Manifest Detailed list of cargo carried.

Manioc (Tapioca or Cassava) A root crop which is widely grown in the tropics. As an Animal Feed Ingredient, its value lies in its high starch content which gives a high energy value. Manioc has a low protein content but this can be offset by using it in conjunction with a higher protein feed ingredient such as soymeal. The root is usually dried and either chipped or pelleted to prevent perishing during transit.

Maquiladora Industry A 40 mile bandwidth South of the U.S./Mexico border where U.S. firms could manufacture products in Mexico and reimport the end product or parts into the U.S. without paying the typical tariffs. See NAFTA.

Marché à Terme International de France See MATIF.

Marché des Options Négociables de Paris See MONEP.

Margin Account An account enabling a market participant to trade futures contracts without having the full amount of funds available. Both counterparties (buyer and seller) are required to settle a downpayment to the brokerage firm or the clearing house of the futures exchange once a futures contract is concluded. This downpayment is known as the initial margin. The futures position is thereafter marked to market on a daily basis against closing prices and an unrealised profit or loss is calculated (Variation Margin). Should an unrealised loss be reported, the margin account will subsequently be reduced. Should the account fall below the minimum maintenance margin, the brokerage firm or exchange will make a margin or maintenance call to demand the counterparty to bring funds back to the required level. Opposite to Cash Account.

Margin Call A call made by the clearing house of a futures exchange to a counterparty whose margin account has fallen below the minimum requirement or the Maintenance Margin. Also referred to as a maintenance call.

Margin Trading Trading without having to settle the full amount by the use of a Margin Account.

Marginal Field Oil or gas field whose development depends on whether it will generate enough net income at a given time. If conditions change later then it may become commercial.

Mark to Market The process by which the clearing house of a futures exchange or brokerage firm calculates the value of a position based on the daily closing price, thereby reflecting the unrealised profit and loss on an outstanding position. The margin account is adjusted accordingly. See Margin Account.

Markdown The amount or percentage deducted from the bid price when a customer sells to a broker or market maker in the OTC market, which is regarded as a type of commission. Also used to describe market makers adjusting their prices down to reflect changing market conditions. Opposite to Markup.

Marker Crude Market term referring to any crude oil which is used as a reference for pricing lesser known grades.

Market Capitalisation Total value of a company's securities at current prices as quoted on a stock exchange. Hence, it is the total number of shares issued multiplied by the market price. Also, can denote the total valuation of the whole of a stock exchange's securities or the total value of one sector of a stock exchange's securities.

Market Economy Occurs where demand and supply in free markets determine the allocation of resources. However, most countries impose some limitations within this economic system. See Mixed Economy, Planned Economy, State Planning, Parastatal.

Market Forces Conditions of supply and demand which operate in a free market to determine prices through the decisions of buyers and sellers, lenders and borrowers.

Market if Touched Written as MIT. An order to sell or buy at a specific price if the market reaches that price.

Market Maker Recognised financial institution or individual making buy and sell quotations in the secondary market.

Market Profile Price forecasting tool that provides an on-line graphic representation summarising the day's activity, showing volume that occurs at specific price levels broken down to the nearest half hour.

Market Profile Analysis The market profile analysis is built from letters representing opportunities to buy or sell at a given time and price. These time price opportunities (TPOs) are organised into a stem and leaf plot graph. This graph tends to form a bell curve distribution pattern as the market moves to satisfy supply and demand within one price range, before moving to a new price range.

Market Risk See Systematic Risk.

Market Sentiment Signals the mood of the market. In an uptrend, buyers are stronger than sellers and prices continue to advance. This type of market sentiment is bullish and the market is on a bull run.

In a downtrend, sellers are stronger than buyers and prices continue downwards. Here, market sentiment is bearish and the market is on a bear run.

Market Tone There are various descriptions, or tones, used to report the strength of a whole market, a sector of that market or individual prices. They include such terms as weak, soft, steady, firm and strong.

Market Trend General direction, ignoring short term fluctuations, of price movements overall in a market.

Market Value Weighted Index A stock index giving due consideration to the different market values and hence the different relative price changes of the component shares.

Marketing Loan U.S. scheme where a crop loan can be repaid at the world market price - and not the original loan rate - if the world price is lower. Used mainly for U.S. rice and cotton.

Marketing Year Period during which a commodity - usually agricultural - is sold. Generally starts with the harvest.

Markup The amount or percentage added to the offer price when a customer buys from a broker or market maker in the OTC market, which is regarded as a type of commission. Also used to describe market makers adjusting their prices upwards to reflect changing market conditions. Opposite to Markdown.

Master Agreement The initial agreement signed between two parties proposing to enter into swap agreements, which defines all criteria for future transactions such as references for fixing rates, status of counterparties, and so forth.

Master Note These are notes issued by the major issuers of directly placed commercial paper. It is a variable rate demand note issued to bank trust departments who often have various small sums to invest in the market. These notes provide a convenient way to combine these investments.

Matador Bond A bond issued in Spain by a foreign borrower and denominated in pesetas. A type of foreign bond.

Matched Book A book where the maturity dates for a bank or trader's liabilities match those of the assets. Also, where borrowing costs equal the interest earned on investments. See Mismatch.

MATIF Marché à Terme International de France (MATIF), the Paris financial futures exchange, opened in 1986 and whose development and success has contributed significantly to the increased liquidity of the French government bond market. One third of its members are foreign. Contracts include the Three Month PIBOR future and option, the Long Term Notional Government Bond future and option and the CAC 40 stock index future.

Maturity The date on which payment of the principal is made.

Maturity Value The amount to be paid back at maturity; in bond trading also called principal.

May Day The day, May 1 1975, on which U.S. fixed brokerage commissions were ended, leading to the expansion of the brokerage industry and electronic operating systems.

MCF Means thousand cubic feet (Latin mille, for thousand). Used in connection with U.S. natural gas prices. MMCF means million cubic feet.

Meal Physical form of a feed in which all ingredients are ground or processed into small particle size.

Medium Term Notes See MTN.

Medium Term Treasury Bonds - Japan In Japan there are two types of this bond, discount and coupon bearing.

Coupon bearing bonds have maturities of two to five years and are issued almost every month. The discount bond bears a maturity of five years and is issued quarterly.

Medium-Dated Gilts - U.K. U.K. Treasury debt issues with a maturity between five and 15 years.

Members' Voluntary Liquidation See Liquidation.

Mercato Italiano Futures See MIF.

Merchant A merchant - as opposed to a broker or agent of a producer - sometimes acts as a principal. He buys from producers and others and then sells. Sometimes he retains on his account either waiting for a rise in market price or waiting for a customer.

Merchant Bank Similar to an investment bank but merchant banks have traditionally invested some of their own capital when arranging transactions rather than relying solely on the funds from targeted investors. In the U.K., has a broad role as an issuing house for stocks and bonds, raises loans and equity capital and deals in bills and foreign exchange. It advises, and acts on behalf of, companies, often in merger situations. Some deal in bullion.

MERCOSUR Mercado Común del Sur (Southern Common Market). Aims for Latin American free trade zone, to be operational by 1995. Members are Argentina, Brazil, Paraguay and Uruguay.

Merger A fusion of two or more companies. Can also represent an acquisition or takeover.

Metal Account An account where precious metals are often held and where the holder pays a fee to a custodian such as a bank. For this the holder has the right to the delivery of an amount of precious metals corresponding to the balance in the account. The metal account is liquidated by sale or by receiving physical delivery of bars.

Methane Odourless inflammable gas which can form an explosive mixture with air.

Methanol Methyl alcohol. Colourless, poisonous liquid with a faint smell. Used to mix with gasoline to help power vehicles.

Methyl Tertiary-Butyl Ether See MTBE.

Metric Ton (Tonne) 2,204.6223 pounds weight or 1,000 kilogrammes.

Mezzanine Finance A type of second tier funding capital midway between debt and equity in that it offers a higher interest rate than senior debt but provides a lower long term return than equity. This allows large deals to be structured in the best suitable method for investors and lenders. Often used in management buyouts.

MIB Index   Milano Indice Borsa. A capitalisation weighted arithmetic index for the Milan bourse which comprises 306 stocks. Updated continuously. MIBTEL is its associated index for shares traded on the electronic system. Comprises 152 stocks which account for 90 percent of the turnover.

Micro-Economics   Study of the economic action of individual firms and small well defined groupings of individuals and sectors.

Midcontinent Crude Oil   Oil produced in Kansas, Oklahoma and Northern Texas.

Middle Distillates   Hydrocarbons that are in the middle range of refinery distillation such as heating oil, diesel fuel and kerosene.

Middle Office   The part of settlements that most closely liaises with the front office, inputting trades and reporting positions. See Front Office, Back Office.

MIF   The Mercato Italiano Futures (MIF) is the Italian financial futures market located in Rome. Trading began in September 1992. The MIF trades futures contracts on both five and 10 year Italian government bonds (BTPs).

Mike - Base, Weak, Medium and Strong   The Mike analyses are channel analyses. Used in technical analysis. See Channel Lines, Price Channel.

Milano Indice Borsa   See MIB Index.

Milling   Removal of the Endosperm from the other grain kernel constituents and breaking down the structure of the kernel so the end product is flour.

Milo   U.S. term for grain sorghum.

Min / Max Cargo   Volume tolerance on a standard 500,000 barrels Brent cargo is 50,000 barrels therefore allowing a minimum 450,000 barrels cargo or a maximum 550,000 barrels. Traders may nominate for a min or max cargo for either operational or commercial reasons.

Mine   Dealers' language. The dealer takes the offer which has been quoted by his counterparty. It has to be qualified by the amount. Confirms the act of purchasing.

Minimum Lending Rate (MLR) - U.K.   The minimum rate at which the Bank of England will lend money to discount houses, who are the primary players in the Treasury bill market. See U.K. - Key Interest Rates.

Minimum Price Movement   The smallest unit of change possible in the futures contract price. See Tick.

Ministry of Finance (MOF) - Japan   Second largest issuer of government debt in the world after the U.S. Issues are in the form of Treasury bills and Japanese government bonds (JGBs). JGBs are issued in maturity groups. The government also guarantees government agency bonds.

Minor Metals   Antimony, highly poisonous, used mostly in alloys.
   Asbestos, main uses are roofing and friction products, pipe and sheet.
   Barytes, used in drilling.
   Beryllium, has aerospace and defence applications.
   Bismuth, used in pharmaceuticals, cosmetics, fusible alloys.
   Boron, used in glass products.
   Cadmium, a toxic metal, a thin layer on steel giving protection from corrosion.
   Chromium, used as an alloy, also for chromium plating.
   Cobalt, used as an alloy. Cobalt blue (using cobalt salt) injects colour into glass and ceramics.
   Diamond, crystalline form of carbon. The hardest known natural substance. Produced synthetically for industrial applications. A gemstone.
   Fluorspar, used in chemical industry and production of primary aluminium.
   Gallium, used in the electronics industry.
   Germanium, has expanding use for electronic applications.
   Indium, has useful electrical properties.
   Iridium, platinum alloy for high temperature crucibles.
   Lithium, mainly used as lithium compounds in production of primary aluminium, ceramics, lubricants and synthetic rubber production.
   Magnesium, used for aluminium alloys.
   Manganese, used as an alloy.
   Mercury, very heavy, used in batteries, to make chlorine. An alloy.
   Molybdenum, used in manufacture of alloy steels and other materials for defence applications.
   Rare Earth, comprises 15 elements mainly used as petroleum cracking catalysts.
   Selenium, major uses in electronic and photocopier components.
   Silicon, used in electronics.
   Sulphur, main use is in fertilisers.
   Talc, chief use is in ceramics.
   Tellerium, used as an agent in steel and copper alloys.
   Titanium, used in aerospace, military and chemical industries.
   Tungsten, high technology purposes.
   Uranium, used in production of nuclear energy by fission methods.

Vanadium, used in production of many steels and some non-ferrous alloys.

Zirconium, used in foundry sands, refractories and ceramics.

See Precious Metals.

Minority Interest A minor equity interest comprising less than half the shares in a company which is not controlled by the holder company. Opposite to Majority Interest.

Mismatch A mismatch shows when there is a difference in maturities of funds borrowed and funds invested. A mismatched book occurs when short and long positions do not complement each other. See Matched Book.

Mismatch Note A note on which coupon re-fixes and the reference rate are mismatched with one another, e.g. a note re-fixing against six month LIBOR on a monthly basis.

MIT See Market if Touched.

Mixed Economy Midway between a Planned Economy and a Market Economy. Thus the state runs one or more sectors or parts thereof alongside free market activities generally. See State Planning, Parastatal.

MLR See Minimum Lending Rate - U.K.

MMCF See MCF.

MOC Order Market on Close order placed with a futures broker to buy/sell at the best price possible in the closing range (time) period of trade on a futures exchange. Closing range for IPE Brent, for example, is 2010 to 2013 GMT.

Modified Duration The discounted measure of a change in the price of a bond compared with a given change in interest rates. Quoted in percentage terms. A bond with a modified duration of 0.4 would indicate the bond price will change by 40 cents per 10 basis point shift (0.1 percent) in the yield curve. Also known as volatility. See Basis Point Value.

Modified Exponential Moving Average In some analyses a modified version of exponential moving averages is used. The first value of this modification is the simple moving average of the first determined prices. This first value corresponds to the furthest period. For subsequent periods the version is calculated in the same way as the exponential average but with a smoothing factor.

Modules Packages of equipment for unitised installation on production platforms or refineries.

MOF See Ministry of Finance - Japan.

MOFs A Multi-Option Facility which allows a borrower to obtain funds from various short or long term instruments. May include bank advances, commercial paper and Euronotes. A variety of currencies can also be available. See NIFs.

Molasses Syrup remaining after the sugar separated by crystallisation is removed during sugar refining. Also extracted from sorghum. In addition, an animal feedstuff.

Momentum In technical analysis, a type of oscillator that is used to measure the rate of change - as opposed to the actual price level. The momentum indicator is the difference between the price of the instrument today and the price in the previous determined periods. This positive or negative difference is plotted around a zero line. It is used to signal overbought or oversold conditions as well as entry and exit points.

MONEP Marché des Options Négociables de Paris. The Paris Traded Options Market specialising in options on equity indices. Established in September 1987.

Monetarism Theory which advocates strict control of money supply as the major weapon of monetary policy, especially against inflation.

Monetary Committee of the European Community Known as the EC Monetary Committee. After governments have formally agreed to realignment in the Exchange Rate Mechanism, this committee decides the details, with various options considered. Discussions are held in strict secrecy by its members - the top official from each national treasury and a senior central banker from each EC state.

Monetary Policy Management by a central bank of a country's money supply to ensure the availability of credit in quantities and at levels consistent with specific national objectives. The bank's tools include open market operations in the money markets, intervention in foreign exchange and controls over financial institutions via interest rate ceilings and curbs on lending. See separate entries such as "Germany - Key Interest Rates" for the Group of 10 nations and Switzerland.

Money Back Warrant The holder has the right to sell the warrant back to the issuer either at the full amount of the issue price or at a percentage of it.

Money Flow Index Essentially a volume weighted Relative Strength Index which attempts to measure the strength of money entering and leaving the market. It quantifies price/volume momentum in the same way that the strength index quantifies price momentum but differs from that index in two ways: 1) price is the average of the high, low and close rather than the close and 2) price is weighted by the volume.

Money Market A wholesale market for the buying and selling of money. Money market paper is predominantly negotiable and traded just like any other product. The market is nowadays international as opposed to earlier insular domestic centres. At the short end, stretching from one to six months, the field not taken by interbank deposits and treasury paper is dominated by negotiable CDs (Certificates of Deposit), BAs (Bankers Acceptances), CP (commercial paper) and repurchase agreements. Short term money markets are the main determinant of a nation's overall interest rate structure. Maturities extend out to one year.

Money Market Deposits See Fixed Term Deposit.

Money Market Equivalent Yield The calculation which converts a discount yield into a money market yield enabling the comparison of a Treasury bill yield to yields of other money market instruments. Also known as CD-equivalent yield.

Money Market Preferred Stock A type of stock whose dividend is set at more regular intervals to reflect short term interest rates in the money markets. See Adjustable Rate Preferred Stock.

Money Market Yield The yield of a security expressed under the money market daycount convention, normally measured in basis points.

Money Markets - History Certificates of deposit were introduced in 1961 by 10 main New York banks. These banks were not able to take deposits from the regions and were prevented from offering competitive deposit interest rates by the Federal Reserve's Regulation Q, which allowed saving and loans institutions to offer better rates. CDs outstanding total hundreds of billions of dollars but the size of the market can rise and fall sharply depending on what money the banks need at any one time to fund commercial loans. U.K. discount houses began the sterling CD market in 1968.

Bankers Acceptances are one of the oldest short term interest rates in the world, having financed international trade since the 12th century. Sterling was initially the main medium but in the early 1920's trade payments veered towards the dollar while the fledgling BA market in the U.S. mushroomed.

The U.S. commercial paper market grew in the U.S. because the branch network system was not available to U.S. as the 1927 McFadden Act prohibited interstate banking, including transfer of funds within the same network. Thus, firms in credit-starved regions used commercial paper issues in New York to ease temporary cash shortages.

Repurchase agreements came into use after the Second World War via dealers who were financing their positions in money market instruments. Banks then entered the market to finance their inventories of government paper portfolios.

The London interbank sterling market began in 1963 as a spin-off from the developing London based Eurodollar market. Previously, banks traded sterling surpluses and shortages with the discount houses. Thus before 1963 lending into the discount market (the U.K. domestic money market) was short term and secured. By 1963 banks were dealing with each other on an unsecured basis. In 1971 clearing banks were allowed to operate in the market.

Money Supply Total stock of money in an economy according to various definitions, known as M0, M1, M2, M3, M4. See separate entries such as "Germany - Money Supply" for the Group of Five nations.

Moneyback Option An option which compensates the original premium at the expiry date.

Month-End Dealing Trading with spot value as the last business day of the month. Standard periods in the OTC forward markets will automatically mature on the last business day of the appropriate months, regardless of the number of days. Also known as ultimo dealing.

Montreal Exchange Established in 1874 and known as the Montreal Stock Exchange until 1982. Derivative contracts include the Ten Year Canadian Government Bond future and option as well as stock options.

Moral Suasion A term used when central banks and governments aim to influence market participants to do what they wish by persuasion rather than by coercion.

Moratorium The suspension or delay, by the borrower, of principal repayments and possibly interest due, following the need to settle economic, monetary and financial affairs. If it is determined that interest will in fact be paid, then banks can continue to classify the loan as a performing asset.

Mortgage Backed Security A security backed by, or secured by, a pool or package of mortgage loans. Monthly payments of principal and interest from the underlying pool of mortgages is passed along to the holder of the security.

Mortgage Bankers Originate, sell and service mortgages secured by either residential or commercial real estate.

Mortgage Loan   An advance of funds to a borrower secured by the pledge of specific real estate. The pledge ends when the debt is discharged.

Mortgage Originator   The original lender on the mortgages.

Mortgage Pool   Mortgages are packaged, or pooled, and securities are issued representing shares in the pool. The mortgages bear the same maturity date and same interest rate on the same class of property.

Mortgage Warehousing   Mortgages in the pipeline between origination and securitisation.

Mortgage Yield   Yield based on the receipt of monthly cash flows of principal and interest.

Most Favoured Nation   Undertaking by two countries to give each other the maximum tariff concessions on their mutual trade which they already grant to other countries.

Motor Gasoline   Complex mixture of relatively volatile hydrocarbons, with or without small quantities of additives, that have been blended to make a fuel suitable for use in spark ignition engines. Is abbreviated to Mogas to avoid confusion between natural gas and gasoline (known as gas).

Moving Average Convergence / Divergence (MACD)   This technical analysis uses two exponential moving averages to produce two lines which oscillate above and below a zero line. The first line plots the difference between the two exponential moving averages (the MACD W), while the second plots the exponential average of the first line and is called the MACD or signal line. When the MACD W crosses the signal line from above, a sell signal is generated and when the opposite cross occurs it is a buy signal. Such a sell signal is more reliable if the cross occurs well above the zero line, while a buy signal is more reliable if it occurs well below the zero line. Overbought and oversold signals can be indicated when both lines are significantly above or below the zero line respectively.

Moving Average Crossover   The use of two moving averages - one using a short interval and the other a longer interval. 1) When the short moving average dips under the long moving average, and both moving averages are falling, a sell signal is generated. When the short moving average crosses the long moving average from below, and both moving averages are rising, a buy signal is generated. 2) In another method, a buy signal would be seen after a close above both averages. However, this becomes void if the next close then occurs between the two averages. A sell signal is noted when the close comes under the lower line.

Moving Strike Option   An option on which a single strike price is not determined for the life of the option but will vary over time.

MPM Price   Official monthly selling price of Omani crude, notified retroactively by the Ministry of Petroleum and Mines (MPM). Oman decides on the price after monitoring spot prices of its crude.

MR Cargo   Medium range cargo of oil products - 25,000 to 30,000 tonnes.

MTBE   Methyl Tertiary-Butyl Ether. A lead free anti knock chemical compound that is a gasoline additive used to enhance engine performance and cut harmful emissions.

MTN   Medium term notes. Borrowings in the medium term (usually out to about five years) typically issued under a similar borrowing facility as for commercial paper. Also EMTN (Euro MTNs).

MTS - Italy   Mercato Telematico Secondario is a screen based system showing two-way prices of Italian government debt issues by the market makers and is supervised by the Banca d'Italia. This system was introduced in 1988 and has contributed to the dramatic growth of the Italian government debt market.

Multi-Family Housing   U.S. term. A residential structure containing five or more dwelling units.

Multi-Fibre Arrangement   Reached in 1973 by some 50 nations meeting under the auspices of the General Agreement on Tariffs and Trade (GATT) in Geneva. The MFA lays down rules for international trade in textile products of wool, cotton and man-made fibres.

Multi-Option Facilities   See MOFs.

Multinational   A publicly owned company which operates commercially in a number of countries outside its own base. Usually its activities in each country encompass all aspects of production of its goods or services. Such companies are often listed on more than one stock exchange or have shares available via depositary receipts. See American Depositary Receipt, European Depositary Receipt.

Multiples   See P/E Ratio.

Multiplier Bond   A bond which allows the investor to convert coupons into identical bonds and to reinvest coupons on these subsequent bonds. The borrower gains a cash flow benefit because the payouts are being converted into extra debt. For investors, the issue bears some similarities to a Zero Coupon Bond because the risk that falling interest rates will reduce reinvestment income is largely eliminated. However, unlike a zero, if interest rates actually rise and make the existing coupon unattractive, investors can take their annual payment in cash to reinvest at the higher rates. Also known as a bunny bond.

Municipal Notes Short term U.S. securities, typically out to three years maximum, issued by state and local governments and agencies. Commonly known as munis. Types of municipal note include: Tax Anticipation Notes (TANs); Revenue Anticipation Notes (RANs); Grant Anticipation Notes (GANs); Bond Anticipation Notes (BANs); Tax exempt commercial paper.

Mutual Fund U.S. equivalent of the U.K. unit trust. A mutual fund is often an Open End Management Company which pools together funds from many investors to establish a diversified portfolio of investments. After the Initial Public Offering, it continuously sells and redeems its shares while investing the combined contributions from the public at large in various securities and pays them dividends in proportion to their holdings. The shares are managed by a portfolio manager. The price of the mutual fund is calculated as a total portfolio value having taken into consideration the value of each security in the portfolio. This figure, the net asset value, is one unit value of one share in the mutual fund. There are several types of mutual funds. See Closed End Company, Balanced Fund.

N/O A normal order to buy or sell at a certain level, i.e. to sell at higher or to buy at lower levels than prevailing market rates.

NAEGA North American Export Grain Association. Establishes contract, trade, shipping and port rules for its members. Based in Washington.

NAFTA North American Free Trade Agreement, a three member free trade zone between the U.S., Canada and Mexico. Signed into law by President Clinton in December 1993, effective January 1 1994. Mexico is committed to the biggest changes as the U.S. and Canada entered their own free trade agreement in 1989. Key provisions include: most tariffs disappear over 15 years, investors win long-sought protection for their money from Mexico which seeks to draw in huge amounts of new capital, Mexico must improve its health, safety and child labour laws, the U.S. and Mexico will each commit an initial 225 million dollars to clean up border pollution, augmented with other loans. The NAFTA agreement eliminates the Maquiladora Industry.

Naked Position A long or short position that has not been hedged.

Naked Warrant Issued as a stand alone warrant instead of being attached to a bond. Issuers save costs because the exercise period for the warrant

corresponds to the call feature of a previous bond issue and thus a call premium need not be paid.

Naphtha Range of distillates covering the heavier end of the gaseous fuel and the lighter end of the kerosene range. A volatile, colourless product, it is used as a paint solvent, cleaning fluid, a feedstock for ethylene and a blendstock in gasoline production.

NASD National Association of Securities Dealers. An organisation in the U.S. of Over the Counter brokers and dealers that formulates legal and ethical standards of conduct for its members. Founded in 1939.

NASDAQ The National Association of Securities Dealers Automated Quotations System owned and operated by the National Association of Securities Dealers (NASD). A computerised inter-dealer system in the U.S. providing price quotes for Over the Counter shares.

NASDAQ Composite Index Arithmetic capitalisation weighted index based on all shares traded through the National Association of Securities Dealers Automated Quotations system (NASDAQ). Calculated in real time, i.e. as share prices change.

National Association of Securities Dealers See NASD.

National Debt Total indebtedness of a government as a result of cumulative net budget deficits. Normally financed by the sale of government securities and debt instruments.

National Grain & Feed Association Domestic association of several hundred members connected with the feed industry. Establishes contract rules, carries out arbitration and promotes interests of the U.S. feed grain industry. Based in Washington.

National Securities Clearing Corporation Manages back office functions such as clearing and settlement for most securities in the U.S. Owned jointly by the New York Stock Exchange, American Stock Exchange and NASDAQ, the Over the Counter market.

Natural Gas Mixture of light hydrocarbons, predominantly methane, which occurs naturally in the Earth's crust and is frequently found in association with oil.

Natural Gas Liquids Consist of natural gas, liquid petroleum gases and natural gasoline.

Natural Gasoline A light liquid hydrocarbon mixture recovered from natural gas that is similar to motor gasoline but with a lower octane number.

Nautical Mile Varies from 6,045.93 feet on the Equator to 6,107.98 feet in latitude 90 degrees. A mean nautical mile is 6,076.91 feet.

Navigator Bonds   Bonds issued by foreigners in escudos in Portugal. Usually listed in Luxembourg as well as Lisbon.

Near Money   Assets, such as money market fund shares, bank time deposits and government securities which are readily convertible into cash. This also applies to bonds near their redemption date.

Nearbys   Nearest delivery months of a commodity futures contract.

NECIGEF   The Netherlands Centraal Institut Giraal Effectenverkeer B.V. is the administrative and clearing institution of the Amsterdam Stock Exchange.

Negative Carry   Situation where the financing cost of a position is greater than the return.

Negative Pledge   Clause in a bond agreement which restricts the borrower from pledging a greater security or collateral to other lenders.

Negative Stock Split   See Reverse Stock Split.

Negotiable   An item that can be traded or transferred freely. Also refers to any part of a transaction where, for instance, a fee or commission or interest rate can be negotiable, i.e. agreed to the satisfaction of one or more parties.

Net   Any figure from which some liability, such as tax, has been deducted.

Net Asset Value   Valuation of a company, or fund, based on its assets. This can lead to differences of perception depending on how assets are valued, as in differences between book value, market liquidation and replacement value. For mutual funds and unit trusts this is calculated daily by the portfolio manager by dividing the net value by the number of outstanding shares. This is the price at which investors can redeem mutual fund shares. See Mutual Fund.

Net Cash Flow   Retained earnings plus depreciation.

Net Earnings   The company's profit which remains once all coupons on outstanding bonds, all taxes and all dividends on outstanding preferred shares have been settled.

Net Position   Difference between long and short positions held by a dealer in a given market.

Net Present Value   See Present Value.

Net Profit   Trading profits after deducting the charges detailed in the profit and loss account such as tax, depreciation, auditors and directors fees.

Net Transaction   A transaction whereby the investor is not charged a commission. If a company sells new issues, the underwriter's commission is incorporated in the issue price. A commission will only be charged in secondary market trading.

Net Worth   A measure of the difference between the total value of assets and possessions and total indebtedness.

Netback   Refers to the value of a crude oil once it has been refined and the products from it have been sold taking into account freight and refining costs. Thus crude traded in a netback deal is sold at a price that reflects the value of the product it yields. Also used as a generic term for the net FOB (Free on Board) cost after freight charges have been deducted from the CIF (Cost, Insurance, Freight) price.

Netherlands - Key Interest Rates   The rates to watch are:

Special advances rate - sets the tone for money market rates.

Secured loans rate (interest rate on advances) - sets the floor for money market rates.

The special advances rate is the money market intervention rate. It tends to set the tone for money market rates and is usually between 0.1 and 0.5 percentage points above the secured loans rate. It is roughly comparable to Germany's repo rate but usually fixed rather than variable.

The secured loans rate is similar to the German discount rate but there is no equivalent for the Bundesbank's lombard rate. It is the Nederlandsche Bank's lowest rate and is usually changed by a quarter percentage point or a multiple thereof. The discount rate was abolished on January 1 1994.

The money market is in effect a system of central bank windows where commercial banks can obtain funds limited by quotas. Quotas are set such that commercial banks are always short of funds and therefore need to borrow from the central bank's special advances facility.

The Nederlandsche Bank sets monetary policy. Rate decisions are taken by the Bank's executive board (the governor, plus four directors). Under the central bank's statutes, the finance minister has the authority to issue a directive if this is deemed necessary to co-ordinate Bank and government policies. But such a directive has not been issued since the Bank Act of 1948. While the central bank has effective independence in setting interest rates, in practice it has little autonomy given the objective of preserving the link between the guilder and the mark.

Netting   A system whereby outstanding financial contracts can be settled to arrive at a net figure, i.e. receivables are offset against payables to reduce the credit exposure to a particular counterparty and to minimise settlement risk.

Network Architecture   The logistics of building a Super Digital Information Highway using such as fibre optics, existing telephone lines and the facilities of cable television companies.

Neural Network   Massively parallel processing in a computer aimed at simulating the power of the billions of neurons in the human brain which complete an operation at the same time instead of by step by step. Likewise, when a computer has parallel processing it is able to solve a problem by many steps at the same time.

Neutral Budget   See Balanced Budget.

New Crop   Crop about to be harvested or having just been harvested. Can also refer to next crop, i.e. before it has been planted - if it is a listed futures contract.

New Issue Stock   A share which is being offered for sale by a company in the primary market.

New Money   In a refunding operation, the amount by which the nominal value of the new securities is greater than maturing securities, allowing a borrower to take in additional cash.

New Straits Times Industrial Index   Price weighted arithmetic index of the daily closing prices of 30 listed industrial companies on the Kuala Lumpur Stock Exchange.

New York Cotton Exchange   Founded in 1870, is the oldest commodity exchange in New York. Trades futures and options in cotton and frozen concentrated orange juice (FCOJ) contracts.

New York Futures Exchange   See NYFE.

New York Mercantile Exchange   See NYMEX.

Newly Industrialising Countries   Term covering Asian nations with comparatively recent rapid economic growth. Applies to Hong Kong, South Korea, Singapore and Taiwan. Known also as Tigers, Dynamic Asian Economies, Newly Industrialising Economies.

Newly Industrialising Economies   See Newly Industrialising Countries.

Nickel   A base metal. Major consumer market is the steel alloy industry and in particular the stainless steel sector. Producers include the Commonwealth of Independent States, Canada, Australia, New Caledonia, Indonesia, Cuba, the Philippines, Dominican Republic, South Africa, Brazil, Botswana, Greece, Zimbabwe, Finland and the U.S.

NIFs   A Note Issuance Facility allows borrowers to offer short term paper, usually three or six months, in their own names. Fund availability is guaranteed to the borrower by underwriting banks who buy any unsold notes at successive rollover dates or who provide a standby credit. Similar are Revolving Underwriting Facilities (RUFs) and Multi-Option Facilities (MOFs), which are types of Euro-note bank facilities.

Nikkei 225 Average   Benchmark index for the Tokyo Stock Exchange. A price weighted arithmetic average of the 225 most heavily traded shares. Market capitalisation is not taken into account and so a share price change in one of the smaller companies will affect the index the same as a similar price move in one of the larger companies. Calculated every minute. Futures and options are traded on the Osaka Stock Exchange and on the Singapore International Monetary Exchange.

Nikkei 300 Index   A weighted average for the Tokyo Stock Exchange, launched October 1993 and calculated once a day. Consists of 300 issues which are mostly shares with large capital and high liquidity. Options and futures are scheduled to be traded on the Osaka Stock Exchange.

Nil Paid   A new issue of shares on which no payment has yet been made to the company.

NMS   The National Market System is a centralised system in the U.S. for reporting transactions and quotations for Over the Counter shares from all qualified market makers.

No Par Value   Shares with no par value assigned at the time the stock is authorised.

Noble Metals   See Precious Metals.

NOLA   New Orleans, Louisiana, the main export point for U.S. grains, oilseeds and their derivatives and the world's largest grain handling port.

Nominal Interest Rate   The interest rate expressed in money terms. See Real Interest Rate.

Nominal Value   See Face Value.

Nominations   Each month, term contract holders submit nominations to sellers, telling them how much crude they intend to lift that month.

Nominee Account   Securities which are owned by an investor but are registered in the name of the brokerage firm. The certificate bears the name of, and is held in safekeeping by, the brokerage firm. In this case, the records of the issuing company show the brokerage firm as the holder of record. The brokerage firm records the investor as the beneficial owner. Also known as street name.

Non-Callable   A security which does not have a call feature. See Call Feature.

Non-Competitive Bid Auction   Bidding which does not include a yield, only the quantity. The investor then pays the average price determined by the competitive bidders. These bids allow small investors to participate in the auction. Since non-competitive bids are given priority and are awarded the full allocation, they could reduce the amounts available to competitive bidders.

Non-Conforming Mortgages Mortgages not deemed acceptable to the agencies but may be purchased and securitised by private conduits. See Conforming Mortgages.

Non-Ferrous Metals Metals and alloys which contain no iron or where iron is not the main component. See Base Metals.

Non-Financial Debt A U.S. term for a set of reported data. It covers total debt held by U.S. households, businesses and federal, state and local governments. It excludes banks and other financial institutions.

Non-ICO Market See ICO.

Non-Negotiable A transaction where the terms of the contract are fixed and are therefore not negotiable. Also, an instrument which can only be held by the original holder. It cannot be traded or transferred or used as collateral.

Non-Performing Loan A loan on which neither interest payment nor principal repayment is being made. When a bank has such a loan on its books then it can either write it off against profits immediately or make loan loss provisions ready to make such a write-off in the future.

Non-Systematic Risk See Specific Risk.

Non-Voting Stock Securities that do not allow the holder to vote on company resolutions, for example, ordinary "A" shares.

Norinchukin Bank The Central Cooperative Bank for Agriculture and Forestry, a financial institution which is able to borrow from the Bank of Japan, the nation's central bank, for money market purposes.

North-South Dialogue General expression for any discussions that may take place between, loosely, the prosperous industrial nations of the Northern hemisphere and the developing countries of the Southern hemisphere.

Nostro Account "Our account" - meaning a bank's account in a foreign currency at a bank of the corresponding nationality. See Vostro Account.

Note Issuance Facility See NIFs.

Notional Bond A standardised bond with hypothetical terms (coupon and maturity) which represents the basis for a bond futures contract.

Notional Principal The hypothetical amount on which interest payments are based in products such as interest rate swaps, FRAs, Caps and Floors.

NPV See Present Value.

NSPA National Soybean Processors Association. Promotes standardisation of domestic U.S. oil and meal cash trading rules and issues weekly and monthly breakdowns of its membership's total crush rate, capacity, stocks on hand and so forth. Based in Washington.

NYFE The New York Futures Exchange Inc. was established in April 1979 as a fully owned subsidiary of the NYSE. Trades futures and options on the NYSE composite index.

NYMEX The New York Mercantile Exchange (NYMEX) was established in 1872 as the Butter and Cheese Exchange. Renamed the NYMEX in 1882. Trades platinum futures and options, palladium futures as well as crude oil, heating oil and gasoline futures and options. The Exchange trades futures for light crude oil which is an influential benchmark in determining the level of world oil prices.

NYSE Composite Stock Index A capitalisation weighted arithmetic index which calculates, every 15 seconds, all New York Stock Exchange shares on an aggregate market value as of December 31 1965. The New York Futures Exchange - an NYSE unit - trades futures and futures options on the index. Options are traded on the NYSE.

O/N Abbreviation for overnight. Used in swap and deposit transactions when the first value date is today and maturity falls tomorrow. The O/N swap price has an adjustment based on the interest rate differential for that short period.

O/N Funds Funds traded overnight on the interbank market to satisfy commercial banks' reserve requirements at the central bank.

O/N Limit Limits authorising dealers to carry positions overnight. They are therefore not obliged to square the position at the end of the day.

OAPEC Organisation of Arab Petroleum Exporting Countries. Aims to improve economic cooperation in the petroleum industry. Based in Cairo. Members are Algeria, Bahrain, Egypt, Iraq, Kuwait, Libya, Qatar, Saudi Arabia, Syria and the United Arab Emirates.

OAT - France Obligations Assimilables du Trésor are fungible Treasury bonds issued in France with maturities ranging from seven to 30 years and with fixed or floating interest. The 10 year bond (benchmark) is reopened every month and the long bond (15-30 years) is reopened every other month. OATS were first issued in 1985 by auction and have replaced the Emprunts d'Etat. OATs are not callable. Since the existence of OATs, the market for other issues such as exchangeable, extendible, renewable bonds and FELINs has become less liquid. Since 1989 OATs have also been issued in European Currency Units. Since mid 1991 the French Treasury has allowed the stripping of the long bond and from June 1993 the 10 year benchmark has become strippable.

OAT TMB - France Taux Moyen des Bons du Trésor are floating rate bonds issued in France which are indexed to the monthly average yield of 13 week Treasury bill auctions.

OAT TME - France Taux Moyen d'Emprunts d'Etat are floating rate bonds issued in France based on bond yields. The coupon is defined yearly based on an index of government bond yields on issues with maturities greater than seven years (mostly 12 years).

OAT TRB - France Taux Révisable des Bons du Trésor are floating rate bonds issued in France based on bond yields. The coupon is paid quarterly in arrears and is based on the TRB Index; the weighted average yield of the 11th auction of each quarter (auctions are weekly) of the 13 week Treasury bill.

Oats The oat grain is similar physically and chemically to wheat, barley and rye. The coating of the oat grain is known as the bran while inside is the germ or seed. Compared with wheat, the oat grain has one third more protein, nearly four times as much fat but less starch. Edible products of processed oats include rolled oats, steel-cut oatmeal, ground oatmeal and instant oats. Oat hulls, a by-product of the milling process, are used in the mixed feeds industry. Historically, oats have been used when a wheat harvest failed. Oatmeal became a key food in regions with cool, moist climates suitable for oats cultivation.

Obligor One who is legally bound to pay a debt.

OBX Index An Oslo stock exchange index comprising the 25 most heavily traded companies. Futures and options are traded on the Oslo stock exchange. Calculated continuously.

OCO One Cancels the Other. A limit order which consists of two buy orders (or two sell orders) at different levels either side of the current market level. Execution of one order automatically cancels the other.

Octane Number Measure of the resistance of a fuel to pre-ignition (known as knock) when burned in an internal combustion engine.

Odd Coupon This occurs when the first or last coupon period is longer or shorter than the normal coupon period.

Odd Date See Broken Date.

Odd Lot Trade A block of securities or commodities which is smaller or larger than the standard lot size traded in that market. The price can vary from the current market value. See Round Lot Trade.

ODR Official Discount Rate. See Japan - Key Interest Rates.

ODRs See Ordinary Drawing Rights.

OECD Organisation for Economic Cooperation and Development, based in Paris. Consists of the Group of 10 nations (actually 11 as Switzerland is included) plus Australia, Austria, Denmark, Finland, Greece, Iceland, Ireland, Luxembourg, New Zealand, Norway, Portugal, Spain and Turkey. Thus, it has 24 members. Not to be confused with the informal Group of 24.

Off Balance Sheet An obligation entered into by a company which does not have to show on the balance sheet. Examples are leases, project finance and take or pay contracts. With banks, where money earned is fee based, examples include trading of swaps, options and letters of credit.

Off Spec Oil product that does not meet specifications. Refers to those generally accepted in the trade for a particular product or to those specifications laid down in a contract.

Off the Run Issue Benchmark issues which are no longer the most recently issued in that maturity and therefore tend to trade with a wider spread than the On The Run Issues.

Offer See Ask.

Offer Document Official document from a bidder in a takeover battle and which is sent to shareholders in the target company. In the U.S., can be synonymous with Prospectus.

Offer for Subscription A common method of issuing shares. The issue will generally be underwritten and prospective investors are invited to subscribe either at a fixed price or by submitting a price tender. See Oversubscribed, Tender Price.

Offered Market A market in which there is more interest from sellers than buyers. Opposite to Bid Market.

Office of Management and Budget Part of the executive office of the U.S. President. Prepares the President's budget and is headed by the budget director.

Official Development Assistance Defined by the Development Assistance Committee of the Organisation for Economic Cooperation and Development (OECD) as follows: "Those flows to developing countries and multilateral institutions provided by official agencies, including state and local governments, or by their executive agencies, each transaction of which meets the following tests - it is administered with the promotion of economic development and welfare of developing nations as its main objective and that it is concessional in character and contains a grant element of at least 25 percent."

Official Prices - LME Official prices on the London Metal Exchange are the buyer/seller prices at the end of the morning second Ring. See LME.

Official Receiver In the U.K., a civil servant who is an officer of the court who deals with compulsory liquidations.

Offshore Many institutions have subsidiaries located offshore, i.e. in countries where regulatory controls and taxation are favourable enough to attract lenders and borrowers. Such subsidiaries would normally have to conform to the rules of the authorities in their parent's country, thus in these freer offshore locations they remain independent offshore entities.

Offshore Fund Funds based outside the tax system of the country in which prospective investors reside.

Offtake To load or lift crude oil.

Oil Gasification Manufacture of gas from oil for use as a fuel.

Oil in Place An estimated measure of the total amount of oil contained in a reservoir. As such, it is a higher figure than that for estimated recoverable reserves.

Oil Patch Originally used to refer to areas of the southwest U.S. such as Texas and Oklahoma where there had been extensive drilling and production but now used generally for oil producing regions.

Oil Slick Layer of oil floating on the surface of the sea. Generally caused by accident or spillage but can sometimes reflect natural seepage from the ocean floor.

Oil Trap Hydrocarbon retained by a geological structure and resulting in formation of an oil field.

Oils Key products in international commodity and agricultural trade. The major oils are palm and soy. Palm oil is not liquid as it solidifies at room temperature. RBD palm olein (refined, bleached and deodorised) is the edible part of RPO (refined palm oil). Palm stearine is the inedible part of RPO.

Soft oils, or liquid edible oils, are soy, rape, groundnut, cottonseed and sunflowerseed.

Lauric oils are coconut oil (extracted from copra) and palm kernel (extracted from kernel of palm oil nut).

The range of oils includes soybean, cotton, groundnut, sunflower, rapeseed, corn, olive, coconut, palm kernel, fishoil, linseed, castor and palm.

Oilseeds Agricultural products from which vegetable and industrial oils and meals are extracted. The most important are soybeans. Others include cottonseed, rapeseed, sunflowerseed and flaxseed (for linseed).

Old Lady of Threadneedle Street Colloquial name for the Bank of England, the U.K. central bank.

Olein A form of processed palm oil.

Oligopoly Situation where a few firms selling an item control its supply and hence its price.

Oligopsony Situation where a small number of significant purchasers control the buying power and therefore the price and output of an item.

OLOs - Belgium Obligations Linéaires (linear bonds) were introduced in 1989 and are fungible and fixed rate bullet issues. These issues account for the major part of the total bonds outstanding. Their maturities range from two to 20 years with the most recently issued 10 year bond being the benchmark. Recently, stripping of the 15 year OLO was permitted. OLOs are not callable.

OM Stockholm The Swedish Futures and Options Market was established in 1985 and acts as an exchange and clearing house for derivatives. Contracts include the OMX Index future and option, the Government Bond future (Two, Five and Ten Year), the Treasury Bill future and the Three Month STIBOR future. An option contract is traded on the Five Year Government Bond. STIBOR is the Swedish Interbank Offered Rate. See LIBOR / LIBID / LIMEAN.

Omega The currency risk involved when a buyer or seller accounts for the deal in a different currency.

OMX Index The Options Market Index, a capitalisation weighted arithmetic index, consists of the 30 largest companies on the Stockholm stock exchange and represents 70 percent of the value of all trading. Calculated continuously. Futures and options are traded on the OM Stockholm.

On the Run Issue The most recent issue of a security which would be trading with a narrower spread than the older Off The Run Issues. Thus, as an issue gets older, its liquidity decreases and the spread tends to widen.

On-Balance Volume This technical analysis maintains a cumulative volume by assigning a positive value to the volume of an interval when prices close higher and a negative value to the volume of an interval when prices close lower. Buy or sell signals are indicated when a divergence between the on-balance volume and price is followed by a trend break in the on-balance volume.

One Cancels the Other See OCO.

ONIC L'Office National Interprofessionnel des Céréales. French National Cereals Office. State agency that manages the grain market.

OPEC Organisation of Petroleum Exporting Countries. Vienna based, founded in 1960. Holds several meetings a year, sometimes at short notice if the oil price is falling and, when necessary, sets production quotas for its member nations and announces an official price for crude oil. Members are Algeria, Gabon, Indonesia, Iran, Iraq, Kuwait, Libya, Nigeria, Qatar, Saudi Arabia, United Arab Emirates and Venezuela. See Arab Oil Embargo, IEA.

Open End Management Company The legal name for a Mutual Fund.

Open Ended Company Applies to most companies inasmuch as share capital can be increased and shares can be redeemed by the company. Marks the difference between a unit trust in the U.K. and a mutual fund in the U.S., both of which are open ended investment companies, and between investment trusts which are closed end companies.

Open Interest A figure that shows the number of outstanding contracts for a given future which are not offset by an opposing futures transaction or fulfilled by delivery. In most cases, the open interest is measured on a daily basis. Reflects the degree of liquidity in that contract.

Open Interest Chart Technical analysts may chart open interest since it gives an indication of likely purchases and sales before contracts expire and in this respect is perceived as providing a clue to price trends. For instance, when prices are rising and volume and open interest are strong, then the uptrend is perceived as likely to continue. When prices are falling and volume and open interest are strong, then the downtrend is likely to continue. If prices are falling but volume and open interest are weak, then that would be interpreted as a bullish signal and a strengthening of the market.

Open Market Operations Central bank sale or purchase of securities in the domestic money market intended to influence the volume of money and credit in the economy. Chiefly involves short term government securities. Purchases inject reserves into the system, thus expanding credit while sales have the opposite effect.

Open Order Book System - Netherlands Introduced by the Dutch Ministry of Finance in 1990, this is a screen based trading system installed in the ASE (Amsterdam Stock Exchange) which has facilitated trading between the exchange and brokers and is maintained by the jobbers.

Open Outcry A trading method in a central location which requires buyers and sellers to cry out bids and offers to each other.

Open Position A position that has not yet been offset or closed.

Open Spec Naphtha Naphtha or condensate originating from east of Suez or west of the International Dateline and from Algeria, Australia, China, Egypt, India, Indonesia and New Zealand with set specifications.

Operating Profit After tax earnings from a company's ordinary revenue producing activities. Definitions vary. In Germany, for example, the "Betriebsergebnis" of commercial banks covers profit before tax, writedowns and risk provisions. In Japan, operating profit is before tax and after the costs of production, administration and sales.

Operational Balances Commercial banks' funds held on deposit at the central bank to settle the final position at the end of the day between the banking system and the central bank.

Operator An individual, partnership or corporation that has legal authority to drill wells and undertake production if hydrocarbons are found. The operator coordinates a programme of exploration and development of the licensed area and also on behalf of any co-licensees.

Optical Fibre Known also as fibre optic. Microscopic glass fibre through which light is transmitted to carry telecommunications signals. The technique is faster and more compact than copper wire but is more costly.

Option An option gives the buyer (holder) the right but not the obligation to buy (call) or sell (put) a specified financial instrument (the underlying) at a fixed price (strike) before or on a certain date in the future (expiry). The seller (writer) of an option has the obligation to sell (call) or buy (put). The price to have this right (option premium) is paid by the holder of the option to the writer.

Options can be traded Over the Counter (OTC) or on exchanges. Exchange-traded options are standardised contracts on specified underlying instruments in multiples of standard amounts with predetermined strike prices and with standard maturities. OTC options are generally negotiated individually between the writer (usually a bank) and the holder as to the underlying instrument, amount, strike price, exercise rights and expiry. Some OTC options are written to correspond to exchange-traded instruments in strike price and expiry although generally not in amount. See American Option, European Option.

Option Holder An individual who pays a premium for the right to buy or sell the underlying under an option contract.

Option Premium The price paid for an option. The premium is made up of intrinsic value plus time value. The premium is paid by the holder to the writer for value spot.

Option Series Option contracts on the same underlying all having the same expiry date and strike price.

Option Trading Strategies Combinations of calls and puts to create strategies for hedging and speculation purposes. Examples are Bull Spread, Bear Spread, Butterfly Spread, Condor Spread, Risk Reversal, Straddle and Strangle.

Option Writer An institution which sells an option and thereby commits to buy or sell the underlying at a predetermined strike price in exchange for the premium paid by the holder of the option.

Optional Dividend A dividend that is payable either in cash or stock form. The shareholder is allowed to choose which method of payment to take.

Order Driven Trading where the order flow determines prices. See Price Driven.

Ordinary Capital Capital in a company which is entitled to the residue of profits and assets after senior debt and creditors have been satisfied.

Ordinary Drawing Rights (ODRs) Similar to Special Drawing Rights. Also allocated to members of the International Monetary Fund. However, they are credits as opposed to SDRs which are used as currency reserves in addition to a member nation's existing gold and dollar reserves.

Ordinary Share A share which grants the investor voting rights in that company and the right to receive a dividend. However, dividends are neither guaranteed nor regular and, if declared, are only paid after the preferred shareholders. Ordinary shares are the most widely traded of all securities due to continued liquidity and more importantly the ease of transfer of ownership from one investor to another. Ordinary shares may be classed under "A", "B" and so forth for certain companies, the differences being in voting rights and the form of dividend payment. Ordinary shares are known as common stock in the U.S. See Preferred Share.

Ore Any mineral deposit of precious or other metals that is of economic value.

Ore Reserves Can be put into three classes:
- proven, where calculations have been made from drill holes or underground or outcrops together with sampling.
- probable, partly from calculations with some sampling.
- possible, assessed on knowledge of the geological characteristics with a few, or no, samples or measurements.

Orebody An amount of ore large enough to be mined on an economical basis.

Organisation for Economic Cooperation and Development See OECD.

Organisation of Arab Petroleum Exporting Countries See OAPEC.

Organisation of Petroleum Exporting Countries See OPEC.

Origin Producing country. Origin sale is a phrase often used to describe selling by a state marketing board or by an exporter from a commodity producing country.

ORTs See Renewable Bond - France.

Oscillator - Departure / Ultimate Used in technical analysis. The oscillator is an indicator that moves back and forth between an upper and lower boundary. The oscillator as it was originally designed attempts to indicate buy and sell signals by graphing the difference between a short and long term simple moving average. This difference plotted can be either the percentage or points difference. In either case, the oscillator will oscillate between these two limits. Oscillators are generally used only in ranging markets.

Osmium A precious metal produced as a co-product of platinum and palladium.

OSP Official selling price for oil. See Government Selling Price.

OTC Over the Counter. A market conducted directly between dealers and principals via a telephone and computer network rather than via a highly regulated exchange trading floor.

Out of the Money A term used to describe an option whose strike price is less advantageous than the current market price of the underlying instrument. Out of the money options have zero intrinsic value. See In the Money, At the Money.

Outright Purchases Government securities purchased outright by the authorities, i.e. with no agreement to subsequently sell them through a repurchase pact or reverse repo. Purchases are normally made in reserve settlement periods in which there is a particularly large liquidity shortage, such as near tax dates or a year-end with a strong demand for currency and high levels of reserve transactions deposits. Outright sales are much less common since reserve needs tend to grow over time.

Outstanding Shares See Issued Shares.

Over the Bridge Expression used when securities are passing between different clearing systems such as a sale of securities taken from EUROCLEAR and delivered to CEDEL.

Over the Counter See OTC.

Overall Balance of Payments Consists of the basic balance of payments, i.e. current account plus long term capital account, and adding short term capital account.

Overbought A situation whereby prices have risen more than expected by fundamental factors. This could mean that the market is liable to a downward correction. An instrument is overbought when it registers more than 75 percent on its Relative Strength Index. Opposite to Oversold.

Overnight See O/N.

Overseas Private Investment Corp. A U.S. agency that provides assistance to U.S. firms in developing countries through risk insurance and by providing loan guarantees for specific projects.

Oversold A situation whereby prices have dropped more than expected by fundamental factors. This could mean that the market is liable to an upward correction. An instrument is oversold when it registers less than 25 percent on its Relative Strength Index. Opposite to Overbought.

Oversubscribed The situation whereby an issuing house receives more subscriptions for a new issue than are available. The issue will then be allocated, typically, on a pro rata basis and the issue will tend to open at a premium to represent the over-demand. See Stag.

Overvalued A term implying that a security or currency is trading at a price higher than it should be relative to fundamental factors. Opposite to Undervalued.

P and I Club Protection and Indemnity Club. Refers to the various associations of shipping companies which have been formed to provide protection against risks not covered by ordinary marine insurance.

P/E Ratio The price earnings ratio calculated by dividing the share price by the company's earnings per share (EPS). The ratio can be calculated by taking the EPS as announced for the most recent periods, ergo the historical or trailing P/E, or forecasts for the EPS, ergo the prospective or forward P/E. Measures a company's earning power and is one of the most important ratios to determine investment value. The P/E ratio is also referred to as multiples.

PAC Bond Planned Amortization Class bond. Bonds with a greater cash flow certainty, which gives holders of PAC bonds in a CMO (collateralised mortgage obligation) greater priority over all other classes.

Pac Man Defence Tactics used in the U.S. to avoid a takeover whereby the potential victim attempts to take over the predator.

Paddy Rough or harvested rice which has not been husked or processed. Also known as padi.

Paid-Up Capital Shares for which the company has received full nominal value in payment. The part of a share for which the company has not received payment is termed callable capital.

Palladium A precious metal whose main producers are the Commonwealth of Independent States and South Africa. Used in the electronic and dental industries and also as an auto catalyst for exhaust pollution control.

Palm Kernel Oil See Palm Oil.

Palm Oil Second to soybean oil in world vegetable oil production and uses. It is obtained from oil palms grown in tropical countries and yields more per acre per year than any other vegetable oil. Used for edible oils and manufacture of soap. Palm oil comes from a layer of fibrous pulp underneath the outer skin of the fruit. Inside this pulp is the seed which consists of an outer hard shell, used for fuel, and an inner kernel rich in palm kernel oil, used for making margarine. The amount and proportion of the two oils produced depends on the type of palm and the local processing methods. Malaysia accounts for over half of total world production, followed by Indonesia and Nigeria. See Soybean.

Paper Colloquially, refers to any securities.

Paper Barrel A cargo of oil traded for short term hedging or speculative purposes but not usually physically delivered. See Five O'Clocking.

Paper Chain See Daisy Chain.

Paper Profit Apparent and as yet unrealised profit arising out of an increase in the value of an asset.

Par Bond Bond issued at par or, in debt restructurings, swapped for old debt at par to provide debt service reduction.

Par Value See Face Value.

Par Yield Curve   A yield curve indicating the yield to maturity pertaining to series of maturities of bonds trading at or around par.

Parabolic Time Price   Used in technical analysis. Uses stop and reverse points (known as SAR) to suggest entry and exit times in the market. These reversal points occur when the prices range crosses the current stop and reverse point (from above, when the position is long, and from below when the position is short). At such points the current position is closed out and the reverse position set up. Thus the trader always has a position in the market. The aim is to allow more tolerance of contra-trend price fluctuations when a trend begins but to progressively tighten the stop and reverse points as a trend continues and matures. This is achieved by use of acceleration factors which increase (up to a given limit) each time a new extreme is reached in the direction of the expected trend.

Paraffin   See Kerosene.

Parallel Loans   See Back to Back Loans.

Parastatal   An organisation or industry within a country which takes on some of the roles of government and through which a government can operate indirectly. See Mixed Economy, Market Economy, Planned Economy, State Planning.

Pari Passu   Securities issued with a pari passu clause mean they rank equally with existing securities of the same class.

Paris   Dealers' language for the French franc.

Paris Club   An ad hoc forum, which meets in Paris, for Western creditor governments to discuss the renegotiation of debt owed to official creditors or guaranteed by them. Neither the World Bank nor the International Monetary Fund is a member of the Paris Club. To reschedule debt, both the Paris Club and the commercial banks require the debtor country to have agreed on a stabilisation programme with the IMF. See London Club, Paris Donor Group.

Paris Donor Group   Paris Donor Consultative Group meetings are held in Paris under the aegis of the World Bank and concern donor fund aid to countries. The group is not connected in any way with Paris Club discussions.

Parity   Parity occurs when the total market value of the common shares equals the market value of the convertible share. Once both shares are trading and changing prices, disparity will occur.

Participating Preference   Capital whose holders are entitled to receipts of a fixed interest payment out of profits but also to a share in the balance of the profits.

Participation   Part ownership by a company or government in an oil venture or operation. Also refers to a mortgage loan made jointly by two or more lenders.

Participation Certificate   In the U.S., represents an interest in mortgage loans. The buyer receives the cash flows and is the owner financially although the seller remains the mortgagee of record. In Switzerland, a non-voting form of equity issued by Swiss companies. Known in Germany as Genußschein.

Participation Crude Oil   The allocation of crude output - usually a percentage of production - which can be given to a government in a joint venture with an oil firm as payment for granting exploration and development rights.

Partly Paid   A system of payment which allows shareholders or bondholders to pay only part of the determined price for a new issue, with the remainder being settled on a fixed date in the future. U.K. gilts are occasionally issued in partly paid form. Following an initial settlement at purchase, the remainder of the issue is paid in instalments on fixed dates over a period of three months.

Pass Through Certificate   Represents an interest in a pool of mortgages on which payments received on the underlying pool are passed through to the investor by the firm servicing the mortgage payments. Variations are: a) where the holder of the certificate receives interest due - whether collected or not - and principal as collected; b) where the holder gets interest and principal due whether collected or not.

Passing the Dividend   A dividend is passed, i.e. not paid, for various reasons, sometimes lack of funds but also when a company is in a recovery phase. This action may also be taken by a victim company to the disadvantage of a predator company which is making a takeover bid.

Pathfinder   See Red Herring.

Patterns   The formations of various shapes that prices create. Patterns may be used to identify reversals, continuation of trends and the strength of trends. Used in technical analysis.

Pay Date   The date when a dividend is actually due to a shareholder.

Paydown   Amount by which, in a U.S. Treasury refunding, the par value of maturing securities is greater than that of those being sold.

Payer of Fixed   Standard terminology in the interest rate swap market refers to the fixed side of the contract, therefore a payer of fixed is one who pays the fixed amount and receives floating. Opposite to Receiver of Fixed.

Paying Agent   Institution appointed to supervise payment and, in the case of floating rate notes, the setting of rates on bond issues.

Payment in Kind   As part of the U.S. 1982/83 acreage reduction plan grain farmers who took land out of production received as payment grains from Commodity Credit Corporation stocks rather than cash.

   CCC Generic Certificates (called PIK certs by the trade) are issued to farmers who participate in the government programmes. These certificates are redeemable for a fixed dollar value of CCC stocks of any commodity regardless of which one the farmer would have planted. The value of redeemable commodities is set daily by the government. A secondary cash market operates for the certificates.

Payment in Kind Bonds (PIKs)   On these securities the issuer has the right to make coupon payments either in cash or with other securities of a similar value.

PDVSA   Petróleos de Venezuela, the country's national oil company.

Peaks / Troughs   Peaks, or reaction highs, are called resistance points and represent a price level where selling pressure overcomes buying pressure, causing the price advance to reverse. Troughs, or reaction lows, are called support points and represent a price level where buying pressure overcomes selling pressure leading the price fall to turn back. Used in technical analysis.

Pennants   See Flags / Pennants.

Penny Stock   A type of ordinary share which is of negligible value but which may prove to be speculative at some time. In the U.S., a share priced at less than one dollar and in the U.K. at less than one pound.

Pension Benefit Guaranty Corp.   A U.S. government agency that partially covers the pensions obligations of insolvent companies.

Percent R   See William Percent R.

PERCs   In the U.S., Preferred Equity Redemption Cumulative stocks.

Performing Loan   A loan is performing if the borrower is paying the interest on it. See Non-Performing Loan.

Perpetual (Undated) Note   A floating rate note which has no final maturity. For this privilege, the borrower pays a higher margin over a relevant base interest rate. As they will never be paid, the notes assume the characteristics of an equity issue.

Perpetual Gilts - U.K.   See Undated Gilts - U.K.

Petro Dollars   A term prevalent in the 1970s, when the Organisation of Petroleum Exporting Countries (OPEC) pushed up oil prices, to describe the abundance of dollars held, and invested, by the OPEC nations. See Arab Oil Embargo.

Petrochemical   Chemical substance derived from petroleum or natural gas. Examples are ethylene, propylene, benzene and toluene.

Petróleos de Venezuela   See PDVSA.

Petroleum   Mixture of hydrocarbons and other organic compounds including crude oil, natural gas liquids, natural gas and their products.

Pfandbriefe   German bonds issued to refinance mortgages or public projects. Can only be issued by specially authorised banks which are also fully liable for each issue. They are secured by mortgage or public sector loans. They must carry the backing of separate funds with at least matching yields and maturities. Pfandbriefe are monitored by a trustee designated by the state. They are officially quoted on German stock exchanges while issuers maintain a secondary market.

Philippe Bonds - Belgium   A classical Belgian Government Bond (BGB) issued by the state but only three to four times per year. These bonds were introduced in 1990, named after the Belgian Minister of Finance and are particularly aimed at the private domestic investor.

Physicals   See Actuals.

PIBOR / PIBID / PIMEAN   The Paris Interbank Offered Rate (PIBOR) is the rate at which banks are prepared to lend to each other for specified maturities within the Paris market. PIBOR is also fixed daily for reference purposes and is a key interest rate level used for setting rates for loans and floating rate notes and for calculating cash settlements of certain interest rate derivative instruments. PIBID is the Paris Interbank Bid rate, the rate at which banks take deposits from each other. PIMEAN is the Paris Interbank Mean Rate.

Pig   Object placed in a pipeline and propelled by gas or oil flow to clean, clear or check the internal condition of the pipeline.

Pikul   Chinese weight used in Malaysia. It is equivalent to approximately 133-1/2 pounds weight or 60.5 kilogrammes. A long ton equals about 16.8 pikuls.

   The Indonesian pikul is 61.76 kilogrammes.

PIMEAN   See PIBOR / PIBID / PIMEAN.

Pink Book   Official annual publication, The United Kingdom Balance of Payments, which has historic data on the balance of payments.

Pip   Synonymous with point, although may also refer to one tenth of a point. For example, in a T/N swap price quotation of 0.3/0.4 the spread is one pip.

Pit   A section, often self-contained, on an exchange floor for the trading of a particular type of financial instrument or commodity.

Pivot Point   A formula that averages the day's high, low and closing prices which is then used to calculate resistance and support levels. A break of the second support or resistance level is said to indicate a change of trend.

Placing   A method of offering a new securities issue by being passed straight to institutions who usually retain the shares instead of the issue being made available to the public at large. A stock exchange will normally only approve this when significant public demand is not expected.

Plain Vanilla   The term used for standard financial or derivative instruments without special features.

Planned Economy   Economic system where state authorities have direct control over production and prices and, usually, control of the labour force. See State Planning, Mixed Economy, Market Economy, Parastatal.

Plateau Level   Level of peak production reached by an oil or gas field.

Platform   Generic term for a stationary offshore structure typically sitting on, or tethered to, the seabed and which allows development wells to be drilled. Not to be confused with rigs which are mobile drilling or production units.

Platinum   A precious metal which for industrial purposes is mainly used as a catalyst in petrochemical output and pollution control systems as in catalytic converters for car exhausts. The latter use in the auto industry accounts for some 40 percent of world platinum sales. Another 40 percent is used by the jewellery trade in Japan. South Africa and the Commonwealth of Independent States account for over 80 percent of world output.

Platinum Share   Similar to a golden share. One version is for use if an administrator, receiver or liquidator is likely to be appointed to a parent company. The platinum share, relating solely to a relatively stable subsidiary, can be used to safeguard the unit.

Platt's   A U.S. based oil price reporting agency, a unit of Standard & Poor's Information Group, a subsidiary of McGraw Hill. Founded in the 1930s. Established as the leading price reference in the U.S. and world markets. Platt's prices are the basis of crude and products contracts world-wide, including those of virtually every exporter including Saudi Arabia, Iran, Russia, and day to day spot deals. Prices are published in telex format with market news - international crude prices in the Crude Oil Marketwire, products in the European, U.S. and Far East Marketscans. Platt's Oilgram is a daily price compendium in newsletter form. Platt's runs a screen news service - Platt's Global Alert - which also carries prices.

Plaza Agreement   Governments of the Group of Five nations agreed at the Plaza Hotel, New York, in 1985 to promote further depreciation of the U.S. dollar. This followed the dollar's peak early that year after it had already risen sharply the previous year when the U.S. reported record trade and budget deficits.

PLC   In the U.K., a public limited company. Companies whose securities are traded in a market or which invites public subscription for its shares.

Plimsoll Line   Water level on U.K. registered vessels which indicates the maximum permitted loading level.

Ploughed Back   Refers to earnings which are reinvested in the company and not distributed.

Plugging   Sealing of an oil well which is no longer needed.

PMI   Penningmarknads Information (PMI) is a local system in Sweden linking dealers and publishing the results of the government bond auctions.

Point   A term used in foreign exchange equal to one hundredth of one big figure. See Pip.

Points and Figures Chart   A price chart analysis that captures pure price movement with no regard for time or volume. Rising prices are denoted by a column of Xs and falling prices by a column of Os. Subsequent columns are placed to the right of earlier columns. X is only added to an X column if the high is at least one box size greater than the value represented by the last X displayed. O is only added to an O column if the low is at least one box size less than the value shown by the last O displayed.

If a column consists of just one X or O and a reversal occurs then each new O or X is displayed in the current column rather than in a new column. This can only happen when the reversal is one box size. In this case, there is no possibility of an O and X being shown in the same position.

Poison Pill   Covers various methods of outwitting a predator in potential takeover situations. Examples are the issue of high yielding bonds, conditional rights to shareholders to buy shares at a large discount if the takeover succeeds or making massive long term commitments to the company's pension funds.

Polarisation   Measurement in degrees to define purity of sugar. See White Value, Raw Value.

Political Risk   The risk associated with investing in politically unstable countries.

POP   See Public Offering Price.

Pork Bellies   The belly, which yields bacon, accounts for about 15 percent of the carcass weight of a hog. Seasonal trends in production have been altered in recent years by expansion of heated indoor facilities. The Chicago Mercantile Exchange (CME) lists futures and options on pork bellies and live hogs. Contracts are used for normal pricing and hedging purposes. CME hog deliveries are made at designated Midwest stock-yards and pork belly deliveries at cold storage warehouses. Hog production is cyclical with hogs taking eight months to a year from birth to slaughter. Demand factors include competition from poultry, exports, retailer featuring and season.

Portfolio   A collection, or holding, of financial instruments in the possession of an investor.

Portfolio Insurers   Operators who engage in programme trading chiefly by selling stock index futures rather than their stocks to gain protection against a market decline. The operation can feed upon itself to bring a market fall when specula-tors rush to buy the cheaper futures contracts and simultaneously sell the underlying stocks. Profes-sionals can then follow, selling their stocks. The portfolio insurers then sell more futures aiming to safeguard against further market falls in stocks.

Portfolio Manager   Designated advisor who manages a portfolio of investments on behalf of a purchaser, often with full authority to take decisions. Known as acting on a discretionary basis.

Position   Balance of purchases and sales in a given financial instrument for a given maturity. See Short Position, Long Position, Flat Position.

Position Keeping   The monitoring of a dealer's position.

Position Limit   Maximum position, either net long or short, which may be held by a dealer, a group of dealers or a dealing room.

Position Trading   A strategy whereby a trader holds open futures contracts for an extended period of time by rolling expiring contracts forward, as opposed to a day trader who initiates and liqui-dates a futures position in the same trading session.

Positive Carry   Situation where the financing cost of a position is less than the return.

Possible Reserves - Oil / Gas   Oil/gas reserves which the best estimates suggest might eventually be recoverable from undrilled or untested structures but which have not yet been developed.

Postal Saving System   Banking arm of the Japanese Posts and Telecommunications Ministry which takes deposits from individual investors.

Posted Price   Price some oil buyers - especially in the U.S. - will pay for crude of a certain API gravity from a particular field or area. Also, it has been the hypothetical price level on which OPEC governments based their take from foreign producing companies in the form of taxes and royalties.

Pour Point   For petroleum, it is the lowest tempera-ture at which the oil will pour or flow when it is chilled under prescribed conditions.

Power of Attorney   A legal document in which one person is given the power to act on behalf of another person.

PPP   Purchasing Power Parity is a means of comparing living standards between various nations. PPP aims to cut out distortions from translating such as the gross domestic product into one basic currency.

Praecipuum   Part of a management fee assessed on the full principal amount of an issue and which is taken by the lead manager to compensate for taking responsibility for handling a primary market issue.

Pre-Emptive Rights   See Rights.

Pre-Market Trading   Takes place before the official opening of business on the trading floor of an exchange. No set length of time is allocated for pre-market trading, particularly with the advent of electronic screen trading but stock exchanges still have an official opening each day.

Precious Metals   There are eight precious or noble metals - gold, silver, platinum, palladium, rhodium, iridium, osmium and ruthenium. The latter four are produced as co-products of platinum and palladium. See Minor Metals.

Precious Metals Fixings   Official fixings of precious metals take place on a daily basis. For instance, twice a day - 1030 and 1500 London time - the major bullion dealers meet and fix the gold price. The silver price is fixed once a day, in both

London and Zurich. Fixing prices are widely used as reference prices.

Preferential Issue   A certain percentage of a share offer to the public which is set aside for subscriptions from employees.

Preferential Trade Area   Covers Eastern and Southern African states. Aims to improve economic and commercial cooperation and to form a common market. Reserve Bank of Zimbabwe operates a clearing house for transactions of goods and services. Members are Angola, Burundi, the Comoros, Djibouti, Ethiopia, Kenya, Lesotho, Malawi, Mauritius, Mozambique, Rwanda, Somalia, Sudan, Swaziland, Tanzania, Uganda, Zambia and Zimbabwe.

Preferred Share   A share which grants the investor a dividend income on a regular basis. The dividend is fixed at the time of issue. Preferred shareholders always receive the dividend before ordinary shareholders. Typically these shares do not grant voting or pre-emptive rights. Although preferred shares do not have a maturity, due to the fixed dividend they are often considered to be a fixed income security. See Ordinary Share.

Preliminary Prospectus   See Red Herring.

Premium   Amount paid above the normal price level. In the capital markets it is the amount by which a bond sells above par. In foreign exchange terms it is the margin by which the forward rate is higher than the spot. Opposite to Discount. See Option Premium.

Prepayment   In mortgages, any unscheduled principal payment made in addition to the normal amortisation.

Present Value   The current value of a future cash flow discounted at an appropriate interest rate. See Discount Factor.

Presold   Term used when a new security issue has been sold out before all the details of the issue have been announced. In bond issues, this would indicate that sufficient orders for the issue have been placed before the final terms announcement.

Pressure Burst   Sudden bursting of rock due to great pressure in deep mining.

Price Channel   Used in technical analysis. Provides buy and sell signals by indicating when a value moves outside set deviation limits. The channel chart consists of two bands either side of a simple moving average. When an average graph, with the same number of observations, is placed on the same chart it will trace a path exactly midway between the upper and lower deviation, if the deviation limits above and below are equal. By using channel analysis, buy and sell signals will be indicated as the price touches or breaks through the upper or lower channel deviations. Channel charts can also be used on volume and as an overbought/oversold indicator.

Price Driven   Trading where prices set by the market makers determine the order flow. See Order Driven.

Price Earnings Ratio   See P/E Ratio.

Price Volume Index   This analysis is essentially a volume weighted Relative Strength Index and is an attempt to measure the strength of money entering and leaving the market. It quantifies price/volume momentum in the same way that the strength index quantifies price momentum but it differs from that index in that: 1) the price used is the average of the high, low and close rather than the close; and 2) the price is weighted by the volume.

Price Weighted Index   A stock index that weights stocks on the basis of their market price. Typically, the higher the price the greater the weighting.

Primary Commodities   Commodities in the raw or unprocessed state, e.g. iron ore.

Primary Dealer   Dealers who are authorised by the central bank to deal in the primary market for government securities.

Primary dealers in the government bond markets are normally required to make significant contributions to auctions; act as market makers in the secondary market by providing bids and offers on all outstanding Treasury issues and by guaranteeing liquidity; promote government issues to domestic and foreign investors; keep the central bank well informed of market conditions and developments.

Primary dealers can also be known as primary distributors, jobbers, SVTs (France), underwriters and lead managers.

Primary Distributor - Canada   A group of securities dealers and banks designated by the Bank of Canada who are authorised to bid at Treasury auctions although they are not obliged to be market makers in these issues. This role is assured by a smaller group of primary dealers, known as jobbers.

Primary Market   Market for the placing of new securities such as international, domestic and foreign bond issues and shares. Any subsequent resale or purchase is handled on the secondary market.

Primary Market - Belgian Government Debt   The issue timetable for Treasury certificates is published each year by the Treasury. Competitive auctions are held on a regular basis.

There is no official schedule for the issuance of BGBs. The Belgian Treasury relies on the Belgian banks' retail facilities to issue Philippe bonds targeted at the domestic private investors.

OLOs on the other hand are auctioned monthly on a competitive basis. The primary dealers who have access to all auctions are banks and brokers based in Belgium or Luxembourg only. The size of the issue is not announced prior to the auction. Non-competitive bidding is permitted on the second day, although still reserved for primary dealers only. Primary dealers are required to maintain secondary market liquidity in OLOs. Once a month three issues with varying maturities are re-opened.

Primary Market - Canadian Government Debt
Treasury bills are issued by a weekly competitive auction through a group of primary distributors who have both a primary and secondary role in these markets. The Bank of Canada receives bids each Thursday and on the same day announces the results together with the amount of Treasury bills which will be offered the following week. Two year Treasury bonds are issued via quarterly auction (March, June, September, December). Five and 10 year Treasury bonds are also issued via quarterly auction (February, May, August, November). Other maturities have no fixed schedule.

Both competitive and non-competitive bids are accepted with bids being submitted in yield. A new issue may comprise several issues with varying maturities which may be re-opened after one year (two year bonds are not re-opened). Small issues which are not re-opened are known as orphaned issues. The Bank of Canada may also issue bonds via a method known as subscription offering.

Primary Market - Dutch State Loans The Dutch Ministry of Finance has two methods of issuance, Dutch auction and tap issues. The issue size is not normally announced before an auction. Bids are made through authorised banks. The MOF issues longer maturities (up to 30 year bullets) to the domestic market only via the Private Placement Market.

Primary Market - French Government Debt All French government bills and bonds are issued by Dutch auction. An auction calendar is published for all types of issues on a regular basis, indicating the issue size for the forthcoming period. This issue size is then auctioned regularly throughout the period as fungible Treasuries. Bids are made to the Banque de France by stockbrokers, recognised banks and SVTs and are registered electronically.

BTFs (Bons à Taux Fixe). The French Treasury announces the auction calendar on a quarterly basis. The amount to be auctioned is announced on the Wednesday prior to the auction. Bids are placed on a discount basis and the auction results follow two hours later.

BTANs (Bons à Taux Annuel Normalisé). The French Treasury announces the auction calendar on a semi-annual basis. The amount to be auctioned and the coupon rate are announced on the Tuesday prior to the auction. Bids are placed on a clean price basis in percentage of face value. After the initial auction, BTANs are re-opened every month for about six months.

OATs (Obligations Assimilables du Trésor). The French Treasury announces the auction calendar on a semi-annual basis. Bids are made in clean price as percentage of par and must be made by 1000, the results being produced at midday. During the four hours following the auction results, SVTs (Spécialistes en Valeurs du Trésor) have the opportunity to buy, on a non-competitive basis, an additional 25 percent at the average auction price.

Primary Market - German BOBLs BOBLs are issued in tap form by tender. Orders can be placed through domestic or authorised foreign banks. See Bundesobligationen (BOBLs) - Germany.

Primary Market - German Bunds Although there is no regular schedule for the issue of bunds, the 10 year bund is usually issued every month. Since July 1990 the issuing group is the federal bond syndicate (Konsortium).

The issue procedure comprises two tranches. The first tranche is issued to all of the Konsortium. Up to 25 percent of the issue is retained by the Bundesbank for intervention and open market operations. This tranche has fixed terms which include the issue price. The second tranche is dealt on the following day as an open tender with bids (in price) made via eligible members. Both these tranches together with the Bundesbank allocation form one issue. The total issue volume is announced by the Bundesbank once the allocations are complete.

Primary Market - German Schätze Schätze are issued by competitive auction which is managed by the Bundesbank.

Primary Market - Gold Newly mined gold from the producers is sent to primary markets, such as London and Zurich, who then distribute it either directly or through secondary markets.

Primary Market - Italian Government Debt All bonds are issued by Dutch auction. Although there is no official auction cycle, the pattern can be determined as follows: BOTs, BTPs and CCTs - beginning and mid-month auctions, CTOs - mid-month auctions only, CTEs, BTEs - auctioned very irregularly.

All issues can be re-opened.

Primary Market - Japanese Government Debt All instruments are issued on a competitive bid auction basis. Bids are made in price. The auctions tend to be dominated by the four major Japanese securities houses (The Big Four). The auction procedure for the 10 year coupon bond and the five year discount bond is slightly different. A large portion is auctioned as above and the remaining portion is reserved for an underwriting syndicate and allocated according to fixed quotas. The syndicated portion is priced according to the average auction price. In the case of coupon issues, the MOF, the Bank of Japan and the syndicate negotiate the coupon rate and the issue size.

Primary Market - Swedish Government Debt The Swedish National Debt Office announces its funding targets in June and December. It also appoints a small number of primary dealers who are authorised to participate in the auction held twice a month and who are also responsible for maintaining liquidity in the secondary market. Auctions are carried out twice a month on a competitive basis and most issues are re-openings of existing bonds rather than new issues.

Primary Market - Swiss SGBs Swiss government bonds (SGBs) are auctioned on a monthly basis in accordance with the debt calendar announced by the Swiss Treasury. The auction is carried out as a Dutch auction.

Primary Market - Swiss SGNs Swiss government notes (SGNs) are bought deals with the lead manager being selected on the basis of competitive bids.

Primary Market - U.K. Gilts The Bank of England issues gilts by four different methods.

Tender - this has been the traditional method whereby the Bank invites bids based on a minimum tender price. If the tender is unsubscribed, the remaining part will be operated as tap stock. The Bank has occasionally operated fixed price tenders.

Auction - this method has been in operation since mid-1987. Since the details of the auction are issued ahead of the auction date, an active When Issued market is evident. Bidding is invited on both a competitive and non-competitive basis. An auction programme is issued by the Bank before the start of the financial year.

Tap stock - this method is frequently used by the Bank to manage liquidity. Existing stock may be issued for sale through the Bank of England's own dealing room to the GEMS.

Taplet - this method is used if a previously fully allocated stock is extended.

Primary dealers (banks & stockbrokers) deal directly with the Bank of England. Approved gilt edged market makers (GEMS) may also participate in the auctions.

Primary Market - U.S. Treasuries The Federal Reserve issues U.S. Treasuries via competitive auction directly to reporting and primary dealers. The auctions have a regular auction cycle and a fixed procedure. The U.S. Treasury announces in advance the amount of each issue, the scheduled date of the auction, the settlement date and the maturities.

Competitive bids must be submitted to the Federal Reserve by a certain time on the auction day. Non-competitive bids can also be submitted. Additional amounts at the auction average are available to foreign and international monetary authorities and are known as "foreign add-ons".

The results of the auction are announced on the afternoon of the auction day and include the highest yield (stop yield), the lowest yield and the average yield, together with details concerning full and partial allocations and, in the case of Treasury notes and Treasury bonds, the coupon. They also announce the "cover", the ratio by which the auction was oversubscribed.

The success of the auction can be measured by the "tail" which is the difference between the stop yield and the average yield. The smaller the tail, the more successful the auction.

In September 1992 the U.S. Treasury launched a trial Dutch auction for the issuing of two and five year Treasury Notes. As from April 1993 major bidders have been able to submit bids by computer.

Primary Metals Metals produced from ores.

Primary Recovery Recovery of oil/gas from a reservoir purely by using the natural pressure in the reservoir to force the oil/gas out.

Prime Bank A prime bank is one of the highest rank.

Prime Rate The borrowing rate charged by banks to their best customers.

Principal A major party to a transaction, acting as either buyer or seller. The principal buys and sells on his own account. Also means the total amount borrowed or invested.

Print The latest crude price of the corresponding traded month on the New York Mercantile Exchange. This futures market price for oil is used for trading light crude cargoes on the spot market. A hypothetical example could be - December cash light crude traded at the print plus 10 cents a barrel in the Far East.

Prior Charges Charges on senior debt such as debentures, loan stock, notes which rank ahead of ordinary share capital.

Prior Lien A lien (the right to take assets to cover an unpaid debt) that is issued only with the agreement of holders of a first mortgage bond and which has priority over such a first mortgage bond.

Priority Percentage An apportionment of profit earned in any year which is needed to service different classes of capital expressed in order of priority as a percentage of the amount available.

Private Placement Bond issue placed directly with investors, not listed on a stock exchange and without a prospectus. It is usually in large denominations. Without bearing the costs associated with a widespread distribution, a private placement is traditionally cheaper for the borrower than a Public Placement.

Private Placement Market - Netherlands Private market between the Dutch government and domestic investors in the Netherlands only, where longer term maturities (15-25 year bullets) are issued. This market represents 30 percent of Dutch government bond issues.

Privatisation The act of governments selling off to the private sector their state owned commercial and industrial concerns.

Pro Rata Sinking Fund A sinking fund where each investor gives up an equal percentage of holdings to the issuer when the issue is called for sinking fund retirements. Typically only applied to registered securities. See Purchase Fund, Sinking Fund.

Probable Reserves - Oil / Gas Undeveloped oil/gas reserves considered to be recoverable from penetrated formations but lacking information considered sufficient to be classified as proven reserves.

Product Yield Percentages of gasoline, jet fuel, kerosene, gas oil, distillates, residual fuel oil and other products that a refinery can produce from a 42 U.S. gallon barrel of crude. Roughly, the average yield from one barrel is 50 percent gasoline, 21 percent gas oil and distillates, 9 percent residual fuel oil, 7 percent jet fuel/kerosene, 7 percent lubricating oil and 6 percent other products.

Production Platform Platform from which development wells are drilled and which carries all the associated processing plant and other equipment needed to maintain a field in production.

Production Sharing Contract Agreement between an oil firm and a government giving the company - which often bears all costs - the exploration and production rights and giving the government a share of total output.

Profit and Loss Statement A summary of all the expenditure and income of a company over a set period of time. Also called an income statement.

Profit Margin Net profit as a percentage of sales or capital.

Profittaking Realising profits by closing out an existing position.

Programme Trading Computer based trading technique, used in markets, based on the flow of trading, current price levels and movements in futures and options rather than on basics such as earnings or economic indicators. It aims to exploit arbitrage possibilities between U.S. stock index futures/options and underlying equities.

Prolerised Scrap Scrap metal which has been broken up.

PROMINOFI This inter-dealer broker system was established in 1987 in France allowing the SVTs (spécialistes en valeurs du Trésor) to make anonymous quotes for OATs, BTFs and BTANs on a screen. This service is exclusively reserved for the SVTs.

Promissory Note A note representing a promise by the issuer to repay a loan. Promissory notes are not classed as securities. Failure to pay a promissory note renders the borrower immediately liable to be sued for payment.

Prompt Barrel Product which will move or become available within 5-15 days.

Prompt Date The date on which a commodity must be delivered to fulfil a contract.

Propane Key raw material in the chemical and plastics industries. Is a gas but can be easily converted to a liquid. Also used as a domestic fuel. Not to be confused with propene, which is a chemical feedstock.

Prorationing Regulation of oil/gas production by producing states to conserve natural resources. Often is a pronouncement on the number of days in a month that production is allowed.

Prospectus Document provided by the issuing company giving detailed terms and conditions of a new stock or debt offering.

Protection and Push Bids Amendments made by U.S. cash grain buyers to their daily posted basis bids to compensate for expected extreme movements in futures prices when the market opens. A buyer will take protection if futures are expected to open lower or push bids if the market is likely to open higher.

Protectionism Imposition of customs duties on imports so as to protect a domestic industry from cheaper competitive products. It can involve import restrictions, export subsidies and non-tariff moves such as health and environment regulations.

Proven Field - Oil / Gas Field whose physical extent and estimated reserves have been established.

Proven Reserves - Oil / Gas Proven or proved reserves are oil/gas already located and known to be recoverable with existing facilities and present technology and at current cost and price levels.

PSA Public Securities Association. An organisation which represents dealers in U.S. government securities and mortgages. Has produced a standard prepayment benchmark which was devised originally for projecting the cash flows of mortgage backed securities

PSBR - U.K. In the U.K., Public Sector Borrowing Requirement. The disadvantageous difference between the government's revenue and expenditure which means it is still borrowing. See PSDR - U.K.

PSDR - U.K. In the U.K., Public Sector Debt Repayment. The advantageous difference between the government's revenue and expenditure which means it is able to pay back debt. See PSBR - U.K.

Public Law 480 The U.S. Agricultural Trade Development and Assistance Act is better known as Public Law 480, or PL 480. Initially, after the Second World War, PL 480 was regarded as a short term programme to help move growing surpluses of grain to foreign markets. Nowadays PL 480 allows for various export transactions under four titles of the act.

   Title 1 allows for government-to-government export transactions with short or long term financing in the foreign currency.

   Title 2 allows for government-to-government donations of U.S. agricultural commodities in emergency and disaster situations and for economic development.

   Title 3 allows for grain shipments which represent transactions involving government-to-government barter for commodities strategic to the U.S. and also charitable donations.

   Title 4 allows for long term relatively low interest credit arrangements in U.S. dollars between the U.S. and friendly governments. Such exports currently account for some 70 percent of all PL 480 exports.

Public Offering Price The price fixed by the underwriter on behalf of a company at the Initial Public Offering (IPO) of shares. The underwriter's commission is built into the price. Shares in a mutual fund may be purchased at the POP.

Public Placement A public bond placement is offered generally to a market, usually listed on a stock exchange and in relatively small denominations. Usually costs the borrower more than a Private Placement.

Publicly Traded Fund See Closed End Fund.

Pulses Legumes harvested for their seed, such as soybeans, groundnuts (peanuts), lima beans, chickpeas and lentils.

Purchase Fund Similar to a Sinking Fund but not mandatory. The borrower will purchase bonds in the market if available at par or below. See Pro Rata Sinking Fund.

Purchase Price A purchase price becomes legally enforceable, bearing upon both buyer and seller, once a written order to buy has been accepted by the vendor.

Purchasing Power Parity See PPP.

Purgatory and Hell Bond A bond whose proceeds from redemption are tied to the maturity spot exchange rate of another currency against the bond's denominated currency. Redemption receipt is restricted to between zero and 100 percent. See Heaven and Hell Bond.

Put / Call Parity The relationship between a put and a call, both European style, based on the same underlying, exercise price and expiry date.

Put / Call Ratio The number of puts traded in relation to the number of calls traded in the market. This ratio is an indicator of market sentiment.

Put Feature Optional right of the bondholder to oblige the issuer to repurchase the security at a specific date prior to maturity. The repurchase price, which may be at par, a premium or discount, is specified at the time of issue. Also known as a puttable bond. See Call Feature.

Put Option A contract giving the buyer or the holder the right, but not the obligation, to sell the underlying at an agreed price within a specified time. The seller or writer has the obligation to buy. See Call Option.

Put Ratio Backspread An option strategy whereby more puts are bought than sold. All options have the same expiry date.

Put Ratio Spread An option strategy whereby more puts are sold than bought. All options have the same expiry date.

Put Through See Cross.

Puttable Bond See Put Feature.

Putting On the Crush A hedging technique used by a soybean processor. He might consider in, say, August that the Gross Processing Margin for January soybeans versus January oil and meal appears attractive. However, he may think that as the months progress towards January the GPM will narrow or worsen. Thus he will "put on the crush" by buying January soybeans and selling January oil and meal, thereby helping him to establish his gross margin for the particular position. When cash soybeans are bought against the January crush, the long January soybean futures are sold out. As cash oil and meal are sold for January shipment, he buys in his short positions in January oil and meal futures. If the GPM has deteriorated from the level seen in August, then he has safeguarded at the original margin level the amount of crush hedged in the futures market.

Qualified Accounts These are the published balance sheet and accounts of a company, accompanied by the auditors' report, in which the auditors express reservations that they do not feel that a true and fair view of the company's activities has been presented.

Quality of Earnings The quality of a company's earnings can be assessed in various ways. A company might report improved earnings but on a contract which ends shortly. Its current improved earnings might be affected by patent renewal problems. Improved earnings might have been obtained away from the company's core operations. To value the company or shares, it is necessary to be aware of the quality of the company's earnings.

Quanto Option Stands for Quantity Adjusted option. It is an option on an asset or a liability denominated in a currency other than the underlying currency in which it is normally traded.

Quick Ratio An alternative method to assess a current ratio (Current Assets divided by Current Liabilities) which does not include stocks in the assets on the basis that stocks are generally not deemed very liquid.

Quintal Unit of weight equal to 100 kilogrammes. Generally used by Central and Latin American nations in the old Imperial form, i.e. one quintal equals 100 pounds which equals 46 kilogrammes.

Quotation Current price or rate given on the market place or exchange, but not necessarily the price at which a trade will be made.

Quoted Currency The currency quoted against the base currency, i.e. the numerator quoted in terms of the denominator. For example, the quoted currency in the U.S. dollar/German mark quotation is the German mark. See Base Currency.

Rally General trading term, mostly describing a price rise, in a whole market or a sector, which is reversing a previous general fall or is a move up from a narrow trading range.

Rambouillet Summit Leading industrial nations agreed in 1975 at the Chateau de Rambouillet in France to formally endorse floating exchange rates. The previous year the International Monetary Fund moved the basis of valuing Special Drawing Rights to a basket of currencies instead of gold.

Range Forward See Risk Reversal.

Range FRNs Floating Rate Notes which pay a fixed margin above or below a reference rate only when that reference rate falls within a given range. At other times there will be no interest accruing on these securities.

Ranking Denotes where a bond stands in relation to priority claims from a lender upon default by the borrower. Senior debt earns high priority if lenders have to reclaim funds, hence the bond issue terms can be less onerous for the borrower. Subordinated debt ranks a bond lower down the scale, thus a borrower has to offer a lender more advantageous terms. Sometimes claims by governments, government agencies, government tax and customs and excise authorities, banks and various other commercial institutions have priority.

RANs See Municipal Notes.

Rapeseed Major oilseed crop which yields a higher percentage of its weight in oil (as opposed to meal) than soybeans. Rapeseed is known in Canada as canola and in Europe as colza. Rapeoil is a general purpose edible vegetable oil while meal is used as a protein foodstuff. Major producers include France, Germany, the U.K. and Denmark.

Rare Metals See Minor Metals.

Ratchet Option See Cliquet Option.

Rate of Change In technical analysis, the ratio of the most recent closing price to a price in a previous set period. Thus, a five day rate of change oscillator is constructed by dividing the latest closing price by the price five days previous and multiplying by 100. The 100 line becomes the midpoint or zero line.

Rate of Return The return on an investment either in the form of dividends or interest and based on the price paid for the security.

Ratio Spread   An option spread whereby the amount of options or futures contracts purchased is not equal to the amount of contracts sold. See Call Ratio Spread, Put Ratio Spread.

Raw Silk   Traded in Yokohama and Kobe in Japan.

Raw Value   Unrefined sugar traditionally of 96 degrees polarity. See Polarisation, White Value.

Re-Open An Issue   See Tap Issue.

Real Estate Mortgage Investment Conduit   See REMIC.

Real Interest Rate   The actual rate of return calculated by deducting inflation rate from the current rate of interest. Also known as real yield. See Nominal Interest Rate.

Real Return Bond   See RRB - Canada.

Real Yield   See Real Interest Rate.

Realised Gain   The cash profit resulting from the liquidation of a position.

Realised Loss   The cash loss resulting from the liquidation of a position.

Rebalancing Protection   The Uruguay Round accord states that if imports of non-grain feed ingredients into the European Community increase beyond the 1990-92 average then the parties agree to consult to find a mutually acceptable solution.

Receivables   Outstanding debts due to a company.

Receiver   A receiver takes control of a company's assets when appointed by a secured creditor who has a fixed charge over specific assets of the company.

Receiver of Fixed   Standard terminology in the interest rate swap market refers to the fixed side of the contract, therefore a receiver of fixed is one who receives the fixed amount and pays floating. Opposite to Payer of Fixed.

Recession   A period of static or negative economic growth. Various nations have differing definitions. For instance, the U.S. defines a recession as two succeeding quarters of negative growth.

Record Date   The date on which a shareholder must be the official owner of shares to be entitled to the dividend. This date is set by the board of directors. See Ex, Ex Dividend Date.

Recoverable Reserves   Oil/gas known to exist and to be economically recoverable. Of the total hydrocarbons in place, only a proportion can be ultimately recovered. Factors involved are permeability of the rock, properties of the oil and the type of natural drive available. At the extremes, between 10 and 80 percent of the original oil in place can be recovered in the primary phase but the norm is below 30 percent. The success rate can be increased depending on the secondary recovery techniques but the final figure for recoverable reserves will only be known once the field is in production.

Recovery Factor   Ratio of oil/gas reserves which can currently be recovered to estimated total deposits.

Rectangle   Also called a trading range or congestion area. In technical analysis, it represents a pause in a trend in which prices move sideways between two parallel trendlines, thus portraying a consolidation period in the main trend and generally resolved in the direction of the existing trend. A decisive close outside either trendline marks completion of the rectangle and indicates the direction of the trend.

Red Book   In the U.K., it is published by the government in association with the annual government budget and contains detailed information on measures announced. Sometimes has Treasury comments on the economic outlook.

Red Herring   U.S. market jargon. The preliminary prospectus which may be used to obtain an indication of the market's interest in a specific security about to be issued. Key figures are left blank - such as issue price, profit and dividend forecast. Business is not conducted on the basis of a preliminary statement and in the U.S. a red notice is printed to that effect on the face of the document. This is required by law and gives rise to the phrase "red herring". In the U.K., known as a Pathfinder, or the preliminary prospectus.

Redemption   The repurchase of a bond at maturity by the issuer.

Redemption Price   The price at which bonds may be redeemed, either at maturity, or prior to that in the case of callable and puttable bonds or bonds with sinking funds.

Redemption Warrant   The borrower offers the holder a guaranteed redemption price if the warrant is not exercised. This feature is often added to a Harmless Warrant to make it more attractive.

Redemption Yield   Current yield increased or decreased to take account of the capital gain or loss on redemption.

Rediscount   Purchase before maturity by a central bank of a government obligation or other financial instrument already discounted in the money market.

Reef   Lode of gold-bearing quartz.

Reefer   Refrigerated cargo vessel.

Refinancing   The issuing of new debt to replace old. A borrower pays off one loan with the proceeds from another provided by other lenders. If the lenders are effectively the same then it could technically be called a Rescheduling. However, bankers might still use the term refinancing. See Restructuring.

Refinery   Plant used to separate the various components present in crude oil and to convert them into end user products or feedstock for other manufacturing processes.

Refining   Processing of a raw material into a pure state, in particular metals and sugar.

Refunding   Rollover of government debt by replacing one issue with another, the maturity of which is deferred to a later date.

Refunding Operations - U.S.   The quarterly auction of U.S. Treasury securities with maturities of three and 10 years in the months of February, May, August and November together with the semi-annual auction of the 30 year in February and August all form part of the refunding operations of the U.S. Treasury. The latter will make a prior announcement as to the amount to be auctioned, which portion of this amount is to replace maturing Treasury debt and which portion consists of new money.

Regional Banks - Japan   This term applies to 129 banks which have their branches mostly in one region, including 64 banks classified as the first regional banks, and 65 banks as the second regional banks. The division came from a former classification which categorised the second banks as the "sogo" banks. These two types are called common banks and their main business is taking in deposits, lending and foreign exchange.

Registered Form   A security which is registered in the books of the issuer in the name of the owner. Occasionally bond certificates are issued. Securities are kept in either registered or bearer form but government bonds are most commonly registered. See Bearer Form.

Registrar   The body responsible for keeping a record of the company's shareholders. When securities are dealt in book entry form and no certificates are issued, it is particularly important to have an accurate list of shareholders.

Regular Way Settlement   See Corporate Settlement.

Regularity   In the U.S., a processing plant, warehouse, mill, vault or bank that satisfies exchange requirements for financing, handling capacity and location and which has been approved as acceptable for delivery of commodities against futures contracts.

Regulation A   U.S. Securities and Exchange Commission provision for simple registration of small security issues.

Regulation G   U.S. Federal Reserve Board rule regulating lenders other than commercial banks, brokers or dealers who, in the ordinary course of business, extend credit to individuals to buy or carry securities.

Regulation M   Gives the U.S. Federal Reserve Board the power to regulate consumer leasing.

Regulation Q   A U.S. Federal Reserve Board regulation which imposes maximums on the rates that banks can pay on their savings and time deposits.

Regulation T   The regulation giving the U.S. Federal Reserve Board the authority to set the initial margin requirements on most corporate stocks and bonds in the U.S.

Regulation U   U.S. Federal Reserve Board regulation governing the quantity of credit a bank can provide to its clients seeking to buy securities.

Regulation Z   U.S. Federal Reserve Board regulation concerning the Consumer Credit Protection Act (the Truth in Lending Act).

Reid Vapour Pressure   Important test for gasoline. A measure of the vapour pressure of a sample at 100 degrees Fahrenheit. Reported in pounds.

Reinvestment Risk   The risk that future cash flows from a particular investment will be reinvested at a reduced rate of return.

Relative Performance   Compares the performance of a security against an index. The date parameters are used to align the closing prices with the index prices so that corresponding points refer to the closing values of the same date.

Relative Strength   Comparison between a current share price, portfolio of shares or a stock index and the price level of the same instrument at a given point in the past.

Relative Strength Index (RSI)   Like most oscillators, the RSI measures the strength of today's price in relation to a previous period. In short, it is a measure of momentum. The popularity of this index is generally attributed to two facts. 1) The RSI eliminates the erratic movements caused by values being dropped (common to other momentum indicators). 2) The RSI forms within lower and upper boundaries in the range 0-100. This has the benefit of providing a constant comparison range.

It is used to identify overbought and oversold signals as well as to act as a warning when there exists divergence between the direction of the index and price.

REMIC   Real Estate Mortgage Investment Conduit. An issuer of multi-class mortgage backed securities which are similar to collateralised mortgage obligations but which offer tax and accounting advantages.

Renewable Bond - France ORTs. Obligations Renouvelables du Trésor are issued in France with six year maturities with the option to renew within a three year period for a further six years.

Renounceable Certificates In the U.K., these offer the holder the right to renounce and transfer his allotment of shares in a new securities issue.

Repo See Repurchase Agreement.

Repo Rate A simple interest rate calculation to determine how much interest is to be added on to the second leg of a repo transaction. See Repurchase Agreement.

Reporting Dealer In the U.S., primary dealers first have to achieve the status of reporting dealer, whereby they report their positions and trading volumes to the Federal Reserve.

Reporting Limit Size of positions in a market at or above which various daily details are required - by commodity, delivery month and whether it is a hedging or speculative position.

Republic of Italy Issuer of government debt representing the third largest issuer in the world. Various forms of issues include fixed rate bonds (BTPs), puttable fixed rate notes (CTOs), floating rate notes (CCTs) and ECU denominated fixed rate notes (CTEs) and bonds (BTEs). The government also issues Treasury bills (BOTs).

Repudiation A borrower declares that it does not intend to service or repay an existing debt.

Repurchase Agreement Known as RP, repo or sale/repurchase agreement. A repo is in fact an operation consisting of two transactions although it is treated as one.

First transaction: a dealer sells securities to an investor and in return the investor provides funds to the dealer. The securities from the dealer represent collateral for the loan of the funds.

Second transaction: the dealer repurchases the securities and repays the loan.

Through this operation the dealer is effectively a borrower of funds to finance further purchases of securities and pays interest to the investor. It can also be said that by collateralising the loan, the dealer is selling his securities and repurchasing them at an agreed price and date. The difference between the sale and repurchase price would represent the interest payable on the loan.

In the reverse situation, whereby the dealer is a lender of funds, this is known as a reverse repo.

The repo market is, however, much larger than the dealer reverse repo market. The overnight repo market is the largest part of the repo market.

The overnight repo rate is in fact a benchmark and is normally slightly lower than the Federal funds rate since repos are collateralised.

The Federal Reserve, in its open market operations, may transact a repo to add reserves to the system by lending funds to dealers and taking their Treasury securities as collateral. Although known as a Fed repo, it is a repo from the dealer's perspective. See Repo Rate, Reverse Repurchase Agreement, Term Repo.

Rescheduling A process whereby a borrower delays redemption of principal under the terms of a new repayment schedule. Interest continues to be paid but the rate of interest can be raised or lowered. See Refinancing, Restructuring.

Reserve Currency One which is internationally accepted and is used by central banks to meet their financial commitments.

Reserve Requirements Percentage of deposits that, by law, depository institutions must set aside in their vaults or with their central bank. Lowering or raising this requirement effectively influences the money supply. A reduction in reserve requirements enables banks to increase lending while an increase forces them to reduce lending. Sometimes known as minimum reserve requirements, registered reserves or reserve ratio.

Reserves Shareholders' funds, held as cash or in highly liquid assets, which consist primarily of profits retained in the business and accumulated over the years rather than paid out by way of dividends. Shareholders have no rights over reserves so that a company can disburse them or not, as it sees fit, within the usual accounting rules.

Also, official foreign exchange reserves are reserves kept to ensure a government can meet current and near term claims. Official reserves are an asset in a country's balance of payments.

Reservoir Rock Porous and permeable rock, such as dolomite, sandstone and limestone, which contains hydrocarbons.

Residual Fuel Oil Very heavy fuels produced from the residue after the fractional distillation process.

Residual Market See STRIP Market - Canada.

Resistance Point Resistance is a level that for a period of time propels price action. It is a level or area where selling interest is strong enough to overcome buying pressure so that the price does not rise beyond the resistance level. Each time a level of resistance is penetrated it will take on a new level of support. See Peaks / Troughs, Trendline, Support Point.

Restricted Transferability Shares   In Switzerland, registered shares by which Swiss company statutes allow management the right to refuse voting power to some shareholders. German for this is "Vinkulierung."

Restructuring   A process whereby a borrower arranges to replace debt of one maturity with debt of another maturity. See Refinancing, Rescheduling.

Retained Profits   Profits earned for a company's equity holders and which are not distributed to the shareholders. Accumulated retained profits are reserves on the balance sheet.

Retention Scheme   An agreement by producers of a commodity whereby they each hold back an agreed percentage of their exports so as to maintain world prices or to push up depressed world prices. Usually producers continue to retain the percentage until various agreed trigger prices have been reached for a set period of time. As the world price rises, the percentage held back can be reduced. If the price continues to advance then the retention can fall to zero and, eventually, exports could be increased.

Retracement   Percentage retracements can be used to determine price objectives. Markets usually retrace previous moves by predictable percentages such as 33, 50 and 67 percent. The 33 and 67 are Dow Theory minimum and maximum retracements. The 50 retracement is the most important according to Gann. The Fibonacci number sequence refines these numbers to produce retracements of 61.8 (often rounded to 62 percent), 38 and 50 percent. A complete retracement of 100 percent of a prior move should also provide an area of support or resistance. Gann followers also see 12.5, 25, 75, and 87.5 percent as potential market turning points.

Return On Equity   Common financial yardstick expressing earnings as a percentage of equity capital and reserves showing how efficiently they are used.

Revaluation   Formal upward adjustment of a currency's official par value or central exchange rate. Opposite to Devaluation.

Revenue Anticipation Notes   See Municipal Notes.

Revenue Bonds   Municipals specifically issued to finance projects or enterprises.

Reversal   In technical analysis these patterns indicate that a major change in trend is likely to take place. They include the head and shoulders, triple top/bottom, double top/bottom, the rounding bottom/saucer and V-formation/spikes.

Reversal Arbitrage   A strategy combining a short underlying position with the simultaneous purchase of a call and sale of a put. Both options are normally European style with the same strike levels and expiry date. See Conversion Arbitrage.

Reversal Day   Setting of a new high in an uptrend followed by a lower close than the previous day's closing rate (or the previous two days' closing rates). A bottom reversal day would be a new low followed by a close above the previous day's closing rate. All one day reversals are potentially key reversals but only a few actually become such.

The key reversal day marks an important turning point but cannot be correctly identified until prices have moved significantly in the opposite direction to the previous trend.

An island reversal occurs when an upward exhaustion gap has formed, prices have traded in a narrow range for a few days or a week and a breakaway gap to the downside then occurs. This leaves the price action looking like an island which indicates a trend reversal.

Reversals can occur on any kind of bar chart and the longer the period, the more important the reversal. An upside weekly reversal occurs when the market makes a new low but then on a Friday closes above the previous Friday's close.

Reverse Cash and Carry Trade   See Cash and Carry Trade.

Reverse Crush   A hedging spread in which a processor sells soybean futures and buys soybean oil and soybean meal futures. Occurs when the cash market meets high soybean prices reflecting tight supplies and a Gross Processing Margin that is unfavourable or negative. Production is slowed down and this decline in soybean processing eases the tight supply position and curbs the rising prices. However, reduced processing also leads to increased price levels for oil and meal and so these factors together with reversal of hedging operations on the futures market - known as the reverse crush - tend to correct the unfavourable cost/price relationship. Eventually, when the negative margin returns to positive, the reverse crush will be closed out in the futures market, usually at a profit. See Putting On the Crush.

Reverse Repurchase Agreement   Known as a reverse repo or a matched sale/repurchase agreement. This is the reverse of a repo.

First transaction: a dealer purchases securities from an investor and therefore lends funds to an investor.

Second transaction: a dealer sells the securities back to an investor and receives funds back with interest.

By this operation the dealer is effectively a lender of funds and the investor a borrower. One can also say that the dealer lends through the process of purchasing and reselling securities back to the investor.

Reverse Stock Split Reduction of the outstanding shares of a company into a smaller number of shares without cost to the shareholders who retain their proportionate holdings. This is not as common as a stock split and is usually only seen when the share price is low. Also known as a negative stock split. See Stock Split.

Reverse Takeover Either where a company takes over a larger concern or where an unlisted company takes over a concern which is listed on a stock exchange.

Reverse Yield Gap Occurs in periods of high inflation when the yield on bonds rises above that on equities. Opposite to Yield Gap.

Revocable Credit Credit given under a Bill of Exchange which is revocable at any time without prior notice.

Revolving Line of Credit A bank line of credit for which customers pay fees and can then take money according to their needs. Also known as a revolver.

Revolving Underwriting Facility See RUFs.

Rheinisch-Westfälisches Institut Für Wirtschaftsforsch-hung See RWI.

Rho The measure of change in the value of an option compared with a percentage point change in the risk free rate of interest. See Delta, Gamma, Theta, Vega.

Rhodium A precious metal produced as a co-product of platinum and palladium. Main producer is South Africa. Chief use is as an auto catalyst in exhaust pollution control.

Rice An important cereal grain. The seed of a grass which matures at least once a year. Rice which is harvested but unprocessed is known as rough or paddy. Once the husk is removed it is termed brown or cargo. When the husk and outer bran layers have been removed it is known as milled, or polished, rice. Largest producers are China, with some 40 percent of world output and India with over 22 percent. A mere four percent of world output is exported. This is mostly from the U.S. and Thailand to West Asia and Africa.

Rights New ordinary shares which are offered to existing shareholders before the public. Unlike an ordinary share, rights do not have an indefinite life. Existing shareholders are normally granted a certain period to either subscribe to the new share or to sell the rights to another investor. Rights are offered via a rights offering at the subscription price which differs from the current market price (usually lower) to compensate existing shareholders for the increased share dilution. To have the right to subscribe, investors must own the share on the Record Date. The offer to subscribe is known as pre-emptive rights. See Warrant, Capitalisation Issue.

Ring Designated area on the floor of an exchange where futures trading takes place by way of Open Outcry. Also a five minute trading period in a single metal on the London Metal Exchange.

Riser Wide diameter pipeline linking an offshore oil platform to a subsea wellhead or spur line.

Risk The probability that a loss may occur on a trading position.
Various types of risk exist:
Aggregate risk
Basis risk
Business risk
Capital risk
Credit risk / Counterparty risk
Country risk / Sovereign risk
Currency risk
Economic risk
Inflation risk
Interest rate risk
Liquidity risk
Market risk / Systematic risk
Political risk
Reinvestment risk
Settlement risk
Specific risk / Non-systematic risk
Systemic risk
Taxation risk
Translation risk

Risk Factor Risk factors are the influences which affect the level of rates and the level of volatility in markets. In the money markets these can be supply and demand, central bank policy, and so forth.

Risk Free Return The annual rate of return on a high quality investment which is considered to be riskless.

Risk Management Steps taken to avoid loss on an outstanding position held in the financial markets. Most institutions use forwards, futures, options or a combination of these derivatives to hedge, or manage, risk.

Risk Management Adviser Advisers who support sales and trading personnel in the dealing room and who, together with customers, develop cost-effective solutions to risk management problems.

Risk Reversal An option strategy involving the purchase of a put and the sale of a call, or vice versa, with different strike levels. The premium generated from the sale of an option could partly or totally finance the premium to be paid for the purchase of an option. Also known as a cylinder, a break forward or range forward. See Zero Cost Options.

RMA See Risk Management Adviser.

RO / RO Roll on/roll off ships. They allow containers to be driven on and off, avoiding the use of cranes.

Road Fund Bonds - Belgium Bonds guaranteed by the central government and referred to by a number prefixed with a "4". There have been no such issues since 1988.

Robusta See Arabica / Robusta.

Rolled Gold Describes a gold alloy which has been bonded to another metal. The U.S. definition is that the gold alloy proportion to weight of the item is less than one twentieth. If more than that, it is termed gold filled.

Rollercoaster Swap An interest rate swap with a notional principal amount which can fluctuate periodically.

Rolling Settlement Settlement of securities taking place on a recurring cycle of a certain number of days from the trade date. This is the method adopted in the U.S. market, for example, and the opposite to a long running U.K. system of fixed account periods. The U.K. system is undergoing a change. See Account, Corporate Settlement.

Rolling Spot Rolling spot futures contracts mimic activity in spot foreign exchange where spot positions must be renewed or rolled over each day. Rolling spot removes the need to roll positions forward and has the advantage of being backed by a clearing house. Introduced by the Chicago Mercantile Exchange (CME) in June 1993. Rolling spot futures contracts exist for the sterling, German mark, Japanese yen and Swiss franc. Options contracts are also traded on these futures.

Rollover The periodic renewal of a loan, repriced at current market rates.

Rollover Date The date on which Floating Rate Notes pay their previous coupon and from when they start to accrue interest on their next coupon. Will often be used as a flat, i.e. free of accrued interest, settlement date.

Rondelles Cylindrical pellets, mostly used for nickel.

Rotterdam World's largest port, located in the Netherlands. Also a processing centre for soybeans and for producing feed compounds which are transported across continental Europe by barge, rail and road transport.

Rotterdam Market Nowadays a misnomer. With its storage and refinery facilities much of the port's oil business was mainstream carried out by the major companies. Later, prices for crude oil and products were quoted in Rotterdam for resellers and distributors with oil being moved by barge. Then, many of those small trading companies centred in the port moved away, many to London. Actual trading in the port is now either for barges or transfer of oil in tank. Thus, today's telecommunications allows traders around the world to operate in the so-called Rotterdam market because the Rotterdam market quotation is in effect a guide to prices in North West Europe.

Round Lot Trade A block of securities or commodities which is the most common trading unit in that market. In the equities market, practice is to trade in blocks of 100 shares or multiples thereof. However, some preferred shares which are expensive trade in smaller lots of 10, known as cabinet stocks. See Odd Lot Trade.

Round Turn Completed commodity futures transaction through an initial purchase and subsequent sale (or vice versa) of the same month, offsetting each other on the same market. Generally used when referring to commission charges, i.e. 10 sterling round turn.

Rounding Bottom / Saucer Another reversal pattern that is also commonly referred to as the saucer or bowl. It shows a very gradual change and at most times it is difficult to determine whether the rounding process has been completed. No precise measuring rules exist for the rounding formation but the size of the previous trend offers some indication of the potential retracement. The length of time it has been forming is important since the longer it takes, then the greater the potential move.

Royalty Share of the production or revenue reserved by whoever granted the oil lease or licence.

RP See Repurchase Agreement.

RRB - Canada The Real Return bond was launched by the Canadian government at the end of 1991 as an index linked bond. It has since been re-opened and will be issued on a regular basis.

RSI See Relative Strength Index.

RSS Ribbed, Smoked Sheet. A type of rubber.

Rubber World consumption in this market takes over 65 percent from synthetic rubber and over 30 percent from natural rubber. Nearly three quarters of total world natural rubber production is taken by the tyre industry.

Natural rubber producers include Brazil, China, India, Indonesia, Liberia, Malaysia, the Philippines, Sri Lanka and Thailand. The commodity is collected in cups from individual trees and consists of a milky white fluid which is in the form of 30 percent latex and 70 percent water.

Synthetic rubber is made mostly by industrial countries. It is a by-product of mineral oil and can reflect the price levels of that commodity.

RUFs A Revolving Underwriting Facility which allows the borrower to issue short term notes as required but containing an in-built underwriting agreement should the market be unable to provide funds. See NIFs.

Run-Up U.S. term for a quick rise in a share price.

Running Bales Term used in the cotton trade to designate the number of bales of cotton as they come from the gin in varying weights. See Cotton, Cotton Gin.

Rust Plant disease caused by fungi which reduces yields. One example is coffee rust.

Ruthenium A precious metal produced as a co-product of platinum and palladium.

RWI Rheinisch-Westfälisches Institut für Wirtschaftsforschung in Essen. One of six German research institutes which produce regular individual reports and in spring and autumn a joint report on the state of the economy.

Rye Widely grown cereal used for dark bread, alcohol and livestock feed. It is able to withstand cooler temperatures and poorer soils. Major producers are the Commonwealth of Independent States, Poland and Germany. Canada is a relatively small producer but exports a majority of its crop and accounts for a third of world trade. The CIS is the world's largest importer of rye.

S/B Sell after buy limit order. Two orders treated as one, the first order being to buy. If done, the sell order becomes valid. See B/S.

S/L A stop loss order is a limit order to buy or sell which operates only when a given price is reached. Such an order is normally placed to cut the losses on an existing position. Once the stop loss level is reached, the order is often executed at the next market price (particularly in volatile markets).

S/N Abbreviation for Spot/Next. Used in swap and deposit transactions when the first value date is spot value and maturity falls on the next working day. A S/N swap is priced according to the interest rate differential for that short period.

SA French term meaning Société Anonyme. Similar to the U.K. public limited company. Can be quoted on a stock exchange. The term is also used in Belgium and Switzerland.

SADC Southern Africa Development Community. Based in Botswana. Seeks to harmonise development and reduce economic dependence on South Africa. Formed with the aim of becoming a common market with a regional parliament. Replaced the informal Southern Africa Development Coordination Conference. Members are Angola, Botswana, Lesotho, Malawi, Mozambique, Namibia, Swaziland, Tanzania, Zambia and Zimbabwe.

Safe Haven Currency A major traded currency, such as the U.S. dollar or Swiss franc which, in times of political turmoil with world-wide ramifications, is used by investors and fund managers seeking a safe haven for their funds.

SAFEBBA Master Terms Terms and conditions laid down by the British Bankers Association governing the market practice and settlement procedures for Synthetic Agreements for Forward Exchanges (SAFEs), thus SAFEBBA.

SAFEs Synthetic Agreement for Forward Exchange. A collective name for Exchange Rate Agreements (ERA) and Forward Exchange Agreements (FXA). In the U.K., SAFEs are covered by official terms and conditions called SAFEBBA, published by the British Bankers Association.

Sallie Mae Student Loan Marketing Association. A publicly traded stock corporation which guarantees student loans traded on the secondary market.

SAMA Saudi Arabian Monetary Agency. Established in 1952 as the Central Bank of Saudi Arabia.

Sample Grade Usually the lowest quality of commodity acceptable for delivery under a futures contract.

Samurai Bond A bond issued in Japan by a foreign borrower denominated in yen. A type of foreign bond.

Satellite Field A small oil or gas reservoir in proximity to a larger field.

Saudi Arabian Monetary Agency. See SAMA.

SBF 120 Index The Société des Bourses Françaises (French Stock Exchange Association) 120 is an alternative index to the CAC 40 having a total of the 120 most active stocks drawn from both the official and the second market. Shares represent over 80 percent of bourse capitalisation and 90 percent of transactions. Calculated twice a day, at opening and closing. Trading began in December 1993.

Scaledown To buy at regular price intervals in a declining market. Opposite to Scaleup.

Scaleup To sell at regular price intervals in a rising market. Opposite to Scaledown.

Scalpers See Day Traders.

Scatter Chart In technical analysis, these charts illustrate the degree of correlation between two different instruments in a market showing the value for one plotted against the value of the other. The X axis has values for the first instrument and the Y axis portrays corresponding values for the second instrument. Scatter charts cannot be combined with other analyses on the same graph and limit minders cannot be set for them.

Schätze - Germany Officially known as Schatzanweisungen and are fixed coupon bullet bonds with maturities of four years. They are issued by the Bund and Agencies (Schätze), Unity Fund (U-Schätze) and the Treuhandanstalt (TOBLs - Treuhand Obligationen). Schätze have replaced the trading of Kassen.

Schengen Group Nine member nations of the European Community who have agreed to abolish formal passport controls at all internal frontiers. The nine are Belgium, France, Germany, Greece, Italy, Luxembourg, Netherlands, Portugal and Spain. They are in the process of bringing this into effect.

Screen Trading Trading conducted via an electronic system.

Scrip Issue See Capitalisation Issue.

SDRs See Special Drawing Rights.

SEC Securities and Exchange Commission, the official U.S. body responsible for regulatory oversight and administering rules associated with all sectors of the securities industry. Its main aim is to promote full public disclosure. This Federal agency came into being through the 1934 Securities Exchange Act and took over from the Federal Trade Commission.

SEC Filings In the U.S., companies are required to make Securities and Exchange Commission filings on various forms concerning their corporate activities. Some of the forms have also to be filed with the appropriate stock exchange.

Secondary Market Market for the buying and selling of previously issued securities involving non-primary dealers such as dealers and brokers. This market can take place on a regulated exchange or Over the Counter.

Secondary Market - Belgian Government Debt Belgian government bonds are listed on the Brussels Stock Exchange. The computerised system is known as the Obli-Cats system. However, most of the volume is traded OTC.

Secondary Market - BOBLs The initial Bundesobligationen selling period extends over one to three months, after which issues are officially listed on the eight domestic stock exchanges with a daily fixing. The Bundesbank provides liquidity during the fixing. These issues are actively traded in the OTC market.

Secondary Market - Bunds All bund issues are automatically listed on the eight German stock exchanges (Frankfurt, Düsseldorf, Hamburg, Munich, Stuttgart, Hanover, Bremen, Berlin) seven days after issuance, which then become the official market for bund trading, although an OTC market does exist. Prices are fixed at the stock exchange every day. The Bundesbank takes up a certain amount of the issue so as to provide liquidity during the fixing. Most of the bund trading is done on the Frankfurt Stock Exchange.

Secondary Market - Canadian Government Debt Canadian Treasury bills and Treasury bonds are not listed on the stock exchange. They are traded purely Over the Counter. Benchmarks exist in two, three, five, 10 and 30 year Treasury bonds. Treasury bills trade on a yield even though they are discount instruments. Treasury bonds are traded on a price basis. There is also a STRIP market.

Secondary Market - Dutch State Loans Secondary trading is handled domestically on the Amsterdam Stock Exchange. In June 1993 the ASE launched a trading system called the Amsterdam Treasury Bond Market (ATM) which allows direct dealings in government bonds exceeding 2.5 million guilders. Transactions below this amount must still be channelled and executed through jobbers. International trading takes place on the OTC market, particularly in London and Brussels. A grey market in London deals future new issues on a when issued basis. In 1990 the Dutch Ministry of Finance reduced the turnover tax on the ASE and introduced an Open Order Book System in an attempt to be as competitive as the other European stock exchanges.

Secondary Market - French Government Debt New government OATs are listed on the Paris Stock Exchange but most of the trading is dealt on the OTC market managed by the SVTs. The most actively traded bonds are the 10 and 30 year

OATs. The BTANs are not quoted on the Paris Stock Exchange but traded directly on the OTC market managed by the SVTs. The SVTs are most active in the secondary market. In 1987 they established an inter-dealer broker, PROMINOFI. They both quote prices in a when issued market several business days prior to the auction.

Secondary Market - Gold   Centres such as Hong Kong, Tokyo and Dubai are concerned solely with the distribution of gold which they have obtained from the primary market.

Secondary Market - Italian Government Debt   Despite the fact that all government bonds are traded on the Italian stock exchanges six months after issuance, most of the trading occurs OTC. CTEs, which can be stamped payable abroad one year after issue, are listed on the Luxembourg Stock Exchange.

Since new issues are announced five days before the auction, a when issued market commences until the auction date. The secondary market is regulated by 30 market makers who are obliged to show two-way prices on a screen based trading system (MTS) which is supervised by the Banca d'Italia.

A formal benchmark in the Italian market does not exist. The most recent issues per maturity sector is normally the most actively traded and tends to be recognised as a benchmark.

Secondary Market - Japanese Government Debt   The 10 and 20 year JGBs are listed on the Tokyo Stock Exchange. However most secondary trading takes place in the OTC market between securities houses and banks. Among the many market makers in the OTC market, which includes foreign securities houses, the four major Japanese securities houses are dominant. Many securities houses also benefit from a broker's market provided by the Japan Bond Trading Company. Secondary trading occurs in only a small number of issues and is monopolised by the trading in the benchmark issue.

Secondary Market - Schätze   Like bunds, Schätze are automatically listed on the eight German stock exchanges seven days following issuance. However, they are traded in an unregulated market, i.e. the Bundesbank does not influence liquidity at the fixing. OTC trading in this instrument is substantial.

Secondary Market - Swedish Government Debt   All bonds are listed on the stock exchange in Stockholm. Although no trading takes place there, all volumes handled in the OTC market are reported to the stock exchange. Benchmark issues can be represented by several issues.

Secondary Market - Swiss SGBs and SGNs   SGNs are only traded in the OTC market since they are bought deals. SGBs are listed on the stock exchanges in Zurich, Basle and Geneva.

Secondary Market - U.K. Gilts   Secondary market dealing in the U.K. is dominated by the GEMS (gilt edged market makers). Although dealing takes place over the telephone, this market is part of the London Stock Exchange.

Secondary Market - U.S. Treasuries   Primary dealers and brokers constantly provide bid and offers on U.S. Treasury issues in an OTC market. The main activities in the secondary market are the when issued market, the strip market and the repo market.

U.S. Treasuries are also listed on the New York Stock Exchange to accommodate overseas investors. In the when issued market, trading is on a discount basis for bills and on a yield basis for coupon instruments. However, once the results of the auction are announced, when issued trading is conducted on a price rather than a yield basis.

Secondary Metal Dealer   A firm which buys and sells scrap metal in either alloy or fabricated form. Its price can reflect that of the basic metal.

Secondary Metals   Product of refining scrap or alloys as opposed to primary metals produced from ore.

Secondary Offering   Re-offer of a large block of securities. Often undertaken by the sponsor that initially brought the deal to the market.

Secondary Recovery   Technique for recovering oil and gas from a reservoir by artificially maintaining or enhancing the reservoir pressure through the injection of gas, water or other substances into the reservoir rock.

Section 17   In Germany, under Section 17 of the Bundesbank law, the central bank was able to use for brief periods public authority funds that had been deposited with it so as to aid liquidity in the money markets. However, stemming from the terms of the Maastricht Treaty, from January 1 1994, central banks were not allowed to extend credits of any kind to government at any level, except other central banks, which it had done for those deposited funds. The public authority funds are now deposited with ordinary banks.

Sector Fund   A type of mutual fund which invests in one industry or in one geographical area only.

Sector Index   A stock exchange composite index that reflects the market activity of a particular industry.

Secular Trend   A market movement over the long term which does not reflect seasonal or technical factors.

Securities and Exchange Commission See SEC.

Securitising The exchanging of debt, often at below face value, for tradable instruments such as stocks and bonds. See Debt for Equity.

SEGA The Schweizerische Effecten-Giro AG is the Swiss clearing system for bonds and shares on a delivery versus payment (DVP) basis.

Seismic Survey Survey to establish the structure of underground rock by creating shock waves in the strata and then measuring the reflected vibrations.

SELA Sistema Económico LatinoAmericano (Latin American Economic System). Aims to accelerate economic and social development. Cooperates in such fields as technology and food. Members total 27 nations. Based in Caracas.

Selloff A selloff occurs when severe pressures depress prices and so instruments are sold to avoid further falls.

Semi Conductor A material - such as Silicon - whose electrical conductivity is between that of a metal and an insulator.

Semi-Submersible Rig Floating drilling platform that is supported by underwater pontoons and held in place by several anchors at each corner.

Senate Finance Committee Key U.S. Senate committee which is responsible for tax and other revenue bills.

Senior Secured Debt Secured debt which ranks first in terms of repayment in the event of a default.

Senior Unsecured Debt Securities which have priority ahead of all other unsecured or subordinated debt in ranking for payment in the event of default.

Sequestration Bill U.S. Presidential order imposing the spending cuts required to meet Gramm-Rudman-Hollings targets.

Sesame A herb plant whose seeds are used as food and flavouring for foods, notably breads and baked items. Sesameseed oil is used as a salad or cooking oil and also in making soaps, pharmaceuticals and lubricants. The residue after oil extraction is used as cattle feed. Major producers include India, China, Myanmar (Burma) and Sudan.

SET Index Capitalisation weighted arithmetic index of all listed shares on the Securities Exchange of Thailand.

Set-Aside Leaving land idle. It is part of U.S. and European Community policies to curb farm surpluses by encouraging farmers to take land out of agricultural production.

Settlement Date See Value Date.

Settlement Price See EDSP.

Settlement Risk The risk that an expected settlement amount will not be made on time. The establishment of netting systems is a direct consequence of efforts to minimise settlement risk. See Netting.

Severely Indebted Low Income Countries See SILICS.

SGBs - Switzerland Swiss government bonds are the most liquid of the government issues, are in bullet form and have a fixed coupon. Newer issues tend not to have a call feature as before. Maturities range from seven to 15 years and all carry a re-opening clause. Ten year SGBs are issued on a monthly basis.

SGNs - Switzerland Swiss government notes are illiquid since there are only a few remaining outstanding. They have a fixed coupon and are bullet issues.
    The SGBs dominate the Swiss government debt market.

Shale Oil Oil extracted from certain kinds of shale deposits. The shale is heated and resulting vapours are condensed and treated to form shale oil or synthetic oil.

Share A share represents ownership in a company and the right to receive a share in the profits of that company. In the U.S. a share is called a stock. See Ordinary Share, Preferred Share.

Share Discount The amount by which the market value of shares drops below par value. Significant for preferred shares which pay fixed dividends based on par value.

Share Premium The amount charged on the market value of shares in excess of par value.

Share Register The register which contains all relevant details of share ownership.

Shares Per Warrant Ratio A ratio measuring the amount of shares available through exercise of a warrant.

Shelf Registration In the U.S., this occurs when companies register securities they intend to issue in the future when market conditions are deemed to be favourable.

Shell Company Can be a non-trading company with a stock market quote. Also a dormant unquoted company.

Shibosai Bond Yen bond from a non-Japanese issuer, privately placed in Japan.

Shinkin Banks Generic term referring to major credit associations, financial institutions which are able to borrow from the nation's central bank, the Bank of Japan, for money market purposes.

Shogun Bond   Public offering in Japan of a non-yen bond by a non-resident of Japan.

Shoko Chukin Bank   The Central Bank for Commercial and Industrial Cooperatives, a financial institution which is able to borrow from the Bank of Japan, the nation's central bank, for money market purposes.

Short Bill   A bill of exchange payable on demand or within a very short time.

Short First Coupon   The first interest payment on a recently issued bond that includes less than the normal semi-annual or annual payment.

Short Hedge   The sale of a futures or option position to protect against a decrease in price in the corresponding cash market. Opposite to Long Hedge. See Hedge.

Short Margin Account   An account requiring a margin deposit from investors who are involved in short selling as opposed to buying on margin.

Short Position   A position showing a sale or an excess of sales over purchases in anticipation of a fall in prices. A short position can be closed out through the purchase of an equivalent amount. Buying back from a short position is known as shortcovering. Selling into a market without a prior long position is called short selling. See Long Position.

Short Selling   The selling of instruments which are not held, i.e. with no prior long position, in anticipation of a fall in prices. The action of buying back to cover the short position is known in the market as shortcovering.

Short Straddle   An option strategy combining the sale of a call and a put with the same expiry date and strike price in anticipation of very little movement in the underlying. Premium income is generated from both short option positions.

Short Strangle   An option strategy combining the sale of a call and a put with the same expiry date but different strike prices in anticipation of very little movement in the underlying. Since the strike prices are Out of the Money, less premium income is generated than from a short straddle.

Short Term Treasury Bills - Japan   Discount security introduced in 1986 and issued by monthly auction with maturities of three and six months. They are issued for foreign exchange intervention purposes and Treasury revenue. The Bank of Japan purchases any portion which remains unsubscribed.

Short Ton   Ton of 2,000 pounds weight or 0.907 tonne.

Short-Dated Forwards / Deposits   Forward foreign exchange and deposit transactions which show the value date before spot value (O/N, T/N) and from spot (S/N) to one month.

Short-Dated Gilts - U.K.   U.K. Treasury debt issues with a maturity of up to five years.

Shortcovering   The buying back of a financial instrument previously sold so as to close out a short position. Also known as bear covering. See Short Position.

Shout Option   An option which allows the holder to lock in a minimum return if he believes that the market is at its high or low. The shout only operates at the level "shouted" and is thus more restrictive than a lookback where the option can be exercised at the lowest price (call) or highest (put) regardless of subsequent price movements.

SIBOR / SIBID / SIMEAN   The Singapore Interbank Offered Rate (SIBOR) is the rate at which banks are prepared to lend to each other for specified maturities within the Singapore market. SIBOR is also fixed daily for reference purposes and is a key interest rate level used for setting rates for loans and floating rate notes and for calculating cash settlements of certain interest rate derivative instruments. SIBID is the Singapore Interbank Bid Rate, the rate at which banks take deposits from each other. SIMEAN is the Singapore Interbank Mean Rate.

SICAV   Société d'Investissement à Capital Variable. In France and Luxembourg, these are investment funds similar to the U.S. mutual funds and U.K. unit trusts.

SICOVAM   Société Interprofessionnelle pour la Compensation des Valeurs Mobilières is the Paris Stock Exchange clearing organisation. SICOVAM settles the securities side of a transaction whereas the Banque de France settles the cash side.

Sideways Market   Occurs in a market where, for a period of time, price movements up and down are small and restricted to a narrow range. It is also often referred to as a trendless, congested or ranging market.

Sight Draft   See Bills of Exchange.

Sight Money   See Call Money.

Signalling   Since most equity price movements are based on perceptions of future performance, signals sent out by the company are extremely important. Typical signals would be advance information about expected future earnings and dividend payments. The markets will then tend to respond to these signals while also waiting for positive correlation when the actual figures are announced.

Silage   Animal feed made by storing and fermenting green plants including grass and maize (corn).

Silicon Chips   The basis of most memory and logic circuits in computers. Silicon is used because of its properties as a semiconductor and because it is abundant and therefore cheap.

SILICS   Severely Indebted Low Income Countries. The poorest developing nations with heavy debt burdens, mostly located in sub-Saharan Africa. Their debt is owed mostly to governments and international financial institutions.

Silo   A pit or airtight structure in which green crops are pressed and kept for fodder, undergoing fermentation. Also, a pit or tower to store grain.

Silver   A precious metal used extensively in jewellery and silverware and, industrially, in photography, x-ray equipment and electronics. Silver has excellent heat and electricity conducting properties. Major producers include Mexico, Peru, the Commonwealth of Independent States, Canada, Australia and the U.S. Silver, along with gold, is one of the world's oldest traded investment commodities. Traded in lacs. See Silver Lac.

Silver Fix   See Precious Metals Fixings.

Silver Lac   The main trading unit of silver. A standard silver lac in the spot market is 100,000 troy ounces.

SIMEAN   See SIBOR / SIBID / SIMEAN.

SIMEX   The Singapore International Monetary Exchange Ltd. (SIMEX) was inaugurated in 1984 to become the first financial futures exchange in Asia. The exchange has the world's first mutual offset trading link with the Chicago Mercantile Exchange (CME), allowing 24 hour trading as positions at one exchange can be transferred to or liquidated at the other exchange. In 1989, SIMEX also became Asia's leading energy market as the High-Sulphur Fuel Oil futures contract was launched. Other contracts include the Three Month Eurodollar, Euroyen and Euromark future, the Japanese Government Bond future, the Nikkei Stock Average future, dollar/yen, dollar/mark and sterling/dollar future and gold future. Option contracts are traded on the Eurodollar and Euroyen future and the Nikkei Stock Average future.

Simple Interest   Simple interest is the cost of borrowing or the return on lending money. This cost or return is based on three elements: - the amount borrowed or lent which is called the principal, the rate of interest and the amount of time. See Compound Interest.

Simple Moving Average (SMA)   Used in technical analysis. The simple moving average is a trend-following indicator. A moving average is created by adding and then averaging a set of data over a constant number of periods. Calculations usually look at closing prices but can also use High and Lows or a High-Low-Close combination.

A bullish signal exists when prices rise above the simple moving average and the moving average turns up.

A bearish signal exists when prices fall below the simple moving average and the moving average turns down.

Singapore International Monetary Exchange   See SIMEX.

Single Monthly Mortality   A measure - expressed as a percentage - of the outstanding principal prepaid each month on a mortgage backed security.

Sinking Fund   Regular mandatory prepayments by a borrower regardless of price movements in the secondary bond market to redeem a certain amount of an issue through payments to a special account, thus reducing the principal amount due at maturity. See Pro Rata Sinking Fund, Purchase Fund.

SIR   Standard Indonesian Rubber.

Sisal   Plant that produces fibre used for ropes and cords.

Sistema Económico LatinoAmericano   See SELA.

Skip Day Trade   Trade which is settled one day after the normal settlement date.

Slow Stochastics   Slow stochastics uses the fast stochastics method but tends to give less sensitive responses to market movement and, as a consequence, tends to be preferred by traders.

For slow stochastics, the %K is actually the same as the %D in the fast stochastics. The %D for the slow system is a moving average of the slow %K.

Interpretation of overbought and oversold signals, as well as divergences between price and the stochastic analysis, are the same as for fast stochastics. See Stochastics, Fast Stochastics.

Smelting   The initial metallurgical processing of ore or scrap/residues.

SMI   Swiss Market Index. A capitalisation weighted arithmetic index comprising the most important and liquid securities traded on the Zurich, Geneva and Basle bourses. Calculated when a share price changes. Futures and options on the index are traded on the Swiss Options and Financial Futures Exchange (SOFFEX).

Smithsonian Agreement   Major exchange rate adjustments were agreed by the Group of 10 nations in Washington in 1971 as well as a devaluation of the U.S. dollar against gold to 38 dollars per ounce from 35 dollars. A number of key currencies returned to fixed rates relative to the newly devalued dollar with an allowed fluctuation margin of 2.25 percent either side of the new central rates. Some currencies retained their former dollar parity with the overall depreciation of the dollar coming out at around seven percent. Agreement was also reached on suspension of the U.S. import surcharge.

SMR   Standard Malaysian Rubber.

Snake   Preceded the European Monetary System. The aim was for member nations' currencies (including non-European Community) to move together like a snake, within a tunnel, when matched against an outside currency like the U.S. dollar. See European Monetary System (EMS).

Society for Worldwide Interbank Financial Telecommunication   See SWIFT.

SOFFEX   The Swiss Options and Financial Futures Exchange (SOFFEX), based in Dietikon (Canton of Zurich), was founded in 1986 and trading began in May 1988. It provides a fully electronic exchange (no open outcry) for traded options and financial futures. SOFFEX also has a fully integrated clearing system. Contracts include the SMI Index future and option, the Swiss Government Bond future and option and standard stock options.

Soft Loan   Can carry an interest rate below the real cost of borrowing or no interest rate at all. The International Development Association - the World Bank affiliate - provides soft loans to developing countries for long term capital projects.

Sogo Sosha   Very large Japanese trading companies.

Sorghum   Grain grown in warmer climates which competes with maize (corn) and is largely used for animal feed. In the U.S., it is also called Milo. Major producers include the U.S., Mexico, China, India, Argentina and Nigeria.

Sour Crude   High sulphur content crude oil.

Sour Gas   Natural or associated gas which has a high sulphur content.

South African Krugerrand   A gold coin which was first minted in 1967. Its special feature is that it contains exactly one ounce of fine gold which facilitates price comparisons with bullion gold.

South Asian Association for Regional Cooperation   Cooperation has been agreed within a wide range of economic and social sectors. Members are Bangladesh, Bhutan, India, Maldives, Nepal,. Pakistan and Sri Lanka.

South-South   General expression for any liaison that may take place between, loosely, the developing nations of the Southern hemisphere.

Southern Africa Development Community   See SADC.

Sovereign Risk   See Country Risk.

Soybean   The dominant world oilseed taking 50 percent of total world oilseed production. The U.S. soybean crop accounts for a quarter of total world oilseed output. Other major producers are Brazil, China and Argentina. The main value of soybeans is in the products - meal and oil. Soybean meal is the world's leading protein meal with some two thirds of world meal output. It is produced mainly as a high protein ingredient for poultry and animal feed with some being processed further into coarsely ground soy grits, flour or isolated protein for use in human foods. Crude soybean oil is further refined and used in salad and cooking oils, margarines, prepared foods, industrial chemicals. Soybean oil is the world's leading vegetable oil with nearly one third of world vegetable oil output.

SPAN   Standard Portfolio Analysis Risk is a method of assessing margin requirements based on a total portfolio analysis. Originated at the Chicago Mercantile Exchange (CME) but has been adopted by other exchanges.

Special Committee On Agriculture   European Community committee which groups the top agricultural experts in each of the national permanent delegations to the EC with national governmental and European Commission representatives. Its task is to try to establish what is politically feasible in the EC agricultural sector.

Special Drawing Rights (SDRs)   A currency basket with specific weightings of major traded currencies (U.S. dollar, sterling, German mark, French franc and Japanese yen). Created by the International Monetary Fund in 1969 as an international reserve asset to supplement existing reserve assets. The IMF uses SDRs for book-keeping purposes. See Ordinary Drawing Rights (ODRs).

Special Situation Fund   An investment fund offering new investment opportunities by investing in companies which have recently emerged from insolvency or in companies which are candidates for a takeover.

Specialist   A stock exchange member located at the trading post who keeps an orderly market in the shares for which he is listed as a specialist and thus he can buy and sell for his own account as needed. He is also a broker's broker. When a commission broker on the floor has a client order he can leave it, if wished, with the specialist who is obliged to act in the customer's best interest.

Specific Gravity   Ratio of density of a substance at a particular temperature to the density of water at 4 degrees Centigrade.

Specific Risk The risk associated with investing all in only one security. Diversification will protect an investor from this risk. Also known as non-systematic risk.

Specifications Refers to properties of a given crude oil or refined petroleum product. The properties are specified as they often vary widely even within the same grade of product.

Speculation The act of taking a long or short position in the market in anticipation of a favourable move, which should result in a gain when the position is covered. Also refers to investors' general belief that a certain specific event may occur.

Speculative Stock Stock which carries a higher level of risk, in terms of price and company performance.

Speculator A recognised participant in most markets who tries to anticipate price changes with a view to making profits. Generally, the speculator has no long term interest in the underlying physical commodity or financial instrument.

Speedlines Used in technical analysis. An adaptation of dividing a trend into thirds (33, 66 percent and so forth) which are then used as support or resistance areas in retracements. The chief difference is that speedlines measure the rate of rise or fall in a trend, i.e. its speed. A speedline is constructed by finding the high or low point in an uptrend or downtrend and producing a vertical line to where the trend began. This vertical line is then divided into thirds and a trendline is drawn from the trend beginning through the 33 and 66 percent points on the vertical line. In an uptrend, a correction will usually halt at the higher (66 percent) speedline and if not, then prices usually drop to the lower (33 percent). If the lower speedline is broken, prices will probably return to the start of the prior trend. Speedlines reverse roles when they are broken and, in a correction to an uptrend, would change from support to resistance.

Spikes See V-Formation / Spikes.

Spin Off Method used by a company to split its operations and assets by proportionately distributing shares it holds in a company to its own shareholders. Also termed hive off.

Sponsor Term used for the investment or merchant bank that advises on, makes prices and brings a new issue to the market.

Spontaneous Lending New lending which is not intended to provide the funds needed to repay interest and principal on pre-existing loans.

Spot Commodity The actual physical commodity as distinguished from the futures.

Spot Dealer A dealer who specialises in the trading of currencies in the spot market.

Spot Deferred Gold Sales Similar to forward gold sales except that the date of sale usually gets deferred many times before the gold is ulimately delivered. The contango may vary at each deferral or roll forward. The spot deferral contract offers producers considerable flexibility in managing revenue since they need use only as many spot deferred contracts as required to realise a certain gold price on their total sales. See Forward Gold Sales.

Spot Market A market whose trades deliver and settle immediately (normally two working days ahead). Also known as cash market.

Spot Month The nearest dated futures contract.

Spot Next See S/N.

Spot Price Today's market price of a currency. Settlements normally take place two working days from the trade date.

Spot Yield Curve See Zero Coupon Yield Curve.

Spout Trimmed A vessel loaded with a bulk cargo trimmed or levelled off. Commodities such as grains are often spout trimmed which means they are loaded by a spout or chute which ensures level loading.

Spread Difference in a quotation between buying and selling prices. A large spread normally indicates inactive trading of a product and is known as a wide opening.

Can also be used to express the difference in yields between two fixed income securities of the same quality but different maturities or of different quality but same maturities (Ted Spread).

A futures spread is the difference in prices between delivery months in the same or different markets.

An option spread is the combination of two calls or two puts on the same underlying. See Bear Spread, Bull Spread.

Spread Moving Average In technical analysis, uses the basis of a simple moving average but portrays the spread, or the difference, between the corresponding values for two different instruments, such as closing prices, yields, or current market prices.

Spread Trading The purchase of one futures contract and the simultaneous sale of another in order to take advantage of expected price discrepancies. A long spread is created by the purchase of a nearby contract against a sale of a deferred contract. A short spread is created by the sale of a nearby contract and the purchase of a deferred contract. A much followed spread trade is the Ted Spread.

Spudding in   Beginning to drill an oil/gas well by making a hole with a large diameter bit.

Square Position   See Flat Position.

Squeeze   Pressure exerted on one commodity's delivery, usually spot, when the price is exaggerated (upwards) against the rest of the market.

SSAP   Statements of Standard Accounting Practice. They dictate the presentation of a company's financial accounts.

STABEX   European Community programme for helping developing countries under the Lomé Convention by stabilising export commodity earnings, i.e. by providing EC subsidies for those countries in the scheme whose earnings fall below a certain level.

Stabiliser / Budgetary Stabiliser   European Community mechanisms under which farm support prices are cut and/or the co-responsibility levy is increased if EC production exceeds a fixed ceiling.

Stag   Operator who applies for a new security on the chance of selling it, on allotment, at a premium over the issue price. See Oversubscribed.

Stagflation   An economy where rising inflation is accompanied by falling or static industrial production and employment.

Standard & Poor's 100 Stock Index   This index is calculated on the same basis as the S&P 500 and comprises mainly New York Stock Exchange industrials.

Standard & Poor's 500 Stock Index (S&P 500)   A market capitalisation weighted arithmetic index that represents some 80 percent of the market value of all issues traded on the New York Stock Exchange. Thus it comprises 500 shares, mainly NYSE listed firms plus some from the American Stock Exchange and Over the Counter issues. Calculated every 15 seconds. The Chicago Mercantile Exchange (CME) trades futures and futures options on the index. Index options are traded at the Chicago Board Options Exchange (CBOE).

Standard & Poor's Corporation Records   A reference service containing detailed information on a large number of publicly held companies. The section known as Stock Data provides information regarding the privileges and features of each class of ordinary shares issued by each company. This service is updated on a quarterly basis.

Standard Deviation   A mathematical measurement assessing the degree to which an individual value

in a probability distribution may vary from the mean of the distribution. A majority of the calculations fall within one standard deviation which represents 68 percent of the prices. Used as a method of assessing risk factors. See Volatility.

Standard Line Agreement (CP)   The standard back-up facility for commercial paper which when tapped allows the borrowers 90 day notes.

Standard Periods   The most common periods quoted and traded in the forward and deposit markets are, one, two, three, six, nine months and one year. Any other date falling outside these standard periods are broken or odd dates. Short dates are considered to be any value date up to one month.

Standby Boat   Vessel maintaining permanent station near an offshore structure to provide support facilities in an emergency.

Standby Credit   Arrangement with a lender (either a group of banks or the International Monetary Fund in the case of a member country) whereby a fixed amount of credit will be available for drawing during a given period, if required.

Standby Loan   The basic International Monetary Fund sovereign loan, usually over one or two years, aimed at overcoming short term balance of payments difficulties. Loan conditions are focused on macro-economic policies.

State Planning   Regulation by the state of a sector of the economy using state appointed administrators who do not bow to the forces of a free market economy in their sector. See Planned Economy, Market Economy, Mixed Economy, Parastatal.

Step Down Bonds   Debt which has a coupon which decreases over time at given increments on given dates. Opposite to Step Up Bonds.

Step Down Swap   An interest rate swap whereby the notional principal decreases by one or more steps over a period. Opposite to Step Up Swap. See Amortising Rate Swap.

Step Out Well   Oil well drilled away from a discovery well to assess the reservoir area.

Step Up Bonds   Debt which has a coupon which increases over time at given increments on given dates. Opposite to Step Down Bonds.

Step Up Swap   An interest rate swap whereby the notional principal increases by one or more steps over a period. Opposite to Step Down Swap. See Accreting Principal Swap.

Stepped Up Coupon   A bond which pays a below market coupon in the first few years, rising to above market coupon later. These bonds are usually created to minimise investors' near term tax liabilities. Stepped down coupons can also be offered to lenders.

Sterling CDs   Certificates of Deposit issued by the London banks, in sterling, for periods between three months and five years. For periods of less than one year interest is paid on maturity and for issues of over a year paid annually.

Stochastics   Used in technical analysis. The stochastics process is a momentum indicator based on the observation that in a rising market closing prices tend to be closer to the top end of a price range. Conversely, in a falling market they tend to be near the bottom end of the range. There are two types of stochastics methods used. See Fast Stochastics, Slow Stochastics.

Stock   The U.S. equivalent of a share. In the U.K., mainly refers to gilt edged bonds (government stock).

Stock Average   An arithmetic average. Also referred to as an index. See Stock Index.

Stock Derivatives   A generic term for stock options, warrants and rights, both Over the Counter and exchange-traded. A holder of such contracts does not receive the same benefits as the owner of a share.

Stock Dividend   A dividend paid to a company's shareholders in the form of authorised but hitherto unissued shares.

Stock Exchange   A trading floor or screen based auction market, in which members of the exchange come together to buy and sell securities.

Stock Index   A composite measure of the movement of a market as a whole consisting of a large number of shares which are usually representative of various sectors of industry. Indices usually carry some form of weighting which can reflect, for example, the differing importance of components or market capitalisation. See Weighted Index.

Stock Index Fund   A type of Mutual Fund which invests in a group of securities from a particular stock market index.

Stock Index Futures   These contracts, traded on exchanges, are settled on a cash basis at maturity since the underlying index cannot be physically delivered. The cost of the future is adjusted to reflect forthcoming dividends during the contract's life to which the holder is not entitled. The contract cost can also increase when the underlying shares are at a high level. Trading volume in the various futures markets can often be greater than in the underlying cash market. Two leading examples are the Standard & Poor's 500 which is traded on the Chicago Mercantile Exchange (CME) and is the most heavily traded index futures contract. Contender for the volume title is the Osaka Stock Exchange on the Nikkei 225 index.

Stock Lending   Lending of shares by long term holders, such as institutions, when shares are in short supply. Often an investment house will not actually take delivery of the stock but will use it as an underlying instrument in a derivatives strategy.

Stock Option   See Equity Options.

Stock Split   Division of the outstanding shares of a company into a larger number of shares, without cost to the shareholders who retain their proportionate holdings. This is called a positive stock split and is a move made by companies who believe that a lower unit price will promote share liquidity. By increasing the number of shares, they consequently lower the price to attract investors from a broader economic range. Opposite to a Reverse Stock Split.

Stockbroker   A company, or individual, providing execution of trades, and/or investment advice, to the customer base, both individual and institutional while not acting as a principal.

Stockist   Specialised firms who keep semi-fabricated products for sale to actual users. Copper tubing for plumbing is an example.

Stocky   Dealers' language for the Swedish crown.

Stop and Reverse Points   See Parabolic Time Price.

Stop Loss Order   See S/L.

Stop-Gap Bonds   See Government Bonds - Japan.

Stope   A place to extract ore inside a mine.

Stowed   Cargo packed and secured for a voyage.

Straddle   An option strategy involving one call and one put with the same strike and same expiry date. See Long Straddle, Short Straddle.

Straight Bond   See Bullet Bond.

Strangle   An option strategy involving one call and one put with different strike levels but with the same expiry date. See Long Strangle, Short Strangle.

Strategic Metals   See Minor Metals.

Street Name   See Nominee Account.

Strike Price   The price agreed at the opening of an option contract and at which the option may be exercised. Also known as the exercise price.

STRIP Market - Canada   This market was created for Canadian government bonds at the start of 1980. STRIPS are held in registered form with a specific identification number and are therefore not inter-changeable with other STRIPS.

The stripped bond market is known in the Canadian markets as the residual market. See U.S. STRIPS.

Stripped MBS Mortgage Backed Securities which are split and divided into interest only securities (IO) and principal only securities (PO).

Stripper Well Onshore oil well that produces less than 10 barrels per day. It is, nevertheless, uneconomical to shut it down on a temporary basis.

STRIPS See U.S. STRIPS.

Structural Adjustment Reform of the structure of a whole economy. Mostly used in the context of Structural Adjustment Programmes promoted by the International Monetary Fund (IMF) and the World Bank. Designed to bring about open markets, to liberalise trade, to cut deficits generally and so forth. In the case of the IMF, this usually means recipient nations have to agree on such plans, or at least on some broad outline, before funds become available.

Student Loan Marketing Association See Sallie Mae.

Sub-Sea Wellhead Wellhead installed on the sea floor and controlled remotely from a platform or floating production facility or from land.

Subject Order An order given to purchase or sell securities but which cannot be executed without further reference to the customer giving the order.

Subordinated Debt Debt which ranks for repayment of principal behind debt senior to it.

Subrogation Term used when an insurer who has paid a claim assumes all rights of redress against third parties responsible for the loss.

Subscription Purchase of newly issued securities.

Subscription Offering - Canada The procedure whereby the government announces details of a forthcoming issue to the primary distributors. The Ministry of Finance then fixes the issue size based on the initial interest shown by the primary distributors. Once the issue size is announced, the primary distributors are invited to take a part or all of their quota.

Subsidiarity Within the European Community, this is a right sought by member nations to allow their respective governments to take their own decisions in some fields on some occasions.

Subsidiary A company of which more than 50 percent of its voting stock is owned by the parent company.

Sugar Sugar is derived from both sugar beet and sugar cane and traded either raw or white. One

tonne of white (refined) sugar roughly equals 1.087 tonnes of raw sugar.

Cuba is the world's largest single sugar exporter. The European Community is the largest collective producer and India the largest single producer but both are also large consumers. China and Brazil are likewise major producers and consumers. Australia and Thailand are major producers and exporters. The U.S. is a major consumer.

Sugar Beet The most important source of sugar in temperate countries. The crop is harvested in the autumn and early winter. The European Community and the Commonwealth of Independent States are the biggest beet producers.

Sugar Cane Provides more than 60 percent of the world's supply of sugar. The crop is planted by stem cuttings and the first harvest is ready about a year later. After cutting, the plants grow successive crops of stems which take about the same period to mature. Crop years vary widely. This wide variation in national crop years means that output forecasts have to be specified based on the national period and that supply and demand forecasts also have to be period-specified and sometimes include proportions of output estimates from two national crop years.

Sunflowerseed A major oilseed crop yielding more oil and less meal than soybeans per unit weight of oilseed. Major producers include the Commonwealth of Independent States, Argentina, China, France and the U.S.

Sunshine Laws Laws in the U.S. which allow maximum public disclosure on governmental bodies and including organisations in charge of securities trading regulations.

Super Digital Information Highway U.S. vision embracing the multi-media concept which can deliver to the consumer's home via one link full inter-active television, videos on demand, both cable and satellite television, consumer shopping, direct banking, financial services, telephonic communication, fax, bulletin boards, educational services, medical consultation, personal computing time and so forth.

Super Long Term Treasury Bonds - Japan Fixed rate bonds issued in Japan on a regular basis throughout the year with a maturity of 20 years and a semi-annual coupon.

Super Voting Shares A type of share capital structure not often seen outside the U.S. in which certain shares, on being issued, give the holder increased voting rights.

Supplementary Levy Additional levy charged on imports of certain farm products under the

European Community Common Agricultural Policy.

Supply / Demand The amount of sellers, who provide market supplies, and buyers, who create market demand. Supply and demand is a major influence in generating the market price.

Supply Side Economics Theory that tax cuts, and similar measures, will boost investment in production and increase the supply of goods in the economy.

Support Point Support is a level that supports market price action for a period of time. It is a level where buying interest is strong enough to overcome selling pressure so that the market does not break beyond that level. Each time a level of support is penetrated it will take on the new role of resistance. See Resistance Point, Peaks / Troughs, Trendline.

Surplus The difference when income, or revenue, is greater than expenditure. Opposite to Deficit.

Sushi Bond Non-yen bond issued abroad by a Japanese company to Japanese residents. These bonds offer a way for Japanese companies to increase foreign currency holdings.

Suspension A company's shares can be temporarily suspended, either voluntarily by the company or by the relevant stock exchange, when a key announcement is expected shortly. Longer or permanent suspension can be imposed by a stock exchange for failure to comply with listing requirements or numerous other reasons.

SVTs Spécialistes en Valeurs du Trésor, established in 1987, comprises a group of banks and brokers who have a combined role of primary dealers and market makers in the French government bond markets. Officially appointed by the government in an attempt to eliminate the legal monopoly of French stock exchange brokers in these markets. Candidates for the status of SVT are known as CVTs, Correspondants en Valeurs du Trésor.

Swap Yield Curve An interest rate yield curve derived from market swap rates.

Swaps The exchange of one asset for another. See FX Swap, IRS, Currency Swap.

Swaption An option on an interest rate swap, giving the holder the right, but not the obligation, to enter into an interest rate swap as either the payer or receiver of the fixed side of the swap.

Sweden - Key Interest Rates The rate to watch is:
    Marginal lending/deposit rate - sets the tone for money market rates.
    The key rate is the marginal lending/deposit rate at which banks can borrow funds from, or deposit them with, the central bank (Riksbank).

The Riksbank's repurchase agreements relate to the marginal rate since this is an alternative source of funds for commercial banks. Thus, the repo rate follows the marginal rate. From the marginal rate, money market traders derive the overnight interbank rate. Money market and official rates seldom diverge by more than 10 basis points. The marginal rate can either be a lending or a deposit rate depending on whether banks are short of funds or have excess reserves. In August 1993, for example, it was the deposit rate but, out of force of habit, money market traders and the media still called it the marginal lending rate.

Until Spring 1993, the repo was the main window for policy changes. Since then, however, the main forum for marginal rate changes has been the Riksbank's board meeting.

There is an interest rate scale for loans from, or deposits with, the Riksbank set according to each commercial bank's capital base. The more a bank borrows from the central bank, the higher the point on the scale (interest rate) it has to pay.

The Riksbank sets both currency and interest rate policy. It is accountable to Parliament and not just the ruling party in government. Formally, interest rate decisions are taken by the Riksbank council which has eight members including the central bank governor and seven others elected by parliament for three years. Council members can be chosen from inside or outside Parliament and are elected in proportion to the representation of political parties in Parliament. The Riksbank's independence from political pressure, as opposed to just pressure from the government, depends on how many external members are elected.

Swedish National Debt Office (Riksgälden) As part of the Ministry of Finance, the Swedish National Debt Office is a government agency responsible for the Kingdom of Sweden's domestic and international borrowings.

Sweet Crude Crude oil with a low sulphur content such as those from North Africa, Nigeria and the North Sea.

SWIFT The Society for Worldwide Interbank Financial Telecommunication (SWIFT) is jointly owned by over one thousand banks and operates a standard means of effecting international banking transactions over its network. See CHAPS, CHIPS.

SWIFT Codes The coded instructions used by SWIFT, the Society for Worldwide Interbank Financial Telecommunications, for effecting international banking transactions over its network.

Swing Line A credit facility allowing borrowers to take money overnight.

Swiss Confederation   Issuer of Swiss government bonds (SGBs) and Swiss government notes (SGNs). The Swiss government debt market is relatively small due to budget surpluses of the past and a 35 percent witholding tax which traditionally deterred international investors. The government issues represent a very small proportion of the Swiss bond market.

Swiss Market Index   See SMI.

Swiss Options and Financial Futures Exchange   See SOFFEX.

Swissy   Dealers' language for the Swiss franc.

Switch   The exchanging of one security for another. A switch is often used to improve a portfolio, perhaps to enhance the yield or quality.

Switzerland - Key Interest Rates   The rates to watch are:

Overnight rate - indicates the liquidity situation in the money market.

Discount rate - purely of symbolic importance.

Lombard rate (floating) - of limited operational significance.

The Swiss National Bank (SNB) does not set a guiding money market rate but instead controls interest rates by regulating market liquidity. The level of banks' reserves at the central bank (sight deposits, a component of monetary base) and the overall level of money market rates are the key indicators of the SNB's monetary policy stance. Foreign currency operations have long been the main instrument for determining the monetary base and hence the money supply and interest rates. Currency swaps are by far the Bank's favourite tool.

The discount rate is now only symbolic and there are currently no transactions under the discount facility. Nevertheless, the discount rate is still an important way for the SNB to signal or confirm a shift in its views on market rates. If the discount rate is raised or lowered, it indicates that the central bank views a change in money market rates as permanent and unlikely to be reversed immediately.

Lombard borrowings have not been significant since May 1989 when the lombard rate was floated. The lombard rate is set two percentage points above the average money market (call) rate over the previous two days.

The central bank has increasingly used repos to manage the banking system's short term liquidity needs since they were introduced in September 1992.

The SNB sets monetary policy. The statutes under which it operates state that the government and the SNB must inform one another before important decisions are made. However, responsibility for both interest rate and exchange rate policy lies with the SNB.

Syndicate   See Lead Manager.

Syndicated Loan   A large sized loan which will be arranged by a group of banks that form a syndicate, headed by the Lead Manager.

Synthetic Agreement for Forward Exchange   See SAFEs.

Synthetic Long Call   A position synthetically established by the purchase of a put option and a long underlying position. The long position in the underlying offers unlimited profit potential from rising prices. The purchased put ensures limited loss from falling prices.

Synthetic Long Put   A position synthetically established by the purchase of a call option and a short underlying position. The short position in the underlying offers unlimited profit potential from falling prices. The purchased call ensures limited loss from rising prices.

Synthetic Long Spot   A position synthetically established by the purchase of a call option and the sale of a put option with the same strike price and expiry date.

Synthetic Natural Gas   Gas made from coal or oil. It has the same basic chemical composition and burning characteristics as natural gas.

Synthetic Short Call   A position synthetically established by the sale of a put option and a short underlying position.

Synthetic Short Put   A position synthetically established by the sale of a call option and a long underlying position.

Synthetic Short Spot   A position synthetically established by the purchase of a put option and the sale of a call option with the same strike price and expiry date.

Systematic Risk   Risk that cannot be diversified away as it is the risk of market movements or of market segment movements. Also known as market risk.

Systematic Transformation Facility   A temporary facility created by the International Monetary Fund in 1993 to provide special financial assistance to the states of the former Soviet Union and Eastern Europe during their transition to market economies.

Systemic Risk   The risk associated with a change in the overall financial system.

T/N   Abbreviation for tomorrow/next or tom/next. Used in swap and deposit transactions when the first value date is tomorrow (tom) and maturity falls on the next working day (spot). The T/N swap price has an adjustment based on the interest rate differential for that short period.

Tael   The traditional Chinese unit of weight for precious metals. Normal bar sizes are one and five taels. One tael equals 37.429 grammes.

Taft-Hartley Act   Key law in U.S. labour management giving the government wide powers to prevent and settle labour disputes. The powers include imposing a cooling-off period, usually 90 days, and the determination of collective bargaining procedures.

TAIEX Index   Capitalisation weighted arithmetic index of 216 companies which constitute nearly 90 percent of the market capitalisation of the Taiwan stock exchange. Calculated every five minutes.

Takedown   To receive and accept an allotment of securities in the primary market.

Taken   Dealers' language mainly heard through a broker's box when the offer has been lifted.

Takeover   Acquisition of a controlling interest in a company through the purchase of its shares.

Takeover Bid   The initial offer by a predator company for another. The bid can be in cash, shares or a combination. Often a counterbid comes from a third party. Bids may then be increased by either predator in which case the situation becomes a takeover battle. Bids usually have a closing date for acceptance but these are often extended. Usually, one predator withdraws and may sell the accumulated shares to the victor.

Taking a Position   The act of buying and selling to show a long or short position.

Talked at   In the oil industry, a general range within which buyers and sellers are discussing business.

Tan Book   The U.S. Federal Reserve perception of the economic outlook. Published every six weeks. Also known as the beige book.

Tangibles   See Assets / Liabilities.

Tankan   The Bank of Japan's quarterly corporate survey which checks companies' expectations for future business, capital spending, profits and a wide range of other corporate data. It includes the closely watched diffusion index for major manufacturers which compares the ratio of those who expect business to improve to those who expect it to worsen. The lower the index, the gloomier the outlook. The tankan is an important reference for the central bank in formulating monetary policy.

Tankoku   Japanese government paper with maturities of three and six months. Introduced in 1986 as a way of helping to smooth out refunding of huge amounts of previously issued 10 year government bonds.

TANs   See Municipal Notes.

Tanshi   Money brokers in Japan.

Tap Issue   Existing issue of government debt not fully allocated and which may be re-issued at a later date on a demand basis (turned on like a tap).

Taplet   A new issue or extra tranche which follows a previously fully allocated debt issue. A system used in the U.K.

Target Price   In the U.S., a price level established by law for wheat, feedgrains, rice and cotton. If the market price falls below the target price, an amount equal to the difference - but not more than the difference between the target price and price support loan levels - is paid to farmers who participate in commodity programmes.

In the European Community, the target price is fixed by the authorities as the desirable wholesale price for grain delivered to the area of greatest deficit in the Community.

Tax Anticipation Bill - U.S.   Short term money instrument sold by the U.S. Treasury to smooth the inflow of corporate tax payments.

Tax Anticipation Notes   See Municipal Notes.

Tax Exempts   See FOTRA Bonds - U.K.

Taxation Risk   The risk that tax laws relating to dividend income and capital gains on shares are changed, making stocks a less attractive investment vehicle.

Tea   Major producers include India, Bangladesh, China, Sri Lanka, Kenya, Uganda and Tanzania as well as a number of other African nations. Major world importer is the U.K. A key factor for the market is that the more economical tea bags - as opposed to the original packet tea - now account for some 70 percent of the total market.

Technical Analysis   The study of past market action, taking into account the market price, volume and open interest, with the aid of charts. Used to estimate future price trends. Also known as Chart Analysis. See Open Interest, Fundamental Analysis.

Ted Spread   Abbreviation for Treasury Eurodollar Spread. This is the yield difference between U.S. Treasury bill and Eurodollar futures contracts and is a regularly followed spread trade. See Spread Trading.

Tel Quel   Weight of sugar in metric or long tons, given without regard to whether it is in white, raw or crystal form.

Temporao   See Main Crop.

Tender   In the securities market, it is the process whereby all allocations are assigned at the same price.

In commodities trading, it is the notice of intent to deliver physical goods against a futures contract. Also, an invitation to acquire or sell a physical product. In a buy tender, a country sets out the terms under which it will purchase a commodity. In a sell tender, a country states that it wishes to sell a commodity, e.g. a specific quantity of a crop for delivery at a specified time.

Tender Panel   Panel of banks who bid for notes under an issuance facility such as a NIF, RUF or MOF.

Tender Price   Price put forward by an investor at which they are willing to buy a new issue of securities. The tender price will usually be placed within predetermined limits set down by the issuing house. See Offer for Subscription.

Tenderable Grades   Refers to grades designated as deliverable to settle a futures contract. Also called deliverable grades.

Term CDs   Certificates of deposit that carry maturities from two to five years. See CDs.

Term Customer   Buyer in long term oil contract agreements.

Term Liftings   Oil lifted under a long term contract.

Term Repo   A Repurchase Agreement lasting for 30 days or longer used to hedge a position for a similar amount of time. See Repurchase Agreement.

Term Sheet   Document which legally defines all the details of a loan or rescheduling agreement and which is signed by all participants.

Terminal   Onshore installation designed to receive oil/gas from a pipeline or from tankers. It is not a refinery.

Terminal Market   Commodity market where physicals are exchanged for cash and are deliverable against maturing futures contracts.

Tertiary Recovery   Oil/gas recovery from a reservoir in excess of that possible by primary and secondary recovery and requiring special techniques.

The Commonwealth   Based in London. Voluntary association of 50 independent states comprising about one quarter of world population. Also includes 28 dependencies and associated states. Includes the U.K. and most of its former dependencies. Has no written constitution. Members are each responsible for their own policies and can be aligned or non-aligned to any grouping. Holds discussions on international affairs, economic and technical cooperation.

Thermal Cracking   Occurs when basic hydrocarbon feedstock is broken down, or cracked, to produce light products. The method is through the sole use of heat and pressure without using a catalyst.

Theta   The measure of change in the value of an option compared with the continuous decrease in time to expiry. The time to expiry includes bank holidays and weekends. Also known as time decay. See Delta, Gamma, Rho, Vega.

Thin Market   A market in which there is little buying or selling interest, with low volume or activity. Can apply to a whole market or a single instrument.

Three Box Reversal   In technical analysis, a much used point and figure chart for intermediate analysis which needs only the high and low prices for the day.

Threshold Price   In the European Community, minimum price at which grain from a non-member state can enter the EC market. Import levies are imposed to bridge the gap between (usually) lower world prices and the threshold price. The aim is to prevent low-priced grain from outside the EC disrupting the Community market.

Throughput   Total volume of raw materials processed by a plant such as an oil refinery in a given period. Also, the total volume of crude oil and refined products handled by a storage facility or pipeline.

Tick   The minimum movement possible in the price of a financial instrument. See Basis Point.

Tick Value   Expressed in the currency of the futures contract, reflecting the value of the tick size. For instance, a 0.01 tick size on a Eurodollar futures contract of one million dollars would represent a tick value of 25 dollars. This means that one tick move in the price of the underlying would affect the value of the contract by 25 dollars.

Ticker Symbol   Letters that identify a stock traded on a stock exchange. See Ticker Tape.

Ticker Tape   An electronic display showing prices at which each successive trade is executed on a stock exchange, the trading volume and the share symbols. See Ticker Symbol.

Tier One   Under the capital adequacy standards set for commercial banks by the Bank for International Settlements, at least half of the eight percent of capital required to be set against risk weighted assets must be core capital. This comprises equity and disclosed reserves. So-called supplementary capital, or tier two, constitutes the rest. This includes undisclosed reserves, general provisions against loan losses, subordinated term debt and hybrid capital instruments combining characteristics of debt and equity. Also known as core capital.

Tier Two See Tier One.

TIFFE The Tokyo International Financial Futures Exchange was founded in April 1989. Specialises in futures contracts for currencies and interest rates, including dollar/yen and Three Month Eurodollar and Euroyen. An option contract is traded on the Three Month Euroyen future.

Tigers See Newly Industrialising Countries.

Tight Hole Exploratory oil well which has been drilled but whose drilling results are withheld by the operator for confidential commercial reasons.

Tight Money See Dear Money.

TIGRs - U.S. Treasury Investment Growth Receipts - a zero coupon instrument which was created by Merrill Lynch in 1982 as a result of trading note and bond coupons and principal repayments. This process is known as coupon stripping. Similar instruments are CATs and LYONs. See U.S. STRIPS.

Time Charter Hiring of a vessel for a fixed period, usually for a minimum three months. The charterer has the use of the vessel with the shipowner supplying specific services such as crew and provisions.

Time Decay See Theta.

Time Deposit See CDs.

Time Draft See Bills of Exchange.

Time Value The component of an option premium which takes into consideration the time to expiry and the volatility of the underlying. See Intrinsic Value.

Tin A base metal. Major consumer market is the canning industry where cans are made of steel sheet, plated with a thin layer of tin. However, tin is facing increasing competition from aluminium. Tin is a key constituent of most solders and other alloys such as bronze. There is limited recovery for scrap tin. China is the largest producer with others including Indonesia, Brazil, Bolivia, Malaysia, Thailand and Australia. A key factor in market trading is the strategic stockpile of the U.S. Defense Logistics Agency (former General Services Administration) which has made sales from time to time. At one stage, its stockpile equalled one year's total world consumption. Penang, in M alaysia, produces more than half the world's refined tin metal which is the top quality Straits tin. The two chief pricing centres are the Kuala Lumpur tin market, which is the main physical market, and the London Metal Exchange (LME).

TLP (Tension Leg Platform) An offshore platform tethered to the seabed, typically used in deep water development projects.

TOCOM The Tokyo Commodities Exchange was established in November 1984 as a result of the merger of the Tokyo Gold Exchange, the Tokyo Rubber Exchange and the Tokyo Textile Commodities Exchange. The TOCOM is the largest commodity exchange in Japan and is one of the most important for platinum and palladium futures contracts.

Tokkin Tokutei Kinsen Shintaku. Special money trust accounts operated by Japanese trust banks for institutional investors. The institutions or investment advisers specify in detail how the funds will be invested. Returns are in cash. Corporations poured money into tokkin in the late 1980s because they were a way to invest in securities without reassessing the book value of their other securities holdings and because tokkin profits are free from capital gains taxes for the life of the account. Many firms have extensive shareholdings in affiliated companies for the purpose of cementing business ties and revaluing such shares at market prices would subject them to massive taxes.

Tokyo Commodities Exchange See TOCOM.

Tokyo International Financial Futures Exchange See TIFFE.

Tokyo Stock Exchange See TSE.

Tola The traditional Indian unit of weight for precious metals. One tola equals 11.1 grammes. Normal bar size is 10 tolas.

Tom Next See T/N.

Tombstone A notice to the public, such as an advertisement in a newspaper, announcing the names of banks, investment and finance houses who have organised and provided funds for a security issue. It describes the terms and appears as a matter of record and not as an invitation to subscribe.

Ton Mile For air cargo, a ton mile means one ton of cargo flown one mile.

Tonne Measurement for crude oil in many countries. One tonne of oil is equal to approximately 7.3 or 7.4 barrels of crude. Exact conversion depends on temperature, specific gravity and other physical factors.

Top / Bottom In technical analysis, tops and bottoms refer to their positions relative to chart formations and not to highs or lows.

Top 5 Index A capitalisation weighted arithmetic index based on the five largest international companies traded on the Amsterdam bourse - Akzo, KLM, Philips, Royal Dutch Petroleum and Unilever. The European Options Exchange (EOE) runs the Top 5 index and calculates it in real time, i.e. whenever a price changes on any of the five shares. Futures are traded on the Amsterdam Financial Futures Market (ATF) and options on the European Options Exchange (EOE).

Top Reversal A top reversal day would be the setting of a new high in an uptrend followed by a lower close than the previous day's closing rate (sometimes the previous two days).

TOPIX Index A capitalisation weighted arithmetic index comprising all the companies - some 1,100 - listed on the first section of the Tokyo stock exchange. Calculated every minute. Index futures and options are traded on the Tokyo stock exchange.

Toronto 35 Index A capitalisation weighted arithmetic index based on 35 companies selected from the TSE 300 index (Toronto Stock Exchange). Calculated every 15 seconds. Index futures and options are traded on the Toronto Futures Exchange.

Total Return Combination of the dividend income and the capital gains made on any investment.

Touch The best (highest) bid and (lowest) offer in a security currently available in the market. This need not be the two-way price of one market maker but is taken by looking at the market prices submitted by all market makers.

Trade Barrier Artificial restraint on the free exchange of goods and services between countries, usually in the form of tariffs, subsidies, quotas or exchange controls.

Trade Bills See Bills of Exchange.

Trade Weighted Used in reference to foreign exchange rates with currency movements weighted in accordance with their importance in a country's trade. This trade weighting is then formulated in an index.

Trading House Concern that buys and sells futures and physicals for the account of customers as well as for its own account.

Trading Post In the U.S., the structure (the post) on the floor of a stock exchange at which securities are bought and sold.

Trading Range The high and low trading points of an instrument over a period of time, e.g. one day. Often referred to as the hi/lo. Chartists watch to see if the price of a financial instrument breaks through its trading high or low since this can be a portent for its future trend.

Trading Volume A generic term used to describe the total number of contracts traded in any particular period.

Tramp Vessel Vessel engaged in casual trade.

Tranche French word for a slice. Used widely. An agreed instalment of a credit or loan which may be drawn down as required. Also refers to a country's drawings from the International Monetary Fund, which are made in tranches. Also the subsequent part, or parts, of a public debt offering by a government.

Tranche One Part of a series of two or more issues bearing the same coupon rate and redemption date but with different issue dates.

Trans-Shipment Occurs when a vessel from the loading port discharges cargo at an intermediate port and the goods are loaded into another ship bound for the final destination.

Transaction Fees Charges payable by investors on purchases and sales of shares.

Translation Risk A form of currency risk associated with the valuation of balance sheet assets and liabilities between financial reporting dates.

Treasury Bill Short term government security issued in domestic currency with maturities not exceeding one year and therefore considered to be a money market instrument. Treasury bills are sold at a discount from par and do not bear a coupon. The investor's return is measured by the difference from the par value at maturity and the discount price paid.

Treasury Bills - Canada Discount paper issued on a weekly basis with maturities of one, two, three, six and 12 months. The three month Treasury bill is traded by the Bank of Canada to implement its monetary policy and these rates are watched closely by the market. Cash management bills with maturities up to three months are occasionally issued.

Treasury Bills - U.K. Discount paper issued by the Bank of England on the last business day of each week. Bills are offered by tender normally with a maturity of 91 or 182 days. Treasury bills with a remaining maturity of usually less than one month are bought back by the Bank of England from discount houses to balance daily cash shortages in the market and therefore act as a liquidity management tool. The rate at which the Bank of

England buys the Treasury bills back is an important indicator of its monetary policy.

Treasury Bond   Government debt security issued with a maturity of 10 years or more (maximum 30 years to date) traded in the capital markets. Treasury bonds are issued with a fixed coupon.

Treasury Bonds - Canada   Fixed coupon bonds issued with maturities from two to 30 years. Auction schedule depends on the maturity of the bond. All new bonds are in bullet form although there is one outstanding bond denominated in Canadian dollars with a call feature.

A second type of bond issued by the government is known as the Canadian Savings Bond (CSB). At the end of 1991 the government also launched the Real Return Bond (RRB).

Treasury Bonds - Sweden   Swedish government bonds are in the majority bullet issues with coupons paid annually and maturities of between two and 16 years. There are a few low coupon bonds which bear semi-annual coupons. Bonds are referred to by a serial number. Notes and bonds were previously distinguished by different serial numbers but current practice consolidates all issue types under the name Treasury bonds (Statsobligation).

Treasury Certificates - Belgium   Treasury certificates with maturities of up to one year are issued on a regular basis by competitive auction.

Treasury Note   Government debt security issued with maturities of two to 10 years and traded in the capital markets. Treasury notes bear a fixed coupon.

Trend Reversal   See Reversal Day.

Trendline   In technical analysis, a trendline is a line that connects specific points of price action in order to identify the direction of the market. The longer the trendline has been in place, tested but not broken, the more significant the trendline. Trendlines are used to identify the following characteristics about trends:
- direction of the trend
- trend reversals
- trend continuation
- support and resistance

General theory is that once a trendline is penetrated it is a signal for a consolidating market and, depending on what happens after that, a possible change in trend.

Trésor Français   The French Treasury. Issuer of Treasury debt in the form of BTNs and OATs which are fully guaranteed by the French government. Maturities ranging from three months to 30 years. The introduction of OATs in 1985 has made the French government securities market one of the most active in the world. The French Treasury has simplified the issue procedure by regularly publishing auction calendars and introducing fungible Treasuries. Foreign investors hold one third of outstanding French government debt.

Treuhand Bonds - TOBLs - Germany   Bonds issued by the Treuhandanstalt which carry a guarantee from the government and bear the same characteristics as BOBLs.

Treuhandanstalt - Germany   The official vehicle set up by the government in 1990 for the privatisation of East German companies. It issues German government bonds (bunds) known as Treuhand bonds which carry the express guarantee of the government. The Treuhandanstalt will cease to exist at the end of 1994 when its outstanding debt will be passed to the government.

Triangles   Used in technical analysis.

Three types exist - symmetrical, ascending and descending, with the latter two also termed right angle triangles.

The symmetrical shows two converging trendlines, the upper line descending and the lower line ascending. A close outside either trendline completes the pattern. This triangle is usually a continuation pattern representing a pause in the existing trend after which the original trend is resumed. The minimum price objective is obtained by measuring the height of the triangle and projecting that distance upwards from the breakout point.

The ascending triangle has a rising lower line with a flat or horizontal upper line and is usually bullish.

The descending triangle has the upper line falling with a flat or horizontal bottom line and is usually bearish.

A broadening triangle, also termed a five point reversal, is turned backwards so that the trendlines diverge to create an expanding triangle. It occurs most often at market tops and is thus usually bearish. The pattern is completed and the major bear signal given when the reaction from the third peak breaks below the bottom of the second trough.

Triangles usually take longer than a month to form but generally less than three months. A triangle lasting less than a month is probably a different pattern such as a pennant.

Trigger Option   A type of barrier option. See Down and In, Up and In.

Trigger Price   The price level at which buy/sell mechanisms, provided for in commodity agreements, take effect.

Trinidad Terms A U.K. proposal that the stock of official debt owed to Western governments by poor developing nations carrying out market oriented economic reform programmes should be reduced by two thirds. It was envisaged that the reduction would apply to the entire stock of official debt and not to selected maturities.

Triple Nine The highest degree of gold purity - 99.9 percent pure gold.

Triple Top / Bottom In technical analysis, similar to the Head and Shoulders pattern except that the three peaks or troughs are at about the same level. The triple top is not complete until support levels along both of the intervening lows have been broken. The measuring implication is that the price will usually move by a distance at least equal to the height of the pattern.

Triple Witching Occurs every quarter and is the simultaneous expiry of stock index futures contracts, stock index options and options on individual stocks. It can often increase volatility, notably on the U.S. stock markets.

Tropical Growers Association Formerly the Rubber Growers Association. Has some 200 members in 20 countries controlling or managing the production of rubber, cocoa, coffee, coconuts, palm oil, tea, pepper and bananas. Based in London.

Troubled City Bailout Bonds Created specifically to service and repay general obligations issued by entities with major budget deficits. U.S. term.

Troughs See Peaks / Troughs.

Troy Ounces The unit of weight of precious metals. One troy ounce equals 31 grammes and there are 12 troy ounces to the pound (weight). See Avoirdupois.

TRs - U.S. U.S. Treasury Receipts are Zero Coupon instruments traded from stripping coupon and principal repayments from Treasury bonds and notes. See U.S. STRIPS.

Trunk Line A large diameter pipeline gathering oil or gas from several fields in a given production area.

Trust Banks - Japan Seven banks which mainly do trust business but are also allowed to undertake common bank business.

Trustee The institution appointed to ensure all terms and conditions of the bond indenture are fully adhered to.

TSE The Tokyo Stock Exchange Co Ltd was established in 1878. Since 1985, the Exchange has commenced trading in the 10 year Japanese government bond futures contract, the first financial futures contract in Japan. Other contracts include the U.S. Treasury Bond future, the 20 Year Japanese Government Bond future, the Tokyo Stock Price Index (TOPIX) future and option and the 10 Year Japanese Government bond futures option.

TSE 300 A capitalisation weighted arithmetic average comprising all companies traded on the Toronto Stock Exchange. Calculated continuously.

Turnaround Usually spring and autumn refinery maintenance. Alters configuration of refinery to cope with seasonal shifts in oil product demand.

Turning Wet See Daisy Chain.

Two-Way Market Market where dealers actively quote both buying and selling rates.

U.K. - Key Interest Rates The rates to watch are:
Money market dealing rate - dictates the level of bank base rates in normal circumstances.

Minimum lending rate - dictates the level of bank base rates in special circumstances.

The Bank of England typically signals changes in commercial banks' benchmark base rates through its daily money market operations by changing the dealing rates at which it buys bills from the discount houses. But the Bank is increasingly resorting to the announcement of a new minimum lending rate to make its views on interest rates absolutely clear.

The U.K. money market is unlike any other. The key players are the central bank and the commercial banks, as in other countries, but the U.K. also has discount houses which are unique. The discount houses are highly specialised institutions which trade and make markets in sterling money market instruments.

The Treasury controls monetary policy. However, since the debacle of Black Wednesday on September 16 1992, when sterling was withdrawn from the Exchange Rate Mechanism, the Bank of England has been granted a limited amount of independence: the governor of the Bank of England has said that he will speak out if he believes government monetary policy threatens its inflation target; the minutes of monthly meetings between the chancellor and the governor are now published, albeit with a six week delay; and the Treasury has yielded the decision over the precise timing of interest rate changes to the Bank. The Treasury still sets interest rate policy but Bank of England comments carry more weight now than they used to.

U.K. - Money Supply There are three main monetary aggregates. M0 is chiefly notes and coins in circulation. M4 is non-bank, non-building society holdings of notes and coins and sterling deposits.

It does not include deposits held by banks and building societies with each other. M4 lending measures loans made by banks and building societies to the M4 private sector. The financial markets tend to focus on the seasonally adjusted monthly and year on year changes in M0, M4 and M4 lending.

U.K. Treasury   Issuer of Treasury debt in the form of U.K. government securities or gilts (gilt edged stock) which are fully guaranteed by the U.K. government. Considered to be part of the second tier of the government bond market in size alongside Germany, France and Italy, and following the U.S. and Japan. U.K. gilts are issued to fund the PSBR. The U.K. Treasury also issues Treasury bills to control daily liquidity, which are not considered to be part of the government debt issues. Up until 1990 the U.K. Treasury reported a budget surplus and the Bank of England was therefore engaged in buying back debt via reverse auctions and secondary market activities.

U.S. - Key Interest Rates   The rates to watch are:
Federal (Fed) funds rate - sets the tone for money market rates.

Discount rate - usually sets the floor for the Fed funds rate.

The Fed funds and discount rates are the two key interest rates. Depository institutions hold non-interest bearing reserve accounts at the Fed to meet reserve requirements and handle interbank transactions. Deposits above the minimum required are traded overnight and the Fed funds rate is what banks charge each other for these overnight loans. The Fed has an objective for the funds rate which is never formally published. However, so-called Fed watchers can usually tell what the target is by observing where the funds rate trades in conjunction with the Fed's money market operations.

The first time the Fed announced a rise in interest rates at the time it took place was on February 4 1994 when it issued a statement saying that the Federal Open Market Committee had decided to increase slightly the degree of pressure on reserve positions. However, a series of rate rises in early 1994 were accompanied by formal Fed statements which the markets believe were designed to make its intentions clear. What is not clear is whether this will become the standard method by which rate changes are signalled. Traditionally, Fed watchers had to wait until the release of the minutes of the regular Federal Open Market Committee meetings, which are published six weeks afterwards, for confirmation of any perceived change in monetary policy.

All institutions with reservable deposits can borrow at the discount rate from the Fed's discount window for short term adjustment purposes and limited other uses. The Fed funds rate is usually above the discount rate. When the funds rate is at, or below, the discount rate there is little use of the discount window by healthy banks which have access to the funds market.

(There is no U.S. equivalent of the lombard rate which other central banks use to penalise institutions requiring emergency funds. However, there are circumstances when the Fed may charge a market rate above the basic discount rate. For example, borrowing under the seasonal programme is at a market rate average of Fed funds and certificates of deposit (CDs). Extended credit borrowing by banks in difficulty can also be at an above market rate.)

Open market operations are conducted with a group of primary dealers in government securities (about 40) which are mainly subsidiaries of bank holding companies and securities houses. Eligible paper includes Treasury bills, notes, bonds and, for repos, government agency securities.

Basically, the Fed controls U.S. monetary policy. It is often described as independent and in a narrow sense this is true: the Fed is self-financed and does not require presidential approval to change interest rates.

However, the Fed can be abolished or have its terms of reference changed by Congress. The chairman is appointed by the President for a four year term only and is conventionally a political appointee. In practical terms, therefore, it is virtually impossible for the Fed to follow an interest rate policy significantly at odds with that desired by the U.S. Administration.

U.S. - Money Supply   There are two main monetary aggregates. M1 measures funds readily available for spending, basically currency and transactions (current) accounts. M2 is M1 plus relatively liquid savings-type balances held largely by households. The financial markets focus on the percentage and dollar change in weekly and monthly seasonally adjusted M1 and M2.

U.S. Department of the Treasury   The largest single issuer of debt in the world in the form of U.S. Treasury securities. The volume and size of the issues make the Treasury market the most active and most liquid in the world.

U.S. Street Method   The standard yield to maturity calculation used by the U.S. market participants except the U.S. Treasury, whereby the yield is compounded semi-annually despite the coupon frequency.

U.S. STRIPS   Separately Traded Registered Interest and Principal Securities. Zero coupon instruments which are created as a result of trading note and bond coupons and principal repayments separately. This process is known in the market as coupon stripping. STRIPS were registered and authorised by the U.S. Treasury in 1985 and have replaced the trading of TIGRs, CATS and LYONs.

U.S. Treasury Bills Short term U.S. government bearer securities with maturities of three, six and maximum 12 months.

Sold on a regular basis and commanding a dominating position on money markets. Nearly one third of marketable U.S. Treasury debt is concentrated in Treasury bills. The purchase and sale of such bills, i.e. through open market operations, form a key part of monetary policy. In the U.S., auctions of 91 day and 182 day bills take place weekly and their yields are watched closely for clues to interest rate trends. The 12 month Treasury bill is known as the year bill and is auctioned monthly.

U.S. Treasury Bonds Long term U.S. Treasury securities with maturities of 10 years or more. Treasury bonds make up 15 percent of marketable debt. Like Treasury notes, they pay a semi-annual coupon, so they are also known as coupon securities. Many outstanding Treasury bonds are callable within five years of maturity. However, since February 1985, the Treasury no longer issues callable bonds. The yield on the 30 year Treasury bond is watched closely by the market for long term interest rate trends. The 10 year bonds are auctioned on a quarterly basis and as from mid-1993 the 30 year bond was moved from a quarterly to a semi-annual auction cycle.

U.S. Treasury Method The yield to maturity used by the U.S. Treasury to price Treasury bonds at an auction, whereby partial periods are discounted using the simple rather than the compound interest.

U.S. Treasury Notes U.S. Treasury securities with maturities from two to 10 years. Notes are non-callable and make up more than 50 percent of marketable debt. They pay a fixed semi-annual coupon and mature at par. Two and five year notes are auctioned monthly and the three year notes on a quarterly basis. The seven year note which was issued as a mini-refunding operation on a quarterly basis is no longer auctioned (mid-1993) and the remaining notes will mature in April 2000.

U.S. Treasury Securities Issued by the U.S. Department of the Treasury via the Federal Reserve System. Guaranteed by the U.S. government, therefore considered to have no credit risk. The majority of U.S. government marketable debt is in three types of instruments: Treasury bills,

Treasury notes and Treasury bonds. Many U.S. Treasuries are stripped.

UCITS Undertakings for Collective Investments in Transferable Securities. A European Community regulation governing any collective fund, such as a unit trust, sold within the Community.

ULCC Ultra Large Crude Carrier. In the U.K., usually taken to mean a crude oil tanker carrying a minimum of 320,000 long deadweight tons.

Ullage Distance between the top of the cargo when stowed and the hatches.

Ultimo Dealing See Month-End Dealing.

Ultra Large Crude Carrier See ULCC.

UNCTAD United Nations Conference on Trade and Development. Formed in 1964 to establish better international trading conditions for developing countries and to help raise their standard of living. It is also a forum for most commodity price stabilisation pacts. See Common Fund.

Undated Gilts - U.K. U.K. Treasury securities with an undefined maturity, also known as irredeemable or perpetual gilts. These gilts can be called after a stipulated date with three months' notice from the government. However, since these gilts were issued at a deep discount, the market does not expect to see them called. War Loan 3-1/2 percent, for example, was issued in 1930 without a maturity date and is still live.

Under Reference A deal cannot be finalised without reference to the institution which placed the order, whose name should not be mentioned until reference has been made to it.

Undercapitalised Term used when a business has not been supplied with enough funds by its owners to support its activities and to provide for any needed expansion.

Underlying The financial instrument which is the subject of a derivatives contract.

Undersubscribed The situation whereby an issue of debt instruments is not completely bought up by investors in the market. Opposite to Oversubscribed.

Undervalued A term implying that a security or currency is trading at a price lower than it should be relative to fundamental factors. Opposite to Overvalued.

Underwater Expression used to describe a security with a market value below the holder's cost price, or a coupon paying less than current market rates.

Underwriter See Lead Manager.

Underwriting The act of purchasing a fixed quota of a bond or share issue for resale to the secondary market. The quota may be purchased outright through an underwriting syndicate which shares the resale risk.

Underwriting Syndicate - Japan A group of major banks, credit and savings institutions, securities houses and a few foreign participants, who receive fixed allocations in the auction of the 10 year coupon and five year discount bond and who, prior to all auctions, negotiate the coupon and issue size with the Ministry of Finance.

Unencumbered An asset which is fully owned, having no lien against it.

Unit Trust See Mutual Fund.

Unitary Tax Favoured in some U.S. states. Taxes foreign firms on a percentage of their world-wide income, rather than only on income earned in the U.S. state in which the firm is located. See Water's Edge.

United Nations Conference On Trade and Development. See UNCTAD.

Unitisation Owners of oil/gas reserves pool their individual interests in return for an interest in the overall unit. Following this, the unit is operated by a single company on behalf of the group, thus increasing efficiency.

Unity Fund Bonds - Germany Also known as Einheit-sanleihen or Unities and issued by the German Unity Fund following East and West German reunification in October 1990. These bonds carry a guarantee from the Federal government.

Unlimited Liability Term used where no restriction applies to an owner's losses in a business.

Unlisted Stock A security that is not listed or traded on a stock exchange floor.

Unmatched Book One in which the maturities of assets and liabilities do not correspond, specifically when the average maturity of the liabilities is less than that of the assets.

Unofficial Prices - LME Unofficial prices on the London Metal Exchange are the buyer/seller prices at the end of the afternoon second Ring.

Unrealised Gain The profit which would be reported, should a position be liquidated.

Unrealised Loss The loss which would be reported, should a position be liquidated.

Unwinding a Position A position (long or short) is unwound, or reversed, by an offsetting transaction to result in a square or flat position.

Unwrought Metals Forms of metal such as wirebars, billets and ingots before semi-fabrication into tube, wire and sheet.

Up and In A trigger option that is activated when the price of the underlying rises to a predetermined level. A type of barrier option.

Up and Out A knockout option that is cancelled when the price of the underlying rises above a predetermined level. A type of barrier option.

Up Average Used in technical analysis. The indication in a moving average divergence that shows an oversold situation and, hence, a buy signal. See Moving Average Convergence / Divergence (MACD).

Upgrading Upward regrading of credit status for a borrowing institution or its debt instruments. Opposite to Downgrading.

Uplift Amount of oil that can be recovered from a field before taxes have to be paid.

Upstream Prospecting, drilling for, and production from, the wellhead to the pipeline or to the tanker loading terminal of crude oil or natural gas.

Uptrend / Downtrend In technical analysis, both an uptrend and a downtrend require a minimum of four points. An uptrend needs a higher low price and a higher high price. A downtrend needs a lower high price and a lower low price.

Uruguay Round World trade negotiations which began in 1986 and ended successfully in 1993, held under the General Agreement on Tariffs and Trade. They are due to be ratified by the respective governments during 1994. All aspects of international trade problems have been thrashed out to allow further expansion and liberalisation of world trade as well as encompassing fresh sectors such as trade related investment and financial services. See GATT, World Trade Organisation.

USAC U.S. Atlantic Coast. Term used in shipping.

USDA U.S. Department of Agriculture. Responsible for implementing agricultural policy. It is also a major source of forecasts and statistics on agriculture in the U.S. and world-wide.

USG U.S. Gulf ports.

USNH The U.S. north of Hatteras which is a cape in North Carolina on the U.S. Atlantic Coast. USNH covers ports such as New York, Boston, Philadelphia, Baltimore, Norfolk, Newport News and Portland, Maine. Also known as U.S. Northern Range.

USNP U.S. North Pacific ports.

USSH U.S. ports south of Hatteras, North Carolina.

Utilities State or private sector enterprises providing services of public interest such as gas, electricity and water. Listed utilities companies were historically funded by bonds but later turned to the equity market.

V-Formation / Spikes In technical analysis, this is an abrupt reversal pattern that usually gives little warning to the trader. It mostly occurs after a bull trend - and its abruptness is attributed to the fact that there is usually only a few or minor corrections on the way. Though this is a common pattern, it is a difficult pattern to identify.

Vacuum Gas Oil A relatively high boiling point distillate from crude oil obtained by vacuum distillation. It is a prime feedstock for a catalytic cracker.

Value Date The date on which either the security or cash equivalent is settled on completion of a trade.

Value Today Same day value.

Value Tomorrow Value the next working or business day.

Variable Rate / Floating Rate CDs There are two types of variable rate CDs - a six month with interest set, or rolled, every 30 days and a one year with interest set every three months. See CDs.

Variable Rate Note A variation of the floating rate note where not only the coupon but also the margin is reset regularly, often via a Dutch auction process.

Variable Redemption Bond A bond whose redemption value is linked to a variable such as the dollar/yen exchange rate, the performance of the U.S. Treasury 30 year bond, a stock index or the gold price. Often issued in bull and bear portions, or tranches, where the bull redemption price improves on a rise in the variable and declines on a fall in the variable. The bear redemption price declines on a rise but improves on a fall. For the borrower, the locked-in rates, or prices, that this variable redemption creates can effectively be sold to hedgers or speculators as an option. Investors in a bull tranche often obtain a speculative or investment vehicle not readily available in another form (e.g. if their country of residence does not allow options on a stock index) while buyers of a bear tranche can hedge existing holdings of bonds, shares or precious metals.

Variation Margin The amount by which the margin account varies on a daily basis as a result of the marking to market process carried out by the clearing house of a futures exchange.

Vega The measure of change in the value of the option compared with a change in volatility. See Delta, Gamma, Rho, Theta.

Venture Capital Funds used for investment in small companies that are considered to be in their first

phase of growth. Funding is provided by private and institutional investors.

Vertical Spread An option strategy. See Bear Spread, Bull Spread.

Veterans Administration Independent U.S. federal agency set up in 1944 to organise benefits for war veterans. It guarantees small down payment, long term residential mortgages to eligible veterans. These mortgages form a key part of the mortgage pools which are packaged and sold as securities by the Government National Mortgage Association and by the Federal Home Loan Mortgage Corporation.

Viscosity Measures the resistance of a fluid to motion or flow. Viscosity normally decreases as temperature rises.

Visible Supply Usually refers to supplies of a commodity in recognised distribution centres which have been moved from production areas to shipping centres. Varies with different commodities. Often includes afloats and all other supplies "in sight".

VLCC Very Large Crude Carrier. In the U.K., usually taken to mean a crude oil tanker carrying a minimum of 160,000 long deadweight tons.

Vnesheconombank Was the foreign trade bank of the former Soviet Union when it financed most external trade operations. Many accounts were frozen in early 1992 and Russia has said it will compensate account holders by issuing domestic dollar denominated bonds. The bank is now limited to servicing debts and commercial loans and managing a series of domestic hard currency bonds. See Frozen Taiga Bonds.

Vneshtorgbank Formerly the foreign trade bank of the Russian Federation. Now one of Russia's largest commercial banks. It has taken over the commercial operations of Vnesheconombank.

Volatility The degree to which financial instruments or markets are subject to market fluctuations. Volatility is measured by an annualised Standard Deviation of the underlying. The two most common methods of assessing volatility levels are Historical and Implied Volatility. The volatility level is a main factor influencing option premiums. In the bond markets, volatility refers to modified duration.

Volatility Analysis Volatility analysis measures the rate of random change in market prices. The system offers a choice of three different methods.
 1) Close/Close. Uses a standard geometric deviation for the basic data with a trend estimate automatically factored in. The calculation is made over set periods and reported as an annualised

percentage rate. The system has an automatic smoothing mechanism for uneven time lapses between data, for example tick data.

2) Open/High/Low/Close. Measures the rate of random change in market prices taking into account open, high, low and close values. The calculation is reported as an annualised percentage rate.

3) Zero Trend Close/Close. Reckoned to give a better estimate than the straight Close/Close on which it is based and offers the added assumption that the underlying distribution has a zero trend.

Volatility Index Used in technical analysis. A trend-following analysis that measures the average price movement per interval. It employs stop and reverse points to signal entry and exit positions in the market. These reversal points occur when the closing price crosses the stop and reverse point (from above when the position is long and from below when the position is short). At such points the position is closed and the reverse position is set up. Using this analysis implies always having a position in the market. The system is designed to loosen stop and reverse points (relative to the price line) as volatility increases and to tighten them as volatility lessens.

This index should be used with a line chart of closing prices with the same interval to identify when the stop and reverse points are crossed by the closing price. It is not considered suitable for use in option pricing calculations.

Volume / Price Trend Used in technical analysis. This analysis multiplies volume by the relative change in price and takes the cumulative sum of these values. A buy or sell signal is indicated when a divergence between the volume/price trend and price is followed by a trend break in the volume/price trend.

Vostro Account "Your account" - a term used to describe a foreign bank's account maintained in the domestic currency. See Nostro Account.

Voting Rights Voting rights are granted to ordinary shareholders and provide them with the ability to exert control over the management and policies of a company and the right to take part in electing a company's board of directors.

Voting Trust A trust set up by the company at a commercial bank inviting ordinary shareholders to deposit their shares for a fixed period (maximum 10 years). By doing this, the ordinary shareholder has given up the right to vote but retains the other privileges. The voting rights then belong to the trust which is controlled by the board of directors. In exchange, the bank issues a Voting Trust Certificate (VTC). This procedure is carried out if a company has financial instability

and the board members wish to concentrate voting power in order to make changes in policy rapidly.

Voyage Charter Ship charter arranged for a single voyage only and possibly confined to determined ports and area.

VTC A Voting Trust Certificate is issued by a voting trust and is a negotiable certificate proving that ordinary shares have been deposited into the trust and that ordinary shareholders have consequently relinquished their right to vote.

W/I See When Issued.

Wall Street World-wide colloquial name for the New York Stock Exchange that has loosely come to mean securities trading generally in the U.S. Often the NYSE is referred to as Wall Street, literally part of a street intersection where the exchange is located.

Wall Street Refiner A Wall Street investment firm which buys or sells crude oil and petroleum products - as futures contracts or paper barrels - on a scale similar to real refineries. Typically these investment firms do not own oil refineries and take no actual delivery of oil.

War Risk The risk a shipper may have to pay an extra insurance premium, as a consequence of war, in despatching a specified consignment.

Warehouse Receipt Document providing proof of ownership of a specified quality and quantity of a commodity at a designated warehouse.

Warehousing The process whereby a group of investors independently buy shares in a company but each investor keeps his holding below the official notification threshold. This can be a surreptitious method of mounting a takeover bid. See Acting in Concert.

Warrant A type of security that is attached to a bond but that has a separate life and value. A warrant allows the investor to purchase ordinary shares at a fixed price over a period of time (years) or to perpetuity. The price of the shares is usually higher than the market price at the time of issue. A warrant is freely transferable and can be traded separately. See Rights.

Water Injection Process of pumping water into the reservoir rock to maintain pressure.

Water's Edge An alternative to the U.S. Unitary Tax - favoured by some U.S. states - whereby a foreign firm is taxed by a U.S. state on activities within the U.S.

Wax Solid hydrocarbon found in certain crude oils. Wax deposits in pipelines and equipment can cause exploitation and refining problems.

Weather Window   Time in the month or year when weather conditions are suitable - or likely to be - for various offshore oil operations. An example is platform installation.

Wedding Warrant   Warrant issued with a callable bond. During the period to the first call date of the bond, the warrant can only be exercised by giving up the bond. Following the call date, the warrant can be exercised with cash.

Wedges   Used in technical analysis. This pattern is similar to a symmetrical triangle but has a slant either to the upside or downside. It has two converging trendlines that come together at an apex. The wedge generally slopes against the main trend so that a falling wedge is bullish and a rising wedge is bearish. Wedges are usually seen within the existing trend and are generally continuation patterns. The wedge usually lasts more than a month but not more than three months.

Weighted Average Coupon   The weighted average coupon rate of all the loan rates of the underlying collateral in a pool of mortgages.

Weighted Average Maturity   The weighted average maturity of all the loans making up the underlying collateral in a mortgage pool.

Weighted Close   A weighted average of the high, low and closing prices. High and low are given equal weight while the close is given a user specified weight.

Weighted Index   A stock index that weights one component more heavily than another on a given basis. See Capitalisation Weighted Index, Market Value Weighted Index, Price Weighted Index, Arithmetic Index, Geometric Weighted Index.

Weighted Moving Average   Used in technical analysis. Whereas the simple moving average gives equal emphasis to all the observations, the weighted moving average accentuates the most recent observations. The weights are related in a linear fashion to the age of the observation.

Weighting   The weight, or importance, given to the various constituent components of an index or economic indicator.

Well Logging   Record of data obtained when drilling a well. Provides detailed image of the underground rock formation.

Wellhead   Control equipment fitted to the top of a well casing and incorporating such items as outlets, valves and blowout preventer.

Wellhead Price   Price of crude, natural gas or condensates as they come from the well.

West Texas Intermediate   See WTI.

Wet Barrels   Term used in oil trading which means delivery of a product rather than the transfer of a tanker receipt. Describes oil which has shipping dates ascribed to it.

Wet Natural Gas   Natural gas with large amounts of associated liquids. A wet gas may suggest the gas is being recovered from the vicinity of an oil reservoir.

Wheat   Comprises a wide variety of cereal grasses cultivated throughout the world. Major export grain in world trade. Mostly grown for flour to produce bread, cakes, pasta products. Also used for animal feed. Wheat is a market with many varieties and a wide protein range. The industry takes as its benchmark the U.S. federal grading system which is based on winter or spring growth habits, hardness, softness and colour. Winter wheat is planted in the autumn and harvested in the late spring and summer of the following year. Spring wheat is planted in the spring and harvested the same year. Wheat growing countries include Argentina, Australia, Canada, China, the Commonwealth of Independent States, France, Germany, India, Italy, Pakistan, Spain, Turkey, the U.K and the U.S. See Wheat - Classes.

Wheat - Classes   Five classes of wheat are most frequently grown in the U.S. - Soft Red Winter, Hard Red Winter, White, Hard Red Spring, Durum. Classification reflects planting time, protein content and kernel colour. Each class has different characteristics that make it either suitable or unsuitable for a particular flour. Wheat is also graded as to weight per bushel, defects, foreign materials and the amount of wheat mixed in from other classes. A price factor considered by a buyer is the yield, i.e. the percentage of flour to be obtained from the wheat. This differing yield value is directly related to the weight per bushel and inversely with the moisture content.

Wheat Kernel   There are three main parts:
    - bran, the outer covering that provides the fibre.
    - the endosperm, the flour-like inner part that provides the gluten and starch (and which also makes white flour).
    - the germ, the embryo containing the oil.
    The bran and germ are ground with the endosperm to make whole wheat flour. The bran is also used in livestock feed.

When Issued (W/I)   Means When, as and if Issued. W/I trading starts immediately after the formal announcement of the issues. Instruments are delivered when issued. They are traded on what is known as the Grey Market. No interest accrues during this period. Also known as free to trade.

White Gold Nickel or palladium is alloyed with gold to whiten the metal.

White Knight A potential friendly acquirer sought out by a company to protect them from a hostile takeover. See Poison Pill, Pac Man Defence.

White Metals A collective name for silver, platinum and palladium.

White Value Refers to refined sugar of 99.9 Polarisation. See Raw Value.

Wide Opening Term used when the spread between buying and selling prices is unusually wide.

Wild Well One which is out of control and blowing fluid or gas from the down hole reservoir.

Wildcat Exploration well drilling with no knowledge of what the underlying rock formation may contain.

William Percent R Used in technical analysis. This oscillator is like a stochastic since it measures the latest close in relation to its price range over a set number of days. The last close is deducted from the highest price in the range over a given number of days and the difference is divided by the total range for the same period. The scale is reversed so that an overbought condition is above 20 and an oversold situation is under 80. Named after its originator, Larry Williams.

Windfall Profit An unusual profit, normally as the result of a specific, one-off situation. If too large and too widespread in one industrial sector then a government may impose a one-off windfall profit tax.

Winding Up See Liquidation.

Window Dressing Dates Window dressing dates are ends of periods, usually a year-end but can be three or six months, when banks and companies aim to present their accounts in a favourable light, often helped by raising additional short term funds.

Window Warrant Can only be exercised for a set period - the window - during the life of the relevant bond.

Winter Kill Damage caused to a crop by cold winter weather.

Wintering The period when rubber trees shed leaves and production declines.

Winze In mining, the downwards excavation of a reef made to connect drives on different levels.

Witholding Tax Tax deducted at source on interest or dividend payments to be paid by the investor.

Wool Animal fibre cover, known as a fleece, on sheep. Woollen yarn is used for tweed fabrics and blankets while worsted - made from a longer fibre - is used for suiting and fine dress fabrics. Wool is renowned for its ability to accept dyes. Major producers are Australia, the Commonwealth of Independent States and New Zealand. India is pre-eminent in production of a more coarse variety known as carpet wool.

Working Capital Surplus of current assets over current liabilities which provides the net resources with which a company can finance day to day operations.

Working Control Theoretically more than 50 percent of all voting shares is needed to control a company. However, if the holder has a substantial minority interest then he could have effective (working control) control if the rest of the company's stock was all held in small shareholdings.

World Bank Set up under Bretton Woods in 1944, the official name is the International Bank for Reconstruction and Development. It is the main agency for channelling aid funds, usually medium term, for capital and human resource projects to developing nations. The World Bank can channel private funds and make loans from its own resources. It also raises money by selling bonds on the world capital markets.

World Food Programme Multilateral food aid organisation set up by the Food and Agriculture Organisation and the United Nations in 1962 to help less developed countries and to deal with food emergencies.

World Trade Organisation New title for the General Agreement on Tariffs and Trade, decided December 1993 and effective January 1995. See GATT, Uruguay Round.

Worldscale The Worldwide Tanker Nominal Freight Scale. A freight index designed to express tanker rates, irrespective of vessel size and route, in terms of the costing of a standard vessel. Freight levels for tankers are usually denoted as a percentage of the Worldscale freight rates which are given in dollars.

Write-Off Book-keeping action which at one stroke depreciates an asset out of the balance sheet.

Wrongful Trading Occurs where a director of a company in liquidation allows the company to continue trading when he was aware that there was no reasonable prospect that the company could avoid insolvent liquidation. In other words, the company was not a going concern.

Wrought Metal Metal such as tube, wire and sheet which has been physically transformed from wirebars, billets and ingots.

WTI A light (40 degrees API) sweet blend of crude oils produced in fields in Western Texas (West Texas Intermediate). Used as the benchmark for U.S. crude oil and also in formulas to price imports of foreign oil with differentials to reflect varied quality, e.g. Saudi Arab light at WTI less one dollar per barrel.

Yankee Bond Bond issued in the U.S., by a foreign borrower, in U.S. dollars and registered with the Securities and Exchange Commission. A type of foreign bond.

Yankee CDs Certificates of Deposit issued by the branches of foreign banks in the U.S. These banks rely on dealers to help float their higher yielding issues because their names are not so well known in the U.S. so their funding is more expensive than for U.S. banks.

Yard Currency market term used when dealing one thousand million units of a currency. In foreign exchange, used to refer to yen and lira. Based on the French word milliard.

Year Bill See U.S. Treasury Bills.

Year On Year Rate Compares the current reporting period (e.g. a month or quarter) with the same period a year earlier. However, it suffers from the problem of "base effect", i.e. additions or deletions to the components of the data in an indicator in the periods being compared.

Yearling Bond Issued by a U.K. authority or similar body. Usually for one year.

Yellow Book The rule book of the London Stock Exchange. Officially The Admission of Securities for Listing of the London Stock Exchange.

Yellow Gold Gold which looks more yellow than normal by being an alloy of gold, copper, silver and sometimes zinc.

Yield Percentage return on an investment, usually at an annual rate. A bond's yield may be stated in terms of its return if held to maturity, if held to the call or put date or simply on the basis of the interest the bond pays in comparison to its current market price. See Yield to Maturity (YTM), Yield to Call (YTC), Yield to Put (YTP), Current Yield.

Yield Curve A diagram showing the relationship between yields and maturities for a set of similar securities or interbank deposits. An ascending, positive or normal yield curve slope is characterised by interest rates rising as maturities lengthen. A horizontal or flat slope is characterised by similar yield levels for all maturities. A descending, negative or inverted slope is characterised by interest rates falling as maturities lengthen. Analysis ranges from short term out to about one year and then through to long term, around ten years. See Forward Yield Curve, Zero Coupon Yield Curve.

Yield Gap Also known as yield ratio. Measures the yield, or interest rate earned, on bonds versus equities. Usually assessed as the average yield on equities less the average yield on bonds. Theory holds that equities yield more than bonds when inflation is low because of the greater risk. Conversely - as happened in the U.S. and the U.K. circa 1960 - when inflation rose the capital value of bonds fell as their yields rose, whereas equities prices moved higher and thus their yields fell. This introduced a new term - the Reverse Yield Gap.

Yield to Average Life Yield calculation which takes into consideration a sinking fund provision on a debt instrument, where a percentage of the issue is bought back at regular intervals before the redemption date.

Yield to Call (YTC) Yield calculation which takes into consideration an early redemption via a call facility.

Yield to Equivalent Life Calculation appropriate in the case of bonds with sinking funds since it is the discount rate which equates the present value of the future cash flows to the dirty price, with the cash flows taking into consideration the bond's amortisation schedule. In fact, this calculation is rarely used due to its complexity.

Yield to Maturity (YTM) The interest rate which brings the present value of the future cash flow equal to the present price of the bond including accrued interest, with the assumption that the bond will be held to maturity and that the coupons will be reinvested at the same rate. Factors involved are coupon interest, reinvestment rate and accrual of discount or amortisation premiums.

For example, a yield to maturity of eight percent will only provide a return of eight percent if the coupons are reinvested until maturity at eight percent. The risk that the coupons will not be invested at eight percent is known as the reinvestment risk.

It is the same yield as the current yield if the bond is sold at par. It is larger than the current yield when the bond sells at a discount and smaller when the bond sells at a premium.

If a bond is callable, it is known as the yield to call.

If a bond is puttable, it is known as the yield to put.

Yield to Put (YTP) Yield calculation which takes into consideration an early redemption via a put facility.

Yield Value Percentage of flour that can be obtained from a given amount of wheat.

Yours Dealers' language. The dealer hits the bid which has been quoted by his counterparty. It has to be qualified by the amount. Confirms the act of selling.

YTM See Yield to Maturity.

Zaiteku In Japanese, the science of financial technology. Refers specifically to the investment of funds in financial assets, by industrial companies.

Zenshinren Bank Comprises the National Federation of Credit Associations, a financial institution which is able to borrow from the Bank of Japan, the nation's central bank, for money market purposes.

Zero Cost Options An option strategy whereby the cost of purchasing an option is totally offset by the premium generated from the sale of an option. Both premiums are therefore identical. See Risk Reversal.

Zero Coupon Bond A bond which pays no coupon but is issued at a deep discount to face value. The difference between the issue and redemption prices creates a hefty capital gain which boosts the yield close to market levels. As it does not pay a coupon, investors do not run the risk of reinvesting interest paid at a lower rate, if interest rates fall during the life of the bond. In the U.S. Treasury securities market the only such zero coupon bond issued is the Treasury bill. However, the absence of longer term fixed income securities without a coupon reinvestment risk led to the creation of a market called Coupon Stripping. See U.S. STRIPS.

Zero Coupon Swap An interest rate swap in which one party makes regular payments while the other party makes one lump sum payment, typically at the end of the contract.

Zero Coupon Yield Curve A yield curve showing the Yield to Maturity (YTM) pertaining to a series of zero coupon bonds. Market practice is often to derive this curve theoretically from the par yield curve. Frequently used to derive discount factors. Also known as spot yield curve.

Zinc A base metal. Main uses are in galvanising (covering steel with a layer of zinc for protection from corrosion), die-casting alloys and brass. Galvanising accounts for nearly half of Western world zinc consumption. Dry-cell battery cases are the most important market for zinc sheet while zinc oxide is used in the rubber and paint industries. There is limited recovery for scrap zinc. Major producer is Canada with others including Australia, Belgium, the Commonwealth of Independent States, France, Germany, Italy, Japan, Peru, Poland, Mexico, Spain and the U.S.